LINUX
SYSTEM ADMINISTRATION

Other Linux resources from O'Reilly

Related titles

- DNS and BIND
- Linux in a Nutshell
- Linux iptables Pocket Reference
- Linux Pocket Guide
- Linux Network Administrator's Guide
- Running Linux
- LPI Linux Certification in a Nutshell
- Linux Server Hacks™
- Linux Security Cookbook™

Linux Books Resource Center

linux.oreilly.com is a complete catalog of O'Reilly's books on Linux and Unix and related technologies, including sample chapters and code examples.

ONLamp.com is the premier site for the open source web platform: Linux, Apache, MySQL and either Perl, Python, or PHP.

Conferences

O'Reilly brings diverse innovators together to nurture the ideas that spark revolutionary industries. We specialize in documenting the latest tools and systems, translating the innovator's knowledge into useful skills for those in the trenches. Visit *conferences.oreilly.com* for our upcoming events.

Safari Bookshelf (*safari.oreilly.com*) is the premier online reference library for programmers and IT professionals. Conduct searches across more than 1,000 books. Subscribers can zero in on answers to time-critical questions in a matter of seconds. Read the books on your Bookshelf from cover to cover or simply flip to the page you need. Try it today with a free trial.

SYSTEM ADMINISTRATION

Tom Adelstein and Bill Lubanovic

O'REILLY®
Beijing · Cambridge · Farnham · Köln · Paris · Sebastopol · Taipei · Tokyo

Linux System Administration
by Tom Adelstein and Bill Lubanovic

Published by O'Reilly Media, Inc., 1005 Gravenstein Highway North, Sebastopol, CA 95472.

O'Reilly books may be purchased for educational, business, or sales promotional use. Online editions are also available for most titles (*safari.oreilly.com*). For more information, contact our corporate/institutional sales department: (800) 998-9938 or *corporate@oreilly.com*.

Editor: Andy Oram
Production Editor: Laurel R.T. Ruma
Copyeditor: Rachel Wheeler
Proofreader: Laurel R.T. Ruma
Indexer: John Bickelhaupt
Cover Designer: Karen Montgomery
Interior Designer: David Futato
Illustrators: Robert Romano and Jessamyn Read

Printing History:

March 2007: First Edition.

This book uses RepKover™, a durable and flexible lay-flat binding.

ISBN-10: 0-596-00952-6
ISBN-13: 978-0-596-00952-6
[M]

Table of Contents

Preface

As Bill Lubanovic and I were putting the final touches on this book, I overheard a conversation between two coworkers in our Cisco lab discussing Linux. The senior networking guru of the two made an interesting remark. He said that despite all his knowledge, he felt incomplete as a professional because he had never learned Linux. A moment later he and the other gentleman turned to me and looked me square in the eyes. I smiled and went on working.

That evening, our director of Information Technology made an offhand remark to me during a conference that struck me as unusual. He said that he wanted to learn Apache, and when I asked him why he replied, "I just want to learn it," and left it at that.

Later in the conference, our director requested feedback from the group on a solution for patch management, explaining and using the example of *rsync*. He said he wanted something similar, while launching into a detailed technical discussion of incremental and cumulative patch management. I have a good working knowledge of *rsync*, but hadn't heard such a detailed academic explanation of any open source tool in any forum.

In both of those cases and many others, I wished I had this book ready to hand over to highly trained and skilled people who wanted to learn Linux administration. Perhaps you have had similar experiences and wished you had a book like this one at hand. I venture to guess that conversations like the ones I've just described occur many times in many places daily.

When Andy Oram and I began discussing a Linux system administration book, we had a slightly different idea of what we wanted to accomplish. Andy talked about a book in which each chapter took users through the steps of building and deploying application servers without co-mingling detailed discussions. He suggested that the discussion reside in one place in each chapter and the technical steps in another.

Later, I proposed that we make each chapter a module unto itself and let the reader complete the modules he wanted and/or needed. As this book evolved, we felt that we'd accomplished that objective. You do not have to read this book cover to cover to become a Linux system administrator. Simply start where you have the most interest.

When I first started using Linux, the community consisted mostly of programmers and hobbyists. I don't recall any discussion lists that focused on desktops or commercial applications. We logged onto the Internet by starting a daemon. We didn't have dialers or web browsers like the ones available today. The vast majority of people I knew did their own system administration or were in some stage of learning.

Reflecting on the time when we estimated that 30,000 Linux users existed on the planet, I'm amazed at how many people use Linux today and haven't the slightest idea how to write a configuration file. Linux forums seem to be filled with people asking how to get CUPS or Samba to work. On mailing lists, people hold detailed discussions on the technical details of projects like Postfix, JBoss, and Monit.

Many people still itch to learn the extensive capabilities of Linux as an application platform. If you use Linux and want to take the next step from a power user to an administrator, this book will help you make the transition. We wrote this book with you in mind.

How This Book Is Organized

Chapter 1, *Requirements for a Linux System Administrator*
: Lays out the goals of the book and what you'll gain by reading it.

Chapter 2, *Setting Up a Linux Multifunction Server*
: Gets you started with a nearly Internet-ready server.

Chapter 3, *The Domain Name System*
: Shows you the basics of setting up primary and secondary DNS servers.

Chapter 4, *An Initial Internet-Ready Environment*
: Uses the ISPConfig free software configuration system to get you started with a rich set of services that you can practice while reading the rest of the book.

Chapter 5, *Mail*
: Sets up a Postfix mail server with SASL authentication, a POP server, and an IMAP server.

Chapter 6, *Administering Apache*
: Gives a quick run-through of the popular Apache, MySQL, and PHP combination (together with Linux, known as a LAMP server), including SSL authentication.

Chapter 7, *Load-Balanced Clusters*
: Extends the previous chapter's Apache configuration with IP Virtual Server and *ldirectord* to provide high availability.

Chapter 8, *Local Network Services*
: Shows you how to manage users and configure common networking elements such as DHCP and gateway software on local area networks (LANs).

Chapter 9, *Virtualization in the Modern Enterprise*
: Shows how to set up Xen, VMware on a Linux host and then add guest operating systems.

Chapter 10, *Scripting*
: Shows you some basic techniques for writing robust and powerful *bash* shell scripts that can save you a lot of administration time.

Chapter 11, *Backing Up Data*
: Presents a range of techniques for carrying out this crucial function, from basic *rysnc* and *tar* to the powerful Amanda system.

Appendix, *bash Script Samples*
: Contains a few shell scripts that we've found useful when doing system administration and that might give you tips for how to write your own scripts.

Conventions Used in This Book

The following typographical conventions are used in this book:

Italic
: Indicates new terms, URLs, commands and command-line options, email addresses, filenames, file extensions, and directories.

`Constant width`
: Indicates the contents of files or the output from commands.

`Constant width bold`
: Shows commands or other text that should be typed literally by the user. Also used to highlight key portions of code or files.

`Constant width italic`
: Shows text that should be replaced with user-supplied values.

This icon signifies a tip, suggestion, or general note.

This icon indicates a warning or caution.

Using Code Examples

This book is here to help you get your job done. In general, you may use the code in this book in your programs and documentation. You do not need to contact us for permission unless you're reproducing a significant portion of the code. For example, writing a program that uses several chunks of code from this book does not require permission. Selling or distributing a CD-ROM of examples from O'Reilly books does require permission. Answering a question by citing this book and quoting example code does not require permission. Incorporating a significant amount of example code from this book into your product's documentation does require permission.

We appreciate, but do not require, attribution. An attribution usually includes the title, author, publisher, and ISBN. For example: "*Linux System Administration* by Tom Adelstein and Bill Lubanovic. Copyright 2007 O'Reilly Media, Inc., 978-0-596-00952-6."

If you feel your use of code examples falls outside fair use or the permission given above, feel free to contact us at *permissions@oreilly.com*.

Safari® Enabled

When you see a Safari® Enabled icon on the cover of your favorite technology book, that means the book is available online through the O'Reilly Network Safari Bookshelf.

Safari offers a solution that's better than e-books. It's a virtual library that lets you easily search thousands of top tech books, cut and paste code samples, download chapters, and find quick answers when you need the most accurate, current information. Try it for free at *http://safari.oreilly.com*.

How to Contact Us

Please address comments and questions concerning this book to the publisher:

O'Reilly Media, Inc.
1005 Gravenstein Highway North
Sebastopol, CA 95472
800-998-9938 (in the United States or Canada)
707-829-0515 (international or local)
707-829-0104 (fax)

We have a web page for this book, where we list errata and any additional information. You can access this page at:

http://www.oreilly.com/catalog/9780596009526

Examples, tips, and new procedures will be posted from time to time at the test site set up by the authors for the book:

http://www.centralsoft.org

To comment or ask technical questions about this book, send email to:

bookquestions@oreilly.com

For more information about our books, conferences, Resource Centers, and the O'Reilly Network, see our web site at:

http://www.oreilly.com

Acknowledgments

Books such as *Linux System Administration* come into existence only with the contribution of many people's efforts. Consider it impossible to list them all here.

First, we would like to thank Andy Oram, whose editing, writing, and management efforts to get this book into shape seem remarkable. Apart from working as the overall editor, Andy contributed materially to the content of this book. Andy functioned like a project manager and demonstrated both patience and discipline.

We could not have asked more from the contributions of Falko Timme, Phil Howard, and Herschel Cohen. Falko lent his time and expertise to Chapters 2 and 4. Phil wrote the bulk of Chapter 11 and provided the framework for Chapter 10 and the accompanying appendix of scripts. Herschel wrote sections of several chapters, including Chapters 8 and 10, and contributed his expertise to Chapter 6. All three contributors also reviewed other parts of the book.

Many thanks are also due to our technical experts, who spent countless hours reviewing, testing, and making suggestions about our work: Markus Amersdorfer, Keith Burgess, Robert Day, Ammar Ibrahim, and Yaman Saqqa.

Special thanks go to Yvonne Adelstein and Mary Lubanovic, our wives, who showed remarkable patience. We could not have done this without your total support.

CHAPTER 1

Requirements for a Linux System Administrator

We like Linux. Of all the Unix and Unix-like systems we've used, many now forgotten,* Linux is our favorite. It's an excellent server platform, a good desktop, and the center of much innovation in the current computing world.

Linux probably has the broadest reach of any operating system, from tiny systems the size of phone jacks, to cell phones, to supercomputer clusters bigger than your high school. It has infiltrated the fields of telecommunications, embedded systems, satellites, medical equipment, military systems, computer graphics, and—last but not least—desktop computing.

In a relatively short time, Linux progressed from a Finnish hacker's hobby to a top-tier enterprise-level system backed by high rollers such as IBM and Oracle. The user base has grown from about 30,000 people in 1995 to hundreds of millions today. During the Internet boom of the 1990s, many Unix administrators were surprised to find that Linux on PC hardware could outperform more expensive Unix workstations and servers. Many Windows and Novell administrators saw that Linux could handle DNS, email, and file services more reliably and with less support personnel than their current platforms. The growth of the Internet, and especially the Web, fueled a rapid expansion in the use of Linux servers and the need for people to manage them.

This book is for Linux system administrators. However, you may be a grizzled Unix veteran, a brave MCSE, or a stoic mainframer. You're exploring new territory and need a map and compass. Some of the ground will be familiar, but some will be terra incognita. This book covers many topics that have only recently joined the mainstream, for instance load-balanced clusters and virtualization.

The success of the Internet and open source software is changing business. Google, Amazon, eBay, and others have built huge server farms with commodity hardware and relatively few administrators compared to traditional mainframe and PC installations.

* Our favorite name was *PNX*, pronounced almost like something that would never appear in an O'Reilly book.

The skills needed to develop and maintain such distributed systems and applications are not taught in schools but learned from experience, sometimes bitter and sometimes sweet.

While writing this book we've constantly tested the latest distributions and tools, and we'll keep up our experimentation after the book is released. We invite readers to come to the test site we set up for the book, *http://www.centralsoft.org*, where we'll publish updates to examples, pointers to useful new tools we've discovered, and other tips.

About This Book

System administration books used to be fairly predictable. They showed you how to manage users, filesystems, devices, processes, printers, networks, and so on. They did not tell you what to do when new problems emerged. If your web site became popular, you had to learn quickly about proxy servers, different levels of caching, load balancing, distributed authentication, and other complex issues. If you added a database, you soon needed to scale it and learn to avoid SQL injection attacks. Overnight, sites became mission critical, and you needed the ability to make hot backups on 24×7 systems.

If you've been through these fire drills, you may have become tired of doing everything the hard way, facing new technical challenges nearly every day with few sources of help. Technical documentation—whether for commercial or open source software—rarely keeps up with the technology, and the gap seems to be widening. For example, open source directory servers have become important for managing computers, users, and resources. The original RFC-compliant protocols underlie many commercial products, but good documentation for community projects is surprisingly scarce.

How Can We Help?

Linux people are problem solvers. A typical Linux power user can put together a small server, get a dedicated Internet pipe with static IP addresses into her home, register a domain name, and build a server on the Internet. If you fall into this category, you can simply plow through the other topics in this book and expand your job possibilities.

To some of you, however, all that may sound like the equivalent of rappelling down a 10,000-foot mountain. If you're one of them, just start somewhere. As the saying goes, you eat an elephant one bite at a time, and damn the torpedoes.

You may have certifications for operating systems other than Linux. While you're applying patches and hot fixes, your boss may ask you to deploy an Apache server, or handle your own DNS lookups, or replace Exchange with Zimbra.

Whether you just want to learn or actually *have* to learn, you'll likely need some help climbing the Linux power user curve. That's exactly what we're here for: to help you explore the Linux system landscape without all the hardships our forefathers experienced.

Where Do You Start?

This book summarizes the steps you need to follow to build standalone servers. If you need to build a mail server, create a web server and blogging system, or set up a gateway for your LAN, you can jump right into the middle of the book. You don't have to read *Linux System Administration* from cover to cover.

We start you working right away, presenting a step-by-step guide to building a Linux server in Chapter 2. You can choose whatever path works for you, whether it involves creating a highly available cluster for web services, server consolidation through virtualization using Xen or VMware, or setting up a server for local area networks.

Running a modern operating system is incredibly cheap. You can set up a sophisticated learning center for yourself on hardware that many sites would consider obsolete and give away for free. We started with a used box powered by an Intel CPU two generations older than current models, added older versions of hard drives and memory, and went with a no-frills, free version of Linux.

Do You Need a Book?

Technical books have waned in popularity as the Internet has matured. To write a successful book today, the author has to provide significant value to the reader. An interesting story about one of the first e-commerce sites on the Web helps explain the value a book should deliver. A cheesecake company put up an advertisement in the earliest days of the Web. According to the story, several months passed and the company didn't receive a single order. In an unusual move, the president of the company published the company's secret cheesecake recipe. Within hours, he began receiving calls on his toll-free line. People began ordering cheesecakes in large numbers. Consumers looked at the recipe, considered the effort required to make their own cheesecakes, and saw the value in buying them from the company.

Many of the ingredients for this book were scattered across the Internet, in mailing lists, forums, and discussion groups, while others were mined from books, periodicals, and the experiences of colleagues. We solved a number of problems whose solutions were completely undocumented in the course of researching this book, and we pass our lessons on to you.

Many excellent project sites have inadequate documentation. Developers work hard to provide excellent software for free, but prose often trails code for many reasons: lack of time, lack of resources, lack of interest, language barriers, and so on.

Together with our readers, editors, and reviewers, we hope we've decreased entropy slightly in this little corner of the computing world.

Who Needs You?

A few years ago, most Linux system administrators would have told you that they didn't choose their careers—Linux chose them. In the old days, Linux was like an adolescent Unix. Most Linux system administrators learned the ropes on single workstations and very small networks. Linux inherited some servers from Unix (BIND, Sendmail, Apache), but little office software and few applications. Today, Linux system administration involves thousands of packages and interoperability with other operating systems.

Who needs Linux administrators? The NASA Center for Computational Sciences (NCCS) at the Goddard Space Flight Center does. Its Linux-based high-performance computing (HPC) clusters are designed to dramatically increase throughput for applications ranging from studying weather and climate variability to simulating astrophysical phenomena. Linux supplements NCCS architecture designed to scale to as many as 40 trillion floating-point operations per second (TFLOPS) in its full configuration.

Linux runs more of the world's top supercomputers than any other operating system. In fact, as of this writing Linux runs an astonishing 75 percent of the top 500 supercomputers on the planet.* According to department heads at the Lawrence Livermore National Laboratory in Livermore, CA, Linux runs 10 of their massive systems, all of which are on the TOP500 List. Those systems include BlueGene/L, the world's most powerful supercomputer, and Thunder, which currently ranks nineteenth (*http://www.top500.org/list/2006/11/100*).

Help Wanted

Linux administrators are in high demand. To give you an idea of what's expected of them, we looked at a small selection of the tens of thousands of ads for Linux system administrators on a national job listing agency's web site. Here's a tiny snapshot of some of the jobs' responsibilities:

- Administer and manage large Linux server environment, with an emphasis on performance monitoring, tuning, and management.
- Oversee database physical design, administration, and documentation.
- Provide network troubleshooting, escalated service desk support, and proactive monitoring of mission-critical systems.

* See *http://www.top500.org/stats/28/osfam*.

- Provide guidance and direction of technology solutions for the organization; train and mentor junior-level administrators.
- Supply daily technical support and on-call consulting advice for the hardware and operating system environment supporting the collection platform; administer Linux server infrastructure to maintain stability as well as maximize efficiencies in the computing environment.
- Install, configure, and troubleshoot all hardware, peripherals, and equipment necessary to meet integrated systems objectives; provide support functions on escalated issues.
- Provide effective first/second-level support for a company's Linux environment across 300-plus servers, including Linux blades.
- Manage all aspects of the integrity of the environment, including security, monitoring (capacity and performance), change control, and software management.
- Interface with other internal support groups such as Change Control, Application Development, Engineering, Database Administrators, Web Services, Storage, Security, Operations, and Command Centers.
- Administer infrastructure services—DNS, NIS, LDAP, FTP, SMTP, Postfix/Sendmail, NFS, Samba—and application and database servers, with an emphasis on automation and monitoring.

Linux is now a standard corporate platform, and Linux talent is in short supply. If you want to learn Linux to boost your financial worth, plenty of evidence supports a growing need within the industry for workers with Linux administration skills.

Analyzing Skill Sets

Ask different information system managers to define the role of a system administrator, and you will get a variety of answers. Market inertia has surprised the current crop of managers who lack information about Linux. They do not know what Linux professionals should know, and Linux professionals rarely understand those managers.

Many information system managers who understand Unix attempt to hold Linux administrators to Unix standards. That rarely works. While Unix administrators may believe they can easily transition to Linux, they quickly discover a knowledge gap. Linux administrators have less trouble transitioning to Unix than the other way around. One explanation says Linux administrators have a broader understanding of their systems because of the nature of open source software.

System administration tasks more often than not involve the Internet. The majority of transactions are related to email and web site management, in addition to telecommunications and mobility. Email once represented 70 percent of all traffic on the Internet. Today, broadband applications such as Voice over IP (VoIP) and other forms of communication, including instant messaging, have increased traffic while lowering the percentage devoted to email. But whatever the protocols and media used, the Internet remains the primary domain of Linux.

Let's continue analyzing the job responsibilities described in the previous section. The last set ("Administer infrastructure services") can give you a sense of the standard Linux skill set. Employers want system administrators who can handle what they deem "infrastructure services." Notice the Internet technologies involved. Of the list of Linux components with which familiarity is required, most tasks will involve DNS, LDAP, FTP, SMTP, and Postfix/Sendmail. We will cover most of these components in Chapters 2–6.

The other job descriptions fit mostly into the category of in-house enterprise needs. These include escalated service desk support, technical support, and on-call consulting advice for the hardware and operating system environments. Most Linux system administrators should have the skills required to provide these services, but they are outside the scope of this book because they are not purely technical.

The remaining responsibilities fall under the category of "soft skills." In the past, one would not have expected a typical system administrator to learn to function as a liaison with other internal support groups such as Application Development, Engineering, Database Administrators, or Web Services. However, a system administrator is no longer just a techie with knowledge of some arcane systems; he's a member of the corporate decision-making staff.

One usually gains soft skills and specializations after mastering the basics. We may cover these topics tangentially in this book, but we consider them outside the scope of our focus. Other O'Reilly books and time in the trenches will help you get a hold on these valuable abilities. For now, we'll get you up and running in the areas where system administration has seen the most growth and where documentation seems lacking.

Unlike other areas of computer science and engineering, few schools offer courses in Linux administration, let alone entire degree programs. So, if you want to learn Linux system administration, you will have to look for materials and courses outside the university setting. But much of the existing materials you may find will not include what Linux strategists consider the most critical subject matter.

Most Linux administrators have taught themselves, learning as the need arose. At some point these self-taught administrators moved into jobs. Needs then arose at a faster pace, causing them to learn more, until they could do just about anything a system administrator had to do. This is one area where *Linux System Administration* can contribute, helping you achieve proficiency in a broad range of tasks faster and more efficiently.

What System Managers Should Know About Linux

One of the first things an information technology manager should know is that Linux is not Unix. While Linux can certainly run the vast majority of Unix programs, it also has a wider range of applications in both public and private networks.

Linux administrators can configure distributions by choosing from a vast number of components that do similar jobs. For example, with almost every Unix distribution, Sendmail is the only choice of mail transfer agent (MTA). But with Linux, you can choose from a number of comparable MTAs, depending on whether you want a corporate workgroup application, a large-scale directory-driven corporate mail backbone, or a simple web application for handling "contact us" forms.

A further testament to Linux's flexibility is that it's the first operating system IBM has ever employed that runs on all of its hardware platforms, from the xSeries Intel class server, through the pSeries and iSeries, to the S/390 and zSeries mainframes.

If you want a Linux administrator and you use large IBM systems, your canidate will have to know mainframe architecture and be familiar with terms like "DASD" for hard drive storage, "IPL" for booting up the system, "catalog" for a directory, and "command list" for a shell script. But don't sell Linux administrators short. We once attended a two-day seminar with a group of Linux administrators who went out the day after the class and started deploying Linux on bare-metal IBM zSeries computers.

If Linux people have anything to offer, it's that they learn quickly, adapt quickly, and have a broad knowledge base you will not find with other technologists. They can learn to run your Microsoft boxes in less time than it takes an MCSE to learn a single Linux task.

What's Next

We know you don't like slow-paced learning and scads of fussy background (in fact, we're amazed you've read this far in the chapter), so we want to get started as quickly as possible. We want to provide a working server that will perform many Linux jobs you can learn and use. For this reason, we'll start out with an Internet-ready server in the next chapter. You're going to want Internet tools such as a web server and email no matter how you use your server (probably even if it serves only a LAN), and those tools will be useful to you from the start.

The rest of the book expands on some of the same topics and introduces others that you might not encounter every day. *Linux System Administration* is a combined cookbook and travelogue; you can enjoy a hearty breakfast while you're covering ground. We usually explain topics at the beginning of a chapter and follow with concise steps and applications of those topics. If you just want to follow the step-by-step instructions, go for it. You can figure out what you're doing later. We feel that our approach will keep you headed in the right direction.

Onward and upward. Excelsior!

CHAPTER 2

Setting Up a Linux Multifunction Server

There's a real difference between reading about something and doing it. That's why schools provide laboratories for so many of their courses. If you plan on learning Linux system administration, you need a server. So, the first task in this book involves building a basic server environment. Once you've built one, you'll have a good foundation for practicing and learning Linux.

The Linux operating system resembles the wheelbase of a car, which can take on an enormous variety of different functions depending on the choice of chassis and features. As you add services such as email or a database, the system takes on a different character. Do you need a web server, a development platform, a gateway, or a file and print server? Whatever you need requires a core, which this chapter provides.

We're going to start with a server you might find on the Internet, hosting web sites. Why, you might ask? Because you can adapt an Internet server to do many additional tasks, such as managing user authentication, providing print and file services, handling local email, and providing remote access. You can take the server to a web hosting facility, plug it in, and begin offering web services. You can even keep it in your own home, if you obtain a static IP address from your ISP.

Setting up a server on the Internet may change your perspective about computing. Deploying a wide area network (WAN) differs from using Linux as a desktop, a file and print server, or a simple firewall.

First-time administrators may experience some confusion while configuring the server, due to unfamiliar terms and concepts. You won't have the X Window System's convenient graphical interface, and you'll have to issue commands instead of clicking on icons. Your work will be done in console mode, from the command-line interface.

As part of our strategy to teach you administration, we'll show you how to put a web-based tool on your system in the next chapter (service providers use this web-based tool to manage Linux servers they lease to hosting customers). So, not everything you do will be limited to a black and white screen.

When you follow the instructions in this chapter, you will get a box hosting a web site that you can adapt for other purposes later. Your system will deploy:

- A web server (Apache 2.0.x)
- A mail server (Postfix)
- A DNS server (BIND 9)
- An FTP server (ProFTPD)
- Mail delivery agents (POP3/POP3s/IMAP/IMAPs)
- Webalizer for web site statistics

Although there are many ways to set up a remote web server, following the instructions here provides a good basis for getting a grip on Linux. Once you master this setup, you should have the ability to configure a server to fit your needs.

During the setup process, you will likely see commands and concepts with which you have no familiarity. We will ask you to enter data that may not make any sense. While we will attempt to explain as much as possible about the setup process, you may not feel satisfied with the information in this chapter.

It's difficult for anyone to retain complex information on a first reading. So, while asking you to type commands may seem inefficient, it will allow you to retain enough information about the subject that you will recognize it later. We will cover each topic in greater detail in subsequent chapters, and your exposure now will help you over the course of reading this book.

The threshold to a new Linux world awaits you and your server. So, let's get started!

Server Requirements

You can use almost any distribution of Linux to configure a web server. In this exercise, we'll use Debian. We chose Debian because we wanted to use a stable distribution of Linux. The main commercial distributions—Red Hat Enterprise Linux and Novell's SUSE Linux Enterprise Server—have price tags that put them out of the reach of most users, but you can obtain Debian for free. Also, Red Hat and SUSE use proprietary management tools that create difficulties in transferring knowledge about

Linux. You can learn more about standard Linux behavior by using Debian than by using either SUSE or Red Hat.

To set up a Linux Internet server, you will need a connection to the Internet and a static IP address. If you cannot obtain a static IP address, you can set up the system with the address leased to you by your ISP and configure it statically. Make sure you know how long the lease runs, in case you have to change the IP address while your system is running.

You'll also need a computer with at least a Pentium III CPU, a minimum of 256 MB of RAM, and a 10 GB hard drive. Obviously, a newer CPU and additional memory will provide better performance.

This chapter is based on Debian's stable version. We strongly suggest using a CD with the Netinstall kernel. The Debian web site (*http://www.debian.org*) provides downloadable CD images.

Installing Debian

We assume you know how to do a net installation of Linux. You'll just need a few pointers to set up your base box.

After you boot into the Debian CD-ROM disk, you will see a login screen. Make sure to type in `linux26` to get the most recent Version 2.6 kernel instead of the older version 2.4.

The installer will guide you through a series of installation screens. When you reach the screen called "Configure the Network," Debian first suggests configuring your network with DHCP. You can do that if you have DHCP available. If you do not, Debian will default to a screen that allows you to configure your network manually. You will be asked to provide the hostname of the server, a domain name, a gateway, an IP address, a netmask, and a nameserver. If you have a registered domain and a static IP address, you're ready to go. If you don't have a registered domain name, you will need one.

You can obtain a domain name from a number of sources for as little as $3.00. Search the Internet using the keywords "domain registration." You will see a number of registrars listed. Many vendors provide their services at low prices, and some offer free domain name services. You need two registered DNS servers to obtain a domain name initially. You may also find your registrar's DNS service handy if you do not have another physical server to provide for secondary domain services. Every domain you register requires a primary DNS server and a backup or secondary DNS server.

Now that you have configured your network, you can continue with the installation tasks that complete the base system. The Debian installation script will lead you through the next sections.

Right away, you will reach the hard disk partitioning screens. For the purposes of this book, just create one big partition with the mount point / (just a slash) and a swap partition. Choose the option to put all files in one partition. Finally, choose the finish partitioning option and write the results to disk.

The base Debian installation we're using has two distinct sections. The first installs what some call the GNU/Linux plumbing, which allows you to boot off the hard drive and obtain a root prompt. It also transfers files from the CD-ROM to the hard drive.

Once the first section finishes, it asks you to remove the CD-ROM disk you used to start the installation. From that point on, the installation continues using files stored on the hard drive.

Now proceed through the few remaining installation screens, which eventually ask you to reboot to initialize the kernel and finish the installation.

After the reboot, Debian will want you to add a nonprivileged user during installation. That allows you to log in and use the *su* command to become *root*. For security reasons, system administrators have established a standard practice of not logging into the system as *root* unless they need to recover a failed system.

Name your first user account *Administrator* and give it a user ID of *admin*. Don't use the same password for *admin* as you do for your *root* user. We'll use the *admin* user ID in other chapters as well.

When you reach the Debian software selection screen, move your cursor to the box next to "mail server," press the Space bar, and let the system install the default packages until you reach an option where you see the *libc* client.

You should install the *libc* client with regular Unix mailbox support rather than *maildir* support. Unix mailboxes keep all mail in a single file, whereas *maildir* keeps each message in a separate file. Unix mailboxes are easier to use and configure, so start with them for now.

Debian will also want you to configure Exim as the mail transfer agent (MTA), but don't. We will replace Exim with Postfix a little later in the chapter. In the meantime, when you reach the screen that says "Configuring Exim v4," choose the "no configuration" option. Then answer yes when the installation script asks you, "Really leave the mail system unconfigured?"

Finally, on the last screen involved with configuring Exim, enter the username *admin* as the email recipient for *root* and *postmaster*.

MTAs: Sendmail and Alternatives

Debian's default installation process revolves around Exim, while other Linux distributions generally use Sendmail by default. Sendmail has long been the de facto standard MTA, and early Linux distributions took advantage of that. Nearly all processes in Linux related to mail involve Sendmail configuration files, and most free software applications expect Sendmail to exist on the operating system.

It's possible to fool Linux into thinking it's using Sendmail while replacing it with another MTA. When you install Red Hat, for example, Sendmail is installed by default. However, Red Hat and Fedora both come with a program that allows the user to switch to Postfix, which is what we will do manually.

The Debian project managers chose Exim as the default MTA because its creator licensed it under the General Public License (GPL). Like Postfix, Exim is a drop-in replacement for Sendmail.

The common practice today involves using Postfix, for many reasons that we will cover later in this chapter. You will not mess up your system by replacing Exim with Postfix. In fact, you'll download Postfix from the Debian repositories.

Logging in Remotely

When you finish your installation, you should log into the server from a remote console on your desktop. We recommend you do further administration from another system (even a laptop), because a secure server normally runs in what is called *headless* mode—that is, it has no monitor or keyboard. Get used to administering your server like this, as if you were at a production site. On the remote machine you need only an SSH client, which virtually all Linux distributions have and which can be downloaded for other operating systems as well.

The following printout is typical of what you'll encounter the first time you SSH to your new Linux server:

```
$ ssh admin@server1.centralsoft.org
The authenticity of host 'server1.centralsoft.org (70.253.158.42)' can't
be established.
RSA key fingerprint is 9f:26:c7:cc:f2:f6:da:74:af:fe:15:16:97:4d:b3:e6.
Are you sure you want to continue connecting (yes/no)? yes
Warning: Permanently added 'server1.centralsoft.org,70.253.158.42' (RSA)
to the list of known hosts.
Password: enter password for admin user here
Linux server1 2.6.8-2-386 #1 Thu May 19 17:40:50 JST 2005 i686 GNU/Linux

The programs included with the Debian GNU/Linux system are free software;
the exact distribution terms for each program are described in the
individual files in /usr/share/doc/*/copyright.
```

```
Debian GNU/Linux comes with ABSOLUTELY NO WARRANTY, to the extent
permitted by applicable law.

Last login: Sun Dec 25 19:07:38 2005 from 70.255.197.162
admin@server1:~$
```

At this point, you have established a remote connection and can perform tasks as if you were looking at your system from the monitor of your server. If you wish, you can remove any monitor, keyboard, and mouse you have connected to your server.

Configuring the Network

If you used DHCP during the Debian installation, you should now configure your server with a static IP address so you can perform the testing required later in the chapter. If you had a public IP address and configured it as static, you can skip to the next section.

If you installed Debian with a DHCP client from your router or Internet service provider, you need to reconfigure networking. This is a valuable lesson in its own right for exploring Linux network configuration.

To change the settings to use a static IP address, you'll need to become *root* and edit the file */etc/network/interfaces* to suit your needs. As an example, we'll use the IP address 70.153.258.42.

Our configuration file starts out looking like this:

```
# /etc/network/interfaces -- configuration file for ifup(8), ifdown(8)
# The loopback interface
auto lo
iface lo inet loopback
# The first network card - this entry was created during the Debian
# installation
# (network, broadcast, and gateway are optional)
# The primary network interface
iface eth0 inet dhcp
```

To add the IP address 70.153.258.42 to the interface *eth0*, we must change the file to look like this (you'll have to obtain some of the information from your ISP):

```
# /etc/network/interfaces -- configuration file for ifup(8), ifdown(8)
# The loopback interface
auto lo
iface lo inet loopback
# The first network card - this entry was created during the Debian
# installation
# (network, broadcast, and gateway are optional)
auto eth0
iface eth0 inet static
        address 70.153.258.42
        netmask 255.255.255.248
        network 70.153.258.0
```

```
        broadcast 70.153.258.47
        gateway 70.153.258.46
```

After editing the */etc/network/interfaces* file, restart the network by entering:

```
# /etc/init.d/networking restart
```

You will then need to edit */etc/resolv.conf* and add nameservers to resolve Internet hostnames to their corresponding IP addresses. Though we have yet to configure our own nameserver, we will do so later in this chapter. At this point, we will simply set up a minimal DNS server. The other nameservers should specify the IP addresses of the DNS servers offered by your ISP. Our *resolv.conf* looks as follows:

```
search server
nameserver 70.153.258.42
nameserver 70.253.158.45
nameserver 151.164.1.8
```

Make sure you use the DNS servers that work with your domain site; otherwise, your DNS server will not indicate that it's the authority for your domain.

Now edit */etc/hosts* and add your IP addresses:

```
127.0.0.1       localhost.localdomain      localhost       server1
70.153.258.42   server1.centralsoft.org    server1
```

Ignore the IPv6 information in the */etc/hosts* file. We will show you how to set up an IPv6 server in Chapter 8.

Now, to set the hostname, enter these commands:

```
# echo server1.centralsoft.org > /etc/hostname
# /bin/hostname -F /etc/hostname
```

You'll need to use the same commands regardless of how you set up your networking during installation, substituting your domain name for *server1.centralsoft.org*.

Next, verify that you configured your hostname correctly by running the *hostname* command:

```
~$ hostname
server1
~$ hostname -f
server1.centralsoft.org
```

If you get this result, you're ready to move on to the next section. If not, look in the */etc/hostname* file. You may find that it looks like this:

```
#less /etc/hostname
server1
```

Oops. It should read *server1.centralsoft.org*. You can change it now.

Changing the Default Debian Packages

We started with the packages the Debian maintainers place in their distribution by default. As noted earlier, we need to make some changes—notably, in order to use Postfix. While you might think we're second-guessing the good work of the Debian team, that's not quite the case.

The Debian team has chosen to install, by default, services appropriate for a LAN, such as the Network File System (NFS). But we're putting our server on the Internet, so we'll want to delete NFS and some other services, while adding others such as OpenSSL.

To retrieve the files needed for this chapter, execute the following command:

```
# apt-get install wget bzip2 rdate fetchmail libdb3++-dev \
unzip zip ncftp xlispstat libarchive-zip-perl \
zlib1g-dev libpopt-dev nmap openssl lynx fileutils
```

You will then see Debian downloading files in your console. Soon, the downloading activity will stop and you will see a question such as the following asking you if you want to continue:

```
0 upgraded, 42 newly installed, 0 to remove and 0 not upgraded.
Need to get 12.2MB of archives.
After unpacking 35.8MB of additional disk space will be used.
Do you want to continue? [Y/n]
```

Entering `Y` will complete the installation of the additional files.

Next, you will want to remove services you will not use. Execute the following command, and you will see the output that follows:

```
# apt-get remove lpr nfs-common portmap pidentd pcmcia-cs \
pppoe pppoeconf ppp pppconfig
Reading Package Lists... Done
Building Dependency Tree... Done
Package pcmcia-cs is not installed, so not removed
The following packages will be REMOVED:
  lpr nfs-common pidentd portmap ppp pppconfig pppoe pppoeconf
0 upgraded, 0 newly installed, 8 to remove and 0 not upgraded.
Need to get 0B of archives.
After unpacking 3598kB disk space will be freed.
Do you want to continue? [Y/n] Y
(Reading database ... 22425 files and directories currently installed.)
Removing lpr ...
Stopping printer spooler: lpd .
Removing nfs-common ...
Stopping NFS common utilities: statd.
Removing pidentd ...
Removing portmap ...
Stopping portmap daemon: portmap.
Removing pppoeconf ...
Removing pppoe ...
```

```
Removing pppconfig ...
Removing ppp ...
Stopping all PPP connections...done.
```

Make sure you double-check the commands you type. If you make a typo, Debian will tell you that it can't find the file in question. In this case, simply re-enter *apt-get*, specifying just the name of that package.

Since you have made changes to the package database, you need to change the scripts that start at boot time. Use the following commands to modify the startup scripts:

```
# update-rc.d -f exim remove
Removing any system startup links for /etc/init.d/exim ...
# update-inetd --remove daytime
# update-inetd --remove telnet
# update-inetd --remove time
# update-inetd --remove finger
# update-inetd --remove talk
# update-inetd --remove ntalk
# update-inetd --remove ftp
# update-inetd --remove discard
```

Now you need to restart *inetd*, which is the server process for standard Internet services. *inetd* generally starts at boot time, but because you have changed the services on the system, you need to restart it so it can discover the services in its configuration file. The *inetd* command accepts an argument that points to a configuration file listing the services it provides. But if no argument is given on the command line, *inetd* reads the configuration information from the */etc/inetd.conf* file, which for our purposes is fine. The *update-inetd* commands stored our changes in this file.

To restart *inetd* using t*he default configuration file, enter:*

```
# /etc/init.d/inetd reload
```

You will see the following message in your console:

```
Reloading internet superserver: inetd
```

Setting Up Quotas

Apache's web server gives Linux the ability to provide *virtual hosting*—that is, your server can host several web sites with domain names that differ from the name of the physical server. In the web server configuration file, you can define different domains using virtual hosting clauses. For example, even though the domain name used in this book is *centralsoft.org*, we could have *mothersmagic.com*, *wildbills.info*, or any other domain we register and use the same IP address.

We cover this concept thoroughly in Chapter 6. For now, just think of the IP address like the telephone number for a house where several different people live. When a browser accesses port 80, it can reach whatever domain you set up.

Linux provides a means to manage disk usage for multiple domains via a facility called *quotas*. Originally, Unix provided quotas on user accounts so they wouldn't take up too much room on a server. For instance, if you had 50 users sharing disk space on a file server, without a quota system one user could fill up the disk, causing all of the users' applications to refuse to save any more data.

A quota facility forces users to stay under their disk consumption limits, taking away their ability to consume unlimited disk space on a system. The system keeps track of quotas per user and per filesystem. If you have more than one filesystem where users can create files, set up the facility for each filesystem separately.

You can use the same quota system to limit the space allocated to a domain you host. Various tools allow you to administer and automate quota policies on your system. In this part of the server setup, you'll add a quota facility so you can use it later.

First, install the *quota* packages using *apt-get*:

```
# apt-get install quota quotatool
```

You will encounter a question that reads:

```
Enable this option if you want the warnquota utility to be run daily to alert users
when they are over quota.
Send daily reminders to users over quota?
<Yes>                        <No>
```

At this point, choose <No>.

Debian will install and configure the two packages, but you will have to edit */etc/fstab* to enable quotas on each filesystem where you want them. Because our system has just one partition for all user files, you can just add the *usrquota* and *grpquota* options to the partition with the mount point */*:

```
# /etc/fstab: static filesystem information.
#
# <filesystem>  <mount point>   <type>  <options>       <dump>  <pass>
proc            /proc           proc    defaults        0       0
/dev/sda1       /               ext3    defaults,errors=remount-
ro,usrquota,grpquota 0       1
/dev/sda5       none            swap    sw              0       0
/dev/hdc        /media/cdrom0   iso9660 ro,user,noauto  0       0
/dev/fd0        /media/floppy0  auto    rw,user,noauto  0       0
```

Now run the following commands to add files to the root directory:

```
# touch /quota.user /quota.group
# chmod 600 /quota.*
# mount -o remount /
# quotacheck -avugm
```

The Linux kernel usually has default support for quotas. The kernel sees the quota options in */etc/fstab* and checks *quota.user* and *quota.group* to determine whether users and/or groups have limits to their disk space.

You will now see the following in your console:

```
quotacheck: Scanning /dev/hda1 [/] done
```

You will also see a message in your console stating something like this:

```
quotacheck: Checked 1912 directories and 28410 files
```

You can now execute the next command:

```
# quotaon -avug
```

You will see the following messages:

```
/dev/hda1 [/]: group quotas turned on
/dev/hda1 [/]: user quotas turned on
```

Are you wondering what you just did? This sequence enabled quotas on the system. You can check the manual pages for *quota* if you feel the need to understand more right now. Your server box is now set up to use the quota facility.

Providing Domain Name Services

In Chapter 3, you will learn how to manage domain names for your server and for any virtual domains residing on your system. For now, we will set up a minimal configuration for BIND, the ubiquitous DNS server.

Debian provides a stable version of BIND in its repositories. We'll install and set up BIND and secure it in a *chroot* environment, meaning it won't be able to see or access files outside its own directory tree. This is an important security technique. The term *chroot* refers to the trick of changing the root filesystem (the / directory) that a process sees, so that most of the system is effectively inaccessible to it.

We will also configure BIND to run as a non-*root* user. That way, if someone gains access to BIND, she won't gain *root* privileges or be able to control other processes.

To install BIND on your Debian server, run this command:

```
# apt-get install bind9
```

Debian downloads and configures the file as an Internet service. You will see the following messages on your console:

```
Setting up bind9 (9.2.4-1)
Adding group `bind' (104)
Done.
Adding system user `bind'
Adding new user `bind' (104) with group `bind'.
Not creating home directory.
Starting domain name service: named.
```

You will see similar output as you install or remove other services with the *apt-get* utility.

To put BIND in a secured environment, you need to create a directory where the service can run unexposed to other processes. You will also run it as an unprivileged user, but only *root* will be able to access that directory.

First stop the service by running the following command:

```
# /etc/init.d/bind9 stop
```

Next, edit the file */etc/default/bind9* so that the daemon will run as the unprivileged user *bind*, chrooted to */var/lib/named*. Change the line:

```
OPTS="-u bind"
```

so that it reads:

```
OPTIONS="-u bind -t /var/lib/named"
```

To provide a complete environment for running BIND, create the necessary directories under */var/lib*:

```
# mkdir -p /var/lib/named/etc
# mkdir /var/lib/named/dev
# mkdir -p /var/lib/named/var/cache/bind
# mkdir -p /var/lib/named/var/run/bind/run
```

Then move the *config* directory from */etc* to */var/lib/named/etc*:

```
# mv /etc/bind /var/lib/named/etc
```

Next, create a symbolic link to the new *config* directory from the old location, to avoid problems when BIND is upgraded in the future:

```
# ln -s /var/lib/named/etc/bind /etc/bind
```

Make null and random devices for use by BIND, and fix the permissions of the directories:

```
# mknod /var/lib/named/dev/null c 1 3
# mknod /var/lib/named/dev/random c 1 8
```

Then change permissions and ownership on the files:

```
# chmod 666 /var/lib/named/dev/null /var/lib/named/dev/random
# chown -R bind:bind /var/lib/named/var/*
# chown -R bind:bind /var/lib/named/etc/bind
```

You'll also need to change the startup script */etc/init.d/sysklogd* so that you can still see messages in the system logs. Change the line:

```
SYSLOGD=""
```

so that it reads:

```
SYSLOGD="-a /var/lib/named/dev/log"
```

Now restart the logging process with this command:

```
# /etc/init.d/sysklogd restart
```

You will see the following message:

```
Restarting system log daemon: syslogd.
```

Finally, start BIND:

```
# /etc/init.d/bind9 start
```

Check */var/log/syslog* for any errors. You can page through the file using:

```
# less /var/log/syslog
```

You will be reassured that BIND succeeded in starting if you see:

```
Starting domain name service: named.
```

Now, let's check to see whether *named* is functioning without any trouble. Execute this command, and you should see the results that follow:

```
server1:/home/admin# rndc status

number of zones: 6
debug level: 0
xfers running: 0
xfers deferred: 0
soa queries in progress: 0
query logging is OFF
server is up and running
server1:/home/admin#
```

If DNS is not working correctly, you'll instead see something like this:

```
server1:~# rndc status
rndc: neither /etc/bind/rndc.conf nor /etc/bind/rndc.key was found
server1:~#
```

Fortunately, our DNS system is working correctly.

For the moment, we have not set up our primary zone files or configured DNS for the system for anything other than a caching server, which populates its cache each time someone requests a web page. We'll show you how to configure primary and secondary DNS severs in Chapter 3.

Although many people fail to stress its importance, mastering DNS is crucial because so many other services depend on it. You'll find DNS to be a critical component of almost every Internet service your system performs.

Adding a Relational Database: MySQL

Web sites and web service applications use relational databases to embed objects into web pages. This allows for rapid scaling of web site requests. Web browsers can stimulate 30 requests at once, increasing loads on CPUs, memory, and disk access.

Relational databases, in combination with a web server, can efficiently construct complex web pages on the fly.

We do not cover the complex topic of database administration in this book. However, Linux system administrators often find that developers expect them to set up databases for development use, so we will demonstrate how to configure your Linux server box with the one of the popular open source databases: MySQL. To make effective use of the database, you will need to know how to:

1. Install and start MySQL.
2. Create a MySQL *root* user.
3. Create a regular MySQL user, which the application will use to access the database.
4. Perform backups and restorations of databases.

To install the database server, a convenient client program that you can use to administer the server, and the library needed by both, issue this command:

```
# apt-get install mysql-server mysql-client libmysqlclient12-dev
```

Debian will download MySQL from its repositories and begin the installation process. You'll see the following messages:

```
Install Hints
MySQL will only install if you have a NON-NUMERIC hostname that is
resolvable via the /etc/hosts file. E.g. if the "hostname" command
returns "myhostname" then there must be a line like "10.0.0.1
myhostname".
A new mysql user "debian-sys-maint" will be created. This mysql account
is used in the start/stop and cron scripts. Don't delete.
Please remember to set a PASSWORD for the MySQL root user! If you use a
/root/.my.cnf, always write the "user" and the "password" lines in
there, never only the password!
See /usr/share/doc/mysql-server/README.Debian for more information.
<Ok>
```

Administratively, MySQL is comparable to Linux: each has a *root* user that has control over everything that goes on and can grant or deny privileges to other users. The MySQL *root* user has nothing to do with the Linux *root* user; only the name is the same. Create the MySQL *root* user by entering:

```
# mysqladmin -u root password 'pword'
```

Choose a reasonably difficult-to-guess nonsense string for your password (*pword*). Whenever you want to administer MySQL in the future, you will enter the following command and supply your password at the prompt:

```
# mysql -u root -p
Enter password:
```

Try it now to make sure that the client and server are working and that you can get into the server. You should see output on your console similar to the one shown next:

```
Welcome to the MySQL monitor. Commands end with ; or \g.
Your MySQL connection id is 14 to server version: 4.0.24_Debian-10-log
Type 'help;' or '\h' for help. Type '\c' to clear the buffer.
mysql>
```

Type /q or quit; to exit.

Because the MySQL server is running, you can run *netstat -tap* and see a line like this:

```
tcp     0     0 localhost.localdo:mysql *:*      LISTEN      2449/mysqld
```

MySQL is accessible on the local host (127.0.0.1) on port 3306. If you do not see this line, edit */etc/mysql/my.cnf* (the configuration file that the client and server check for operating parameters) and add a # sign to comment out skip-networking:

```
#skip-networking
```

If you want MySQL to listen on all available IP addresses, edit */etc/mysql/my.cnf* and comment out the bind-address = 127.0.0.1 line:

```
#bind-address              = 127.0.0.1
```

If you had to edit */etc/mysql/my.cnf*, restart MySQL using this command:

```
# /etc/init.d/mysql restart
```

This discussion has not covered all the functions database developers are likely to expect of you. MySQL is now set up to run on your server, however, and that's sufficient for you to take the next steps. We'll do more with MySQL in Chapters 6 and 11.

Configuring Mail Securely with Postfix, POP3, and IMAP

In this section, we'll add email transport and delivery agents and implement tight control over the systems environment. We will demonstrate how to authenticate bona fide users of an email system and prevent fraudulent access to email facilities.

For more than 25 years, Sendmail has served as the Internet's primary MTA. Many applications written for Linux expect to find Sendmail running on the server. Written before the Internet became open to the public, however, Sendmail has many of the security problems listed on the Common Vulnerabilities and Exposures (CVE) list hosted at *http://cve.mitre.org*.

Fortunately, other MTAs have emerged to take Sendmail's place. The main problem these MTAs face is the expectation by core applications that Sendmail will be present on the Linux server. To get around this, MTAs such as Postfix and Exim must be able to appear to applications as if they are Sendmail. We call these *drop-in replacements*, and they can run in a Sendmail mode.

Postfix is our preferred replacement for Sendmail. Postfix is faster than Sendmail, has a more secure, modular architecture, and offers many of the features required by a high-volume mail provider. Postfix doesn't provide deprecated protocols, but uses the Internet-standard Simple Mail Transport Protocol (SMTP), and it has the lowest number of items on the CVE list. For all of these reasons, we'll use Postfix rather than Sendmail as our MTA.

Securing email involves keeping unauthorized users off the server altogether (so they can't use it to send unsolicited bulk email), making sure that nobody can spoof legitimate users, and protecting the content of each email from being snooped on or changed in transit.

Weak email security makes it easy for imposters to spoof users. To promote authentication, we will install Postfix with Transport Layer Security (TLS), a protocol better known as the Secure Sockets Layer (SSL). This prevents the sending of clear-text passwords from an email client to the server.

We also want users to authenticate or log into our mail server. To this end, we will employ the Simple Authentication and Security Layer (SASL). This creates an extension (ESMTP) that allows an SMTP client to authenticate the server.

To install the packages needed by Postfix and the other mail components, enter:

```
# apt-get install postfix postfix-tls libsasl2 sasl2-bin \
libsasl2-modules ipopd-ssl uw-imapd-ssl
```

As Debian installs the packages, it will present some full-screen (*ncurses*-based) boxes that ask you several questions.

When you see the "Configuring ipopd" screen shown in Figure 2-1, select `pop3` and `pop3s`.

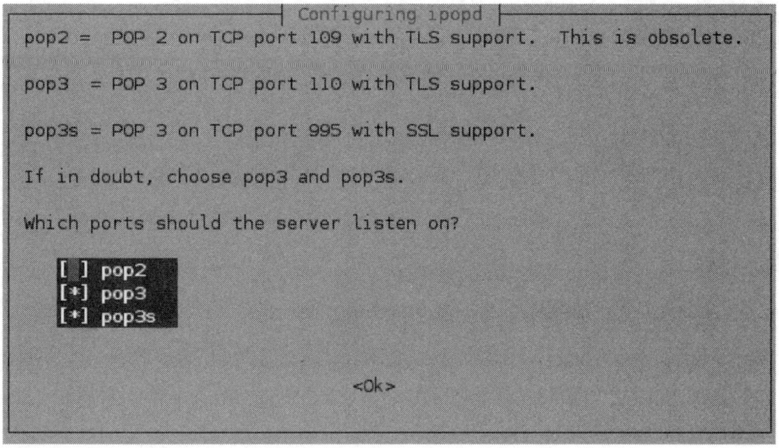

```
Configuring ipopd
pop2 =  POP 2 on TCP port 109 with TLS support.  This is obsolete.

pop3  = POP 3 on TCP port 110 with TLS support.

pop3s = POP 3 on TCP port 995 with SSL support.

If in doubt, choose pop3 and pop3s.

Which ports should the server listen on?

    [ ] pop2
    [*] pop3
    [*] pop3s

                         <Ok>
```

Figure 2-1. Debian mail configuration screen

Next you will see a screen like the one in Figure 2-2, where you should select `<No>` to provide the flexibility to reroute ports if you feel the need later. The default ports work here because we're using TLS and a SASL daemon.

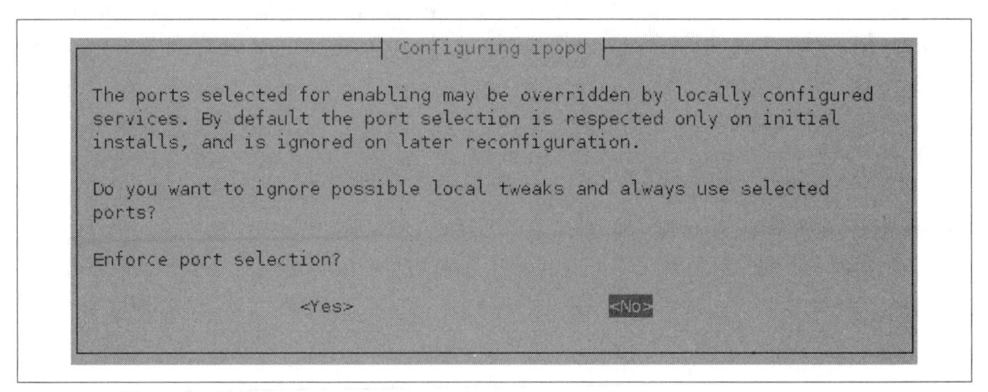

Figure 2-2. Leaving the default ports for mail

Figure 2-3 is informational; the Debian installer is telling you what options you have for a mail configuration. Press OK to get the screen in Figure 2-4, which lets you choose an option. For our purposes, we choose Internet Site, because we will use SMTP for all traffic, either inside a LAN or outside on the Internet. Debian will then provide the kind of configuration file that best fits our needs. We can later add to this default configuration.

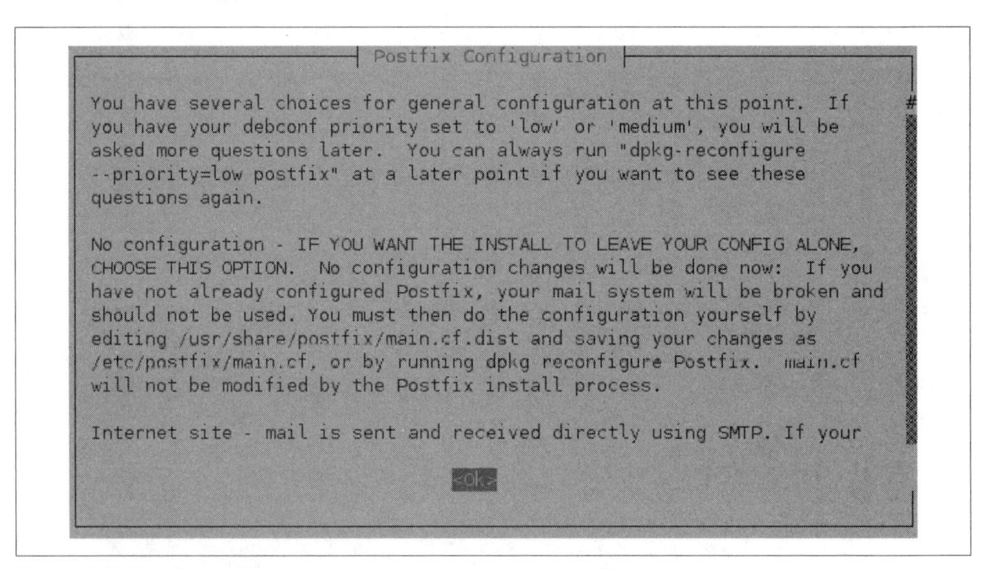

Figure 2-3. Postfix configuration options

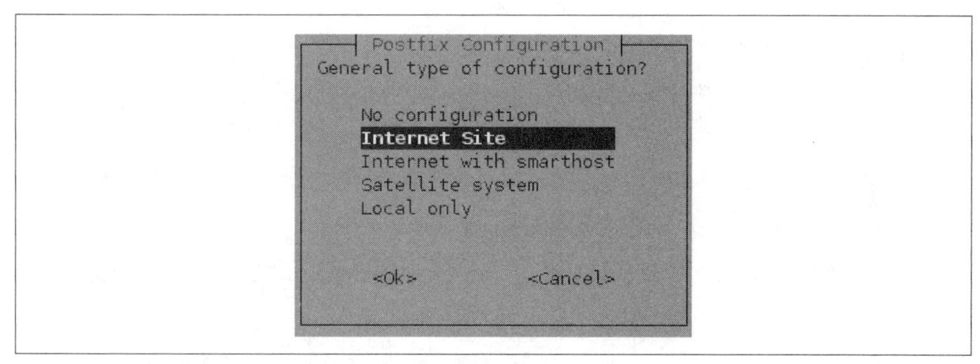

Figure 2-4. Selecting Internet Site from the configuration menu

When you set up Postfix to run mail, it will function as a standard mail transfer agent. You will not choose the option in Figure 2-4 to use another mail server as a smarthost. In other words, your system will be the mail authority for your domain. If you have used another server (such as a popular portal or an ISP) to send and receive mail in the past, your server will take over those chores now.

Next, in the screen shown in Figure 2-5, answer `NONE`. Postfix will then create its own alias file.

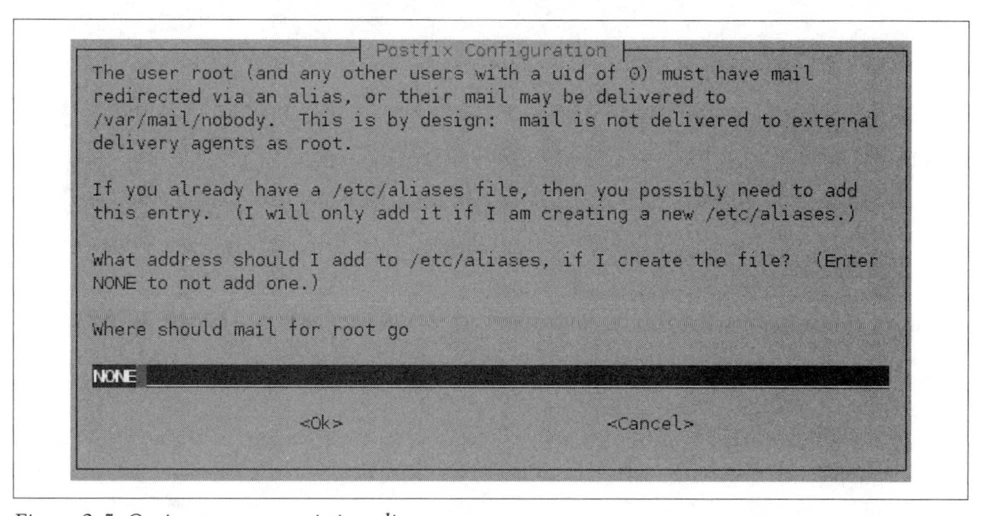

Figure 2-5. Option to use an existing alias account

In Figures 2-6 and 2-7, the Postfix configurator wants to know for whom it will accept and deliver mail. The top domain name is also the "mail name." Postfix will use this name to verify mail directed to the server. When you reach the screens shown in Figures 2-6 and 2-7, they will have default values in the blue text boxes. You can accept Figure 2-6 as it's shown to you.

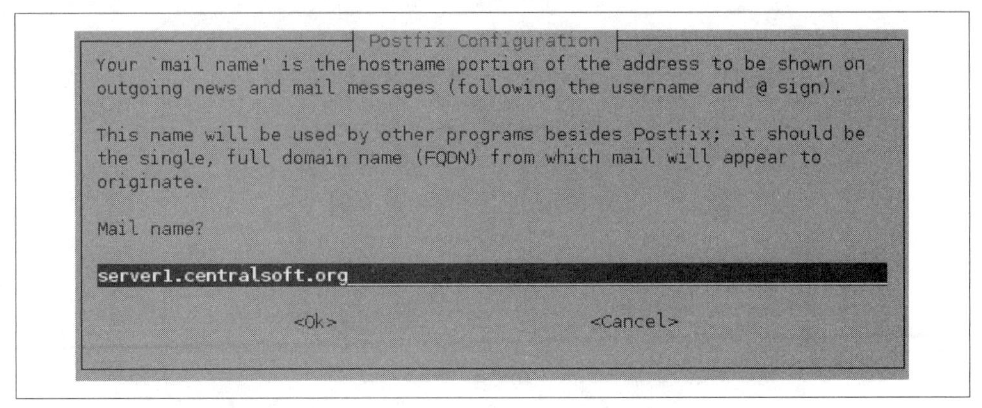

Figure 2-6. Checking the fully qualified domain name set for Postfix

centralsoft.org is the domain name we use in this book, but be sure to substitute your domain name.

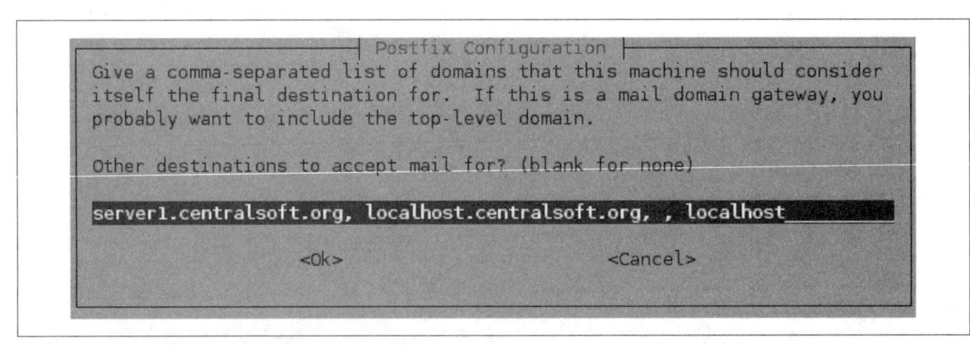

Figure 2-7. Internal domain list in used in Postfix

In Figure 2-7, you will notice that two commas follow the name *localhost.centralsoft.org*. Remove the second comma.

In Figure 2-8, the Postfix configurator inquires about *synchronous updating*. We will cover administering mail servers in greater detail in Chapter 5; for now, answer `<No>` to the question and move along.

After Debian finishes installing and you see the console return to the system prompt, you'll need to start pulling together the various mail components. That means you will write entries to the Postfix configuration file and generate certificates and encryption keys.

We warned you about this part of the setup at the beginning of the chapter. Some of these commands will not make sense to you. Don't worry about that, but you may

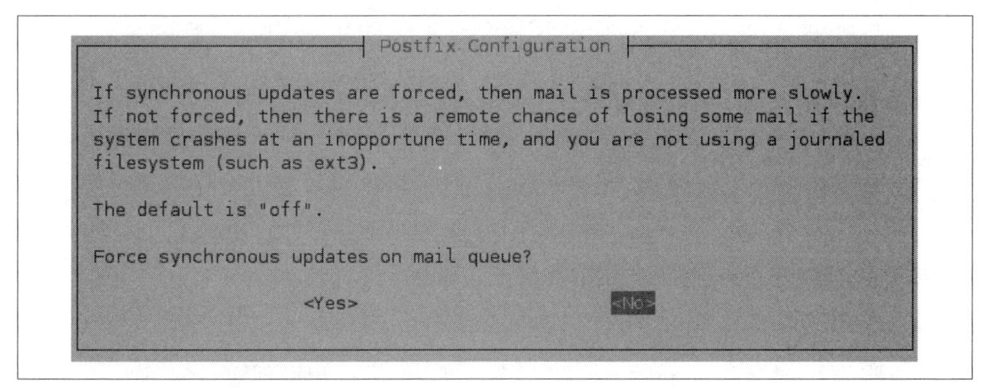

Postfix Configuration
If synchronous updates are forced, then mail is processed more slowly.
If not forced, then there is a remote chance of losing some mail if the
system crashes at an inopportune time, and you are not using a journaled
filesystem (such as ext3).
The default is "off".
Force synchronous updates on mail queue?
<Yes>
<No>

Figure 2-8. Refusing synchronous updates

get some sense of where you're going by looking back at the paragraphs that laid out our tasks at the beginning of this section.

The *postconf* command lives in the */usr/sbin* directory. You'll use it to print the value of a Postfix parameter in the Postfix *main.cf* configuration file.

Since you already installed Postfix and Debian set it up as a service, you need to tell Postfix what to do about secure authentication. Use the following commands:

```
# postconf -e 'smtpd_sasl_local_domain ='
# postconf -e 'smtpd_sasl_auth_enable = yes'
# postconf -e 'smtpd_sasl_security_options = noanonymous'
# postconf -e 'broken_sasl_auth_clients = yes'
# postconf -e 'smtpd_recipient_restrictions = \
permit_sasl_authenticated,permit_mynetworks,reject_unauth_destination'
# postconf -e 'inet_interfaces = all'
```

These commands write text to the *smtpd.conf* file:

```
# echo 'pwcheck_method: saslauthd' >> /etc/postfix/sasl/smtpd.conf
# echo 'mech_list: plain login' >> /etc/postfix/sasl/smtpd.conf
```

Now create a directory for your SSL certificates and generate both the certificates and the encryption keys:

```
# mkdir /etc/postfix/ssl
# cd /etc/postfix/ssl/
# openssl genrsa -des3 -rand /etc/hosts -out smtpd.key 1024
293 semi-random bytes loaded
Generating RSA private key, 1024 bit long modulus
.........................................++++++
.....................................++++++
e is 65537 (0x10001)
Enter pass phrase for smtpd.key:
Verifying - Enter pass phrase for smtpd.key:
```

Then issue this command to change the permissions on the file containing the OpenSSL RSA key:

```
# chmod 600 smtpd.key
```

Next, generate another key and a certificate and change the existing keys to the newly generated ones:

```
# openssl req -new -key smtpd.key -out smtpd.csr
You are about to be asked to enter information that will be incorporated
into your certificate request.
What you are about to enter is what is called a Distinguished Name or a DN.
There are quite a few fields but you can leave some blank
For some fields there will be a default value,
If you enter '.', the field will be left blank.
Country Name (2 letter code) [AU]:
State or Province Name (full name) [Some-State]:
Locality Name (eg, city) []:
Organization Name (eg, company) [Internet Widgits Pty Ltd]: centralsoft.org
Organizational Unit Name (eg, section) []: web
Common Name (eg, YOUR name) []:
Email Address []:
Please enter the following 'extra' attributes
to be sent with your certificate request
A challenge password []:
An optional company name []: cso
# openssl x509 -req -days 3650 -in smtpd.csr -signkey smtpd.key -out \
smtpd.crt
Signature ok
subject=/C=US/ST=Texas/L=Dallas/O=centralsoft.org/OU=web/CN=Tom_Adelstein/
emailAddress=tom.adelstein@centralsoft.org
Getting Private key
Enter pass phrase for smtpd.key:
# openssl rsa -in smtpd.key -out smtpd.key.unencrypted
Enter pass phrase for smtpd.key:
writing RSA key
# mv -f smtpd.key.unencrypted smtpd.key
# openssl req -new -x509 -extensions v3_ca -keyout cakey.pem -out \
cacert.pem -days 3650
Generating a 1024 bit RSA private key
.....................++++++
.........................++++++
writing new private key to 'cakey.pem'
Enter PEM pass phrase:
Verifying - Enter PEM pass phrase:
-----
You are about to be asked to enter information that will be incorporated
into your certificate request.
What you are about to enter is what is called a Distinguished Name or a DN.
There are quite a few fields but you can leave some blank
For some fields there will be a default value,
If you enter '.', the field will be left blank
Country Name (2 letter code) [AU]:
State or Province Name (full name) [Some-State]:
Locality Name (eg, city) []:
Organization Name (eg, company) [Internet Widgits Pty Ltd]:
Organizational Unit Name (eg, section) []:
Common Name (eg, YOUR name) []:
Email Address []:
```

Some debate exists as to whether or not self-generated certificates require the information requested at the prompts. We recommend that you enter the appropriate information for your circumstances.

Now you need to tell Postfix about your keys and certificates, using the following *postconf* commands:

```
# postconf -e 'smtpd_tls_auth_only = no'
# postconf -e 'smtp_use_tls = yes'
# postconf -e 'smtpd_use_tls = yes'
# postconf -e 'smtp_tls_note_starttls_offer = yes'
# postconf -e 'smtpd_tls_key_file = /etc/postfix/ssl/smtpd.key'
# postconf -e 'smtpd_tls_cert_file = /etc/postfix/ssl/smtpd.crt'
# postconf -e 'smtpd_tls_CAfile = /etc/postfix/ssl/cacert.pem'
# postconf -e 'smtpd_tls_loglevel = 1'
# postconf -e 'smtpd_tls_received_header = yes'
# postconf -e 'smtpd_tls_session_cache_timeout = 3600s'
# postconf -e 'tls_random_source = dev:/dev/urandom'
```

The */etc/postfix/main.cf* file should now look like this:

```
# See /usr/share/postfix/main.cf.dist for a commented, more complete
# version
smtpd_banner = $myhostname ESMTP $mail_name (Debian/GNU)
biff = no
# Appending .domain is the MUA's job
append_dot_mydomain = no
# Uncomment the next line to generate "delayed mail" warnings
#delay_warning_time = 4h
myhostname = server1.example.com
alias_maps = hash:/etc/aliases
alias_database = hash:/etc/aliases
myorigin = /etc/mailname
mydestination = server1.example.com, localhost.example.com, localhost
relayhost =
mynetworks = 127.0.0.0/8
mailbox_command = procmail -a "$EXTENSION"
mailbox_size_limit = 0
recipient_delimiter = +
inet_interfaces = all
smtpd_sasl_local_domain =
smtpd_sasl_auth_enable = yes
smtpd_sasl_security_options = noanonymous
broken_sasl_auth_clients = yes
smtpd_recipient_restrictions =
permit_sasl_authenticated,permit_mynetworks,reject_unauth_destination
smtpd_tls_auth_only = no
smtp_use_tls = yes
smtpd_use_tls = yes
smtp_tls_note_starttls_offer = yes
smtpd_tls_key_file = /etc/postfix/ssl/smtpd.key
smtpd_tls_cert_file = /etc/postfix/ssl/smtpd.crt
smtpd_tls_CAfile = /etc/postfix/ssl/cacert.pem
```

```
smtpd_tls_loglevel = 1
smtpd_tls_received_header = yes
smtpd_tls_session_cache_timeout = 3600s
tls_random_source = dev:/dev/urandom
```

If your file matches this one, you can use this command to implement the changes:

```
# /etc/init.d/postfix restart
Stopping mail transport agent: Postfix.
Starting mail transport agent: Postfix.
```

Authentication will be done by *saslauthd*, a SASL daemon, but you'll have to change a few things to make it work properly. Because Postfix runs chrooted in */var/spool/postfix*, enter the following commands:

```
# mkdir -p /var/spool/postfix/var/run/saslauthd
# rm -fr /var/run/saslauthd
```

Now you have to edit */etc/default/saslauthd* in order to activate *saslauthd*. Remove the # sign in front of `START=yes` and add the line `PARAMS="-m /var/spool/postfix/var/run/saslauthd"`, so that the file looks like this:

```
# This needs to be uncommented before saslauthd will be run automatically
START=yes
PARAMS="-m /var/spool/postfix/var/run/saslauthd"
# You must specify the authentication mechanisms you wish to use.
# This defaults to "pam" for PAM support, but may also include
# "shadow" or "sasldb", like this:
# MECHANISMS="pam shadow"
MECHANISMS="pam"
```

Finally, edit */etc/init.d/saslauthd*. Change the line:

```
dir=`dpkg-statoverride --list $PWDIR`
```

to:

```
#dir=`dpkg-statoverride --list $PWDIR`
```

Then change the variables `PWDIR` and `PIDFILE` and add the variable `dir` near the beginning of the file:

```
PWDIR="/var/spool/postfix/var/run/${NAME}"
PIDFILE="${PWDIR}/saslauthd.pid"
dir="root sasl 755 ${PWDIR}"
```

/etc/init.d/saslauthd should now look like this:

```
#!/bin/sh -e
NAME=saslauthd
DAEMON="/usr/sbin/${NAME}"
DESC="SASL Authentication Daemon"
DEFAULTS=/etc/default/saslauthd
PWDIR="/var/spool/postfix/var/run/${NAME}"
PIDFILE="${PWDIR}/saslauthd.pid"
dir="root sasl 755 ${PWDIR}"
createdir() {
# $1 = user
```

```
# $2 = group
# $3 = permissions (octal)
# $4 = path to directory
        [ -d "$4" ] || mkdir -p "$4"
        chown -c -h "$1:$2" "$4"
        chmod -c "$3" "$4"
}
test -f "${DAEMON}" || exit 0
# Source defaults file; edit that file to configure this script.
if [ -e "${DEFAULTS}" ]; then
    . "${DEFAULTS}"
fi
# If we're not to start the daemon, simply exit
if [ "${START}" != "yes" ]; then
    exit 0
fi
# If we have no mechanisms defined
if [ "x${MECHANISMS}" = "x" ]; then
    echo "You need to configure ${DEFAULTS} with mechanisms to be used"
    exit 0
fi
# Add our mechanisms with the necessary flag
PARAMS="${PARAMS} -a ${MECHANISMS}"
START="--start --quiet --pidfile ${PIDFILE} --startas ${DAEMON} --name
    ${NAME} -- ${PARAMS}"
# Consider our options
case "${1}" in
    start)
        echo -n "Starting ${DESC}: "
        #dir=`dpkg-statoverride --list $PWDIR`
        test -z "$dir" || createdir $dir
        if start-stop-daemon ${START} >/dev/null 2>&1 ; then
                echo "${NAME}."
        else
                if start-stop-daemon --test ${START} >/dev/null 2>&1; then
                        echo "(failed)."
                        exit 1
                else
                        echo "${DAEMON} already running."
                        exit 0
                fi
        fi
        ;;
  stop)
        echo -n "Stopping ${DESC}: "
        if start-stop-daemon --stop --quiet --pidfile "${PIDFILE}" \
                --startas ${DAEMON} --retry 10 --name ${NAME} \
                >/dev/null 2>&1 ; then
                        echo "${NAME}."
        else
                if start-stop-daemon --test ${START} >/dev/null 2>&1; then
                        echo "(not running)."
                        exit 0
                else
```

```
                        echo "(failed)."
                        exit 1
                fi
        fi
        ;;
  restart|force-reload)
          $0 stop
        exec $0 start
        ;;
  *)
        echo "Usage: /etc/init.d/${NAME} {start|stop|restart|force-reload}" >&2
        exit 1
        ;;
esac
exit 0
```

Now start *saslauthd*:

```
# /etc/init.d/saslauthd start
Starting SASL Authentication Daemon: changed ownership of
`/var/spool/postfix/var/run/saslauthd' to root:sasl
saslauthd.
```

To see whether SMTP-AUTH and TLS work properly, run the following command:

```
# telnet localhost 25
Trying 127.0.0.1...
Connected to localhost.localdomain.
Escape character is '^]'.
220 server1.centralsoft.org ESMTP Postfix (Debian/GNU)
```

This establishes a connection to Postfix. Now type:

```
# ehlo localhost
```

If you see the lines:

```
server1:/etc/postfix# telnet localhost 25
Trying 127.0.0.1...
Connected to localhost.localdomain.
Escape character is '^]'.
220 server1.centralsoft.org ESMTP Postfix (Debian/GNU)
ehlo localhost
250-server1.centralsoft.org
250-PIPELINING
250-SIZE 10240000
250-VRFY
250-ETRN
250-STARTTLS
250-AUTH LOGIN PLAIN
250-AUTH=LOGIN PLAIN
250 8BITMIME
```

your configuration should work and you have completed this part of the mail setup. You can type **quit** and move to the next section.

Putting Apache to Work

As mentioned earlier in this chapter, we're including a web server in our initial setup because it's important for you to learn some basic server administration, and because the server can be a useful host for other tools. At the end of this chapter we'll use it to serve up web statistics generated by Webalizer.

In November 2006, Netcraft published a report stating that 60 percent of the web sites on the Internet use Apache. That makes it more widely used than all other web servers combined.

Apache is well integrated with most Linux distributions. In this section we will follow a familiar pattern and install and configure Apache by running the following command:

```
# apt-get install apache2 apache2-doc
Setting up ssl-cert (1.0-11) ...
Setting up apache2-utils (2.0.54-5) ...
Setting up apache2-common (2.0.54-5) ...
Setting Apache2 to Listen on port 80. If this is not desired, please edit
/etc/apache2/ports.conf as desired. Note that the Port directive no longer
works.
Module userdir installed; run /etc/init.d/apache2 force-reload to enable.
Setting up apache2-mpm-worker (2.0.54-5) ...
Starting web server: Apache2.
Setting up apache2 (2.0.54-5) ...
Setting up apache2-doc (2.0.54-5) ...
```

Once Debian finishes installing the *apache httpd* server, run:

```
# apt-get install libapache2-mod-php4 libapache2-mod-perl2 \
php4 php4-cli php4-common php4-curl php4-dev php4-domxml \
php4-gd php4-imap php4-ldap php4-mcal php4-mhash php4-mysql \
php4-odbc php4-pear php4-xslt curl libwww-perl imagemagick
```

This command fetches and configures 48 files, so it will take a while. Once it's done, you can move to the next step.

Change the DirectoryIndex directive in the */etc/apache2/apache2.conf* file from:

```
DirectoryIndex index.html index.cgi index.pl index.php index.xhtml
```

to:

```
DirectoryIndex index.html index.htm index.shtml index.cgi index.php
index.php3 index.pl index.xhtml
```

Next, add # marks as shown, to comment out the following lines in the */etc/mime.types* file:

```
#application/x-httpd-php                    phtml pht php
#application/x-httpd-php-source             phps
#application/x-httpd-php3                   php3
#application/x-httpd-php3-preprocessed      php3p
#application/x-httpd-php4                   php4
```

You will also need to comment out two lines in */etc/apache2/mods-enabled/php4.conf*:

```
<IfModule mod_php4.c>
#AddType application/x-httpd-php .php .phtml .php3
#AddType application/x-httpd-php-source .phps
</IfModule>
```

Then make sure that the following two lines are present in the */etc/apache2/ports.conf* file, adding them if necessary:

```
Listen 80
Listen 443
```

Now you have to enable some Apache modules (*SSL*, *rewrite*, and *suexec*) by symbolically linking them to files in the *mods-enabled* subdirectory:

```
# cd /etc/apache2/mods-enabled
# ln -s /etc/apache2/mods-available/ssl.conf ssl.conf
# ln -s /etc/apache2/mods-available/ssl.load ssl.load
# ln -s /etc/apache2/mods-available/rewrite.load rewrite.load
# ln -s /etc/apache2/mods-available/suexec.load suexec.load
# ln -s /etc/apache2/mods-available/include.load include.load
```

As you saw when installing other processes earlier in this chapter, installing the proper modules with *apt-get* automatically starts Apache on the system. Because you've made several changes to the configuration, however, you need to restart Apache so the changes will take place without your rebooting the server. Enter this command:

```
# /etc/init.d/apache2 restart
```

Your web server will restart and enable the new modules, along with your configuration changes.

Adding FTP Services with ProFTPD

Along with the *httpd* server for displaying web pages in a browser, you'll want to implement a File Transfer Protocol (FTP) server. We will use the open source tool ProFTPD for this purpose because it is popular, secure, and configurable.

The FTP server uses a single main configuration file, with directives and directive groups that any administrator who has ever used the Apache web server will understand. ProFTPD has per-directory *.ftpaccess* configuration files similar to Apache's *.htaccess* files, which force users to enter their user IDs and passwords to access individual directories.

ProFTPD allows you to configure multiple virtual FTP servers and anonymous FTP services. It does not execute any external programs at any time and runs as an unprivileged user.

Install ProFTPD by executing this command:

```
# apt-get install proftpd
```

Figure 2-9 shows the screen you'll see once Debian downloads and begins installing ProFTPD. ProFTPD can be run either standalone or as a service from *inetd*. For security reasons, we'll run ProFTPD in standalone mode.

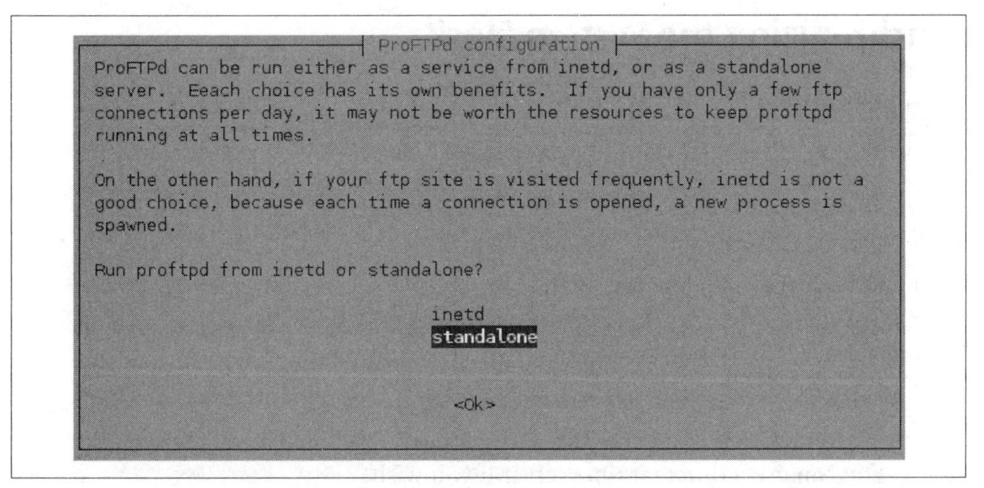

Figure 2-9. Debian configuration screen for ProFTPd

Next, add the following lines to your */etc/proftpd.conf* file:

```
DefaultRoot ~
IdentLookups off
ServerIdent on "FTP Server ready."
```

Now, as we have done with other processes, restart ProFTPD using this command:

```
# /etc/init.d/proftpd restart
```

Summarizing Your Web Statistics with Webalizer

Webalizer develops statistical reports for web server logfiles. You can use it with a standard web browser, and it produces detailed, easily configurable usage reports in HTML format.

The Debian project includes Webalizer in its stable repositories, so you can install it with this command:

```
# apt-get install webalizer
```

During the installation you'll need to verify the installation directory (*/var/www/webalizer*), the name to be used in the titles of the statistical reports (you could specify your domain name, for instance), and the location of the web server's log file (which on our system is */var/log/apache/access.log.1*):

```
Which directory should webalizer put the output in?
/var/www/webalizer
Enter the title of the reports webalizer will generate.
```

```
Usage Statistics for server1.centralsoft.org
What is the filename of the rotated webserver log?
/var/log/apache/access.log.1
```

Synchronizing the System Clock

Computer systems' clocks tend to drift. Therefore, a fairly basic configuration task is to connect your system to a Network Time Protocol (NTP) server that will keep it within a couple of seconds of the correct time.

To synchronize your system clock with an NTP server, add the following lines to */var/spool/cron/crontabs/root*:

```
# update time with NTP server
0 3,9,15,21 * * * /usr/sbin/rdate 128.2.136.71 | logger -t NTP
```

If the file doesn't exist, you can create it with the command:

```
# touch /var/spool/cron/crontabs/root
```

The IP address 128.2.136.71 belongs to Carnegie Mellon University's public time server. You can use a different time server if you wish.

Modify permissions on the *crontab* file by running:

```
# chmod 600 /var/spool/cron/crontabs/root
```

and restart the *cron* service by running:

```
# /etc/init.d/cron restart
```

Installing Perl Modules Needed by SpamAssassin

Many tools depend on the Perl programming language or offer a Perl interface to let you customize them (although other languages are gaining adherents in the open source and Unix worlds). SpamAssassin, a critical tool for mail administrators (and even mail users), is one program we'll use in this book that relies on Perl. As a system administrator, even if you don't want to program in Perl, you should be able to download Perl modules from the most popular and trusted repository, the Comprehensive Perl Archive Network (CPAN).

To give you a feel for installing Perl modules, we'll add a few now using the Perl CPAN shell. This is an environment for searching the archive and installing modules from it.

Log into your command line as *root* and run the following command to start the Perl CPAN shell:

```
server1:/home/admin# perl -MCPAN -e shell
/etc/perl/CPAN/Config.pm initialized.
```

Answer all the questions by pressing the Return key to accept the defaults. Then run the following commands to install the modules we'll use in the next chapter:

```
> install HTML::Parser
> install DB_File
> install Net::DNS
```

At the `enable tests?` prompt, answer `no`.

If a module already exists on your system, you will see a message like `HTML::Parser is up to date`. When a module installs successfully, you will see `/usr/bin/make install - OK`.

Once you're done, simply enter `q` to leave Perl and return to the system prompt.

What's Next

Now that you have completed the tasks associated with setting up your server, you will want to start using it in a production mode. You will need to set up your DNS services and notify the registrar where you set up your domain (the subject of the next chapter). Once you're done with DNS configuration, you can install a web-based application (we'll use ISPConfig) and begin to explore how web applications work.

CHAPTER 3
The Domain Name System

This chapter shows you how to build a Domain Name System (DNS) server using BIND. When you finish this material you should understand how to install, configure, maintain, and troubleshoot a server for any domain you register. We'll begin with an introduction to DNS, which you can skip if you'd rather move directly to the step-by-step installation and configuration section. If you run into problems, you may want to come back and read and/or review the earlier material.

DNS Basics

If you do any research on the Internet's DNS, you are certain to encounter the claim that DNS is the world's largest database. Comparing it to a database like Oracle or MySQL is misleading, though. In fact, DNS is the world's largest distributed digital directory. Like an online telephone directory, you use it to match names with numbers—but with DNS, the numbers are the IP addresses of the multitude of servers connected to the Internet, including those that manage small web sites and gigantic server farms like Google and Amazon.

Like the public library with its master collection of phone books separated by states, DNS separates domains into categories. The master collection of categories lives in what we call *root directories*. This collection is divided into top-level domains (TLDs), in much the same way that the master collection of phone books is divided into states. Instead of looking for a telephone number with a New York area code, DNS looks for names than end in suffixes like *.edu*, *.org*, *.com*, *.net*, *.mil*, *.de*, *.fr*, and so on. The domains within each TLD eventually lead to an address you can use to communicate with a server.

The DNS (originally defined in RFC 882 in 1983, and later revised as RFCs 1034 and 1035) introduced various ideas for managing the mapping of common Internet names to IP addresses. The system distributes data and the naming of hosts hierarchically in a *domain name space*. Each domain resembles a branch of a tree and each branch contains sub-branches. Programs called *nameservers* provide information about their parts of the tree, and *resolvers* request domain information from nameservers on behalf of client programs.

Hierarchical naming schemes like DNS prevent duplication of data. Each domain is unique, and you can have as many servers as you like within a domain—simply prefix their hostnames to the domain name. A site that controls *centralsoft.org*, for example, might have any number of hosts with names like *server1.centralsoft.org*, *ldap.centralsoft.org*, and *mail.centralsoft.org*.

Advantages of Localized DNS Administration

Smaller organizations often let their ISPs handle DNS administration for them. Setting up your own servers has advantages, though. It gives you total control over which systems host your public services (e.g., web services and email), and putting DNS into your infrastructure allows you more scalability: you can add servers as needed and even do load balancing among them. This becomes important if you own and operate several active domains or internal authentication services. You also have more control over keeping your names updated. In short, it's valuable to control your own DNS in today's business environment, instead of having somebody else do it.

Many companies have web-enabled their core business applications. Rather than replacing working systems, they want to make their legacy applications available through snazzy new web interfaces. Businesses do this by adding web frontends while using web-based backends to connect disparate systems together. IT departments use application servers such as JBoss (now owned by Red Hat), IBM's WebSphere, and BEA's WebLogic for the backends and numerous products for the frontends. In every case, DNS becomes an integral part of web-enabling because such systems use directory servers that communicate with one another.

DNS also holds a prominent place in the emergence of web services and an executable Internet, where people can use applications such as those offered by Google, Yahoo!, and others. Resolving IP addresses quickly and dependably is critical to the success of these products outside on the Internet and inside enterprises. Consider DNS configuration and management one of the most valuable system administration skill sets you can have.

So what do you need to do as a system administrator running your own public DNS servers? You must provide the addresses of two or more such servers to your domain registrar (at least two are required, so there's a good chance one will always be running when people request a name). You also must manage the domain names of the systems you want publicly visible: your web servers, mail servers, and so on.

As you begin to learn DNS, you will likely find it unintuitive. In many ways, the jargon feels like a foreign language. It won't make a lot of sense until you've worked with it for a while. We'll show you how to build a DNS server in a moment. Then we'll review some key concepts and terms before diving into the configuration files.

Getting into the BIND

Most of the DNS servers in the world are run by the Berkeley Internet Name Daemon, or BIND. BIND is standard on every version of Unix and Linux. Since administrators are certain to run into it, this chapter covers BIND in detail.

The most popular alternative to BIND is the *djbdns* suite. It works well, is used by many large nameservers, and has an arguably simpler configuration. See *http://cr.yp.to/djbdns.html* for details.

We won't offer a history lesson on BIND, because the subject would put you to sleep. Still, we do need to address one historical concern. Some people continue to use an antiquated, deprecated release of BIND: version 4. In this chapter, we use the newer version 9.

If you work on a system with DNS configuration files that look different from the syntax shown in this chapter, it's probably because the system uses BIND 4. As we said earlier, businesses hate to replace working systems, and it may require a catastrophe to get an IT department to upgrade to BIND 8 or 9. Because of the potential for security exploits in BIND 4, however, you should strongly suggest such an upgrade. (By the way, the version numbering jumped from 4 to 8 to match Sendmail's versions; don't let anyone sell you BIND 5, 6, or 7.)

Components of BIND

BIND comes with three components. The first is the service or daemon that runs the answering side of DNS. This component is called *named* (pronounced *name-dee*). It answers the phone when it rings.

The second item in the BIND bundle is the *resolver* library. This is what web browsers, mail software, and other applications consult when trying to find a server by its DNS name out there in the Internet jungle.

Some folks think of a resolver as a client inside BIND. But unlike the server, the client is no single program; instead, it's a library linked with every web browser, email client, and so on. The resolver code queries DNS servers in an attempt to translate names into IP addresses.

This piece of BIND uses its own little directory called *resolv.conf*, which is present on each computer system. It's your job to configure *resolv.conf*. Here's what the *resolv.conf* file looks like on computers in the *centralsoft.org* domain:

```
search centralsoft.org
nameserver 70.253.158.42
nameserver 70.253.158.45
```

As you can see, the BIND resolver's configuration file is simple. The first line searches for a server in the local domain. The other lines provide addresses of nameservers the administrator knows about, which a resolver can fall back on if the initial search for a server fails.

The third part of BIND provides tools such as the *dig* command for testing DNS. Go to your console and type *dig yahoo.com* (or any known domain), and see what happens. We'll discuss *dig* and the other utilities in this toolkit later.

Setting Up a DNS Server

To build our server, we're going to use a fresh installation of the latest stable version of Debian and configure it with the minimum number of packages.

If you don't already have the net installation disk used in Chapter 2, download it from *http://www.us.debian.org/CD/netinst*. Perform a netinstall and make sure to provide a fully qualified domain name. Then configure Debian as suggested here.

When you acquire the current release of Debian GNU/Linux, you may find differences between it and the version we used to write the following instructions. Linux developers update their distributions frequently, and installation procedures change with updates, patches, and new versions of the Linux kernel. If you do encounter differences in the installation procedures we describe, look for the gist of what we explain and you should have little trouble following along with the latest release.

After the initial stages of the Debian install, you'll see a graphic screen asking you to choose the type of installation you want. The screen will look like this:

```
( ) Desktop Environment
( ) Web Server
( ) Print Server
( ) DNS Server
( ) File Server
( ) Mail Server
( ) SQL database
( ) manual package selection
```

Don't select any of the options; just press the Tab key. Click the highlighted OK button, and Debian's installer will begin downloading and installing packages.

During the downloads, you'll see one more graphical screen. This screen will ask if you want to configure Exim (*Exim-config*). Choose "no configuration." It will then ask you, "Really leave the mail system unconfigured?" Answer yes.

Once you've completed the minimal Debian installation, you should remove some unnecessary programs that may have some use in a LAN but do not belong on an Internet mail server. You can delete them using Debian's *apt-get* utility:

```
# apt-get remove lpr nfs-common portmap pidentd pcmcia-cs pppoe \
pppoeconf ppp pppconfig
```

If you have decided to use SUSE or Fedora instead of Debian, you can delete these packages with your preferred method.

Now, let's snip some out some service scripts and restart *inetd*:

```
# update-inetd --remove daytime
# update-inetd --remove telnet
# update-inetd --remove time
# update-inetd --remove finger
# update-inetd --remove talk
# update-inetd --remove ntalk
# update-inetd --remove ftp
# update-inetd --remove discard
# /etc/init.d/inetd reload
```

To install BIND on your Debian server, run the command:

```
# apt-get install bind9
```

Debian will download the file and configure it as an Internet service. You will see the following messages on your console:

```
Setting up bind9 (9.2.4-1)
Adding group `bind' (104)
Done.
Adding system user `bind'
Adding new user `bind' (104) with group `bind'.
Not creating home directory.
Starting domain name service: named.
```

Using a chroot Environment for Security

Many security administrators recommend running BIND as a non-*root* user in an isolated directory called a *chroot environment*. This protects against the substantial chance that a security flaw will be found in your version of BIND, potentially enabling outsiders to attack the *named* daemon and gain access to your system. Even if *named* is exploited, a chroot environment limits any damage that can be done to name services.

To put BIND in a chroot environment, you need to create a directory where the service can run unexposed to other processes. You will also run it as an unprivileged user, but only *root* will be able to access the directory. This directory will contain all the files that BIND needs, and it will look like the whole filesystem to BIND after you issue the *chroot* command.

First, stop the service by running this command:

```
# /etc/init.d/bind9 stop
```

Next, edit the file */etc/default/bind9* so that the daemon will run as the unprivileged user *bind*, chrooted to */var/lib/named*. Change the line:

```
OPTS="-u bind"
```

so that it reads:

```
OPTIONS="-u bind -t /var/lib/named"
```

To provide a complete environment for running BIND, create the necessary directories under */var/lib:*

```
# mkdir -p /var/lib/named/etc
# mkdir /var/lib/named/dev
# mkdir -p /var/lib/named/var/cache/bind
# mkdir -p /var/lib/named/var/run/bind/run
```

Then move the *config* directory from */etc* to */var/lib/named/etc*:

```
# mv /etc/bind /var/lib/named/etc
```

Now create a symbolic link to the new *config* directory from the old location, to avoid problems when BIND is upgraded in the future:

```
# ln -s /var/lib/named/etc/bind /etc/bind
```

Make null and random devices for use by BIND, and fix the directory permissions:

```
# mknod /var/lib/named/dev/null c 1 3
# mknod /var/lib/named/dev/random c 1 8
```

Then change the permissions and ownership of the files:

```
# chmod 666 /var/lib/named/dev/null /var/lib/named/dev/random
# chown -R bind:bind /var/lib/named/var/*
# chown -R bind:bind /var/lib/named/etc/bind
```

You'll also need to change the startup script */etc/init.d/sysklogd* so that you can still see messages in the system logs. Change the line:

```
SYSLOGD=""
```

so that it reads:

```
SYSLOGD="-a /var/lib/named/dev/log"
```

Now restart the logging process with the command:

```
# /etc/init.d/sysklogd restart
```

You will see the following message:

```
Restarting system log daemon: syslogd.
```

Finally, start BIND:

```
# /etc/init.d/bind9 start
```

Check */var/log/syslog* for any errors. You can page through the file using:

```
# less /var/log/syslog
```

Typically, you'll know that BIND succeeded in starting if the *syslog* file shows:

```
Starting domain name service: named.
```

Unfortunately, *named* can start but fail to load its initial data files, which leaves it nonfunctional. So, check to see whether *named* is functioning by entering:

```
# rndc status
number of zones: 6
debug level: 0
xfers running: 0
xfers deferred: 0
soa queries in progress: 0
query logging is OFF
server is up and running
server1:/home/admin#
```

If DNS is not working correctly, you'll instead see something like this:

```
# rndc status
rndc: neither /etc/bind/rndc.conf nor /etc/bind/rndc.key was found
```

If you get this error, take a look at the "Cannot Connect Using rndc" section toward the end of this chapter.

Configuring an Authoritative DNS Server

If you want to find Jane Doe's telephone number in a digital phone book, the phone company publishes that information. But if you want to be able to find *janedoe.com*, a system administrator has to come forward with the domain name and number (IP address) and make them part of the distributed DNS directory. Administrators do this by creating listings in what DNS aficionados call *zone files*.

A *zone* holds the information for a domain or, continuing with our earlier telephone analogy, for a household. Say there are 15 kids living in your house, and someone who's looking for one of them calls you. Each kid has a cell phone, but you don't know all of their numbers by heart. Instead, you have a listing of your own, a directory you look in to find the cell phone number for the child the caller is trying to reach.

Similarly, you might have 15 servers living in your data center, or 15 web sites hosted on your server. To illustrate this, let's say you administer a server that hosts five different web sites, each with a completely different domain name. Suppose one is *centralsoft.org*, while the others are *linhelp.com*, *supportcall.org*, *jdshelp.net*, and *linuxconf.net*. All the owners of the web sites ask you to manage their DNS records. BIND's versatility allows you to manage several DNS servers at once, and to manage multiple domains independently on one server.

Each web site is in a different domain, so you have to write a zone file for each web site. In the registrars' databases, your DNS server will be listed as the *nameserver* for those domain names. In other words, *server1.centralsoft.org* will be listed as the guy outsiders can contact to find the other kids in the house (*linhelp.com*, *supportcall.org*, and the others).

The file that corresponds to the list of cell phone numbers in our house analogy is */etc/named.conf*. In a sense, */etc/named.conf* is your directory listing of zone files. It provides you with information about the location of each zone on your system.

Your Responsibility in DNS

As stated earlier, DNS distributes its directory. When you pay a fee and register a domain, one of the questions you answer deals with your nameservers. You have to provide the names and addresses of two servers, and they have to be registered in the DNS system.

Now you can get an idea of what the system administrator's work involves. You have to configure any nameservers under your domains so that they conform to specifications set out by the Internet Engineering Task Force (IETF). If you don't follow the specified protocols, your system won't become part of the universal directory service.

Hopefully, the preceding discussion has given you an idea of the "what" of DNS. Now let's take a closer peek at how you get your part of the directory working.

The Distributed Method of Resolving Domain Names

Let's review the DNS directory structure again. The directory has three levels. The first group of servers is called *root* servers, because they provide the starting point for queries. The second group consists of the *top-level domain* servers. TLDs include *.com*, *.net*, *.org*, *.mil*, *.gov*, *.edu*, and so on, as well as country domains such as *.de*. (Incidentally, domain names are case-insensitive: *.com* and *.COM* are the same.)

Figure 3-1 depicts the DNS structure. At the top of the figure, you can see a representation of the Internet's root servers. These servers contain only the names and IP addresses of the next level of servers and are responsible solely for redirecting requests to particular TLDs.

In the center of the figure, you see some of the servers for the *.org* TLD. These servers contain the names and IP addresses of all registered DNS servers with the suffix *.org*. If you register a domain with an *.org* suffix, its IP address will reside in each of *.org*'s TLD servers. You will have to provide the remaining information on any subdomains, including servers within your domain.

The bottom layer in Figure 3-1 represents a primary nameserver called *server1.centralsoft.org*. It functions as the DNS server for a number of domains, as you'll see later. For now, just know that *server1.centralsoft.org* represents the part of the DNS system that you will have to manage.

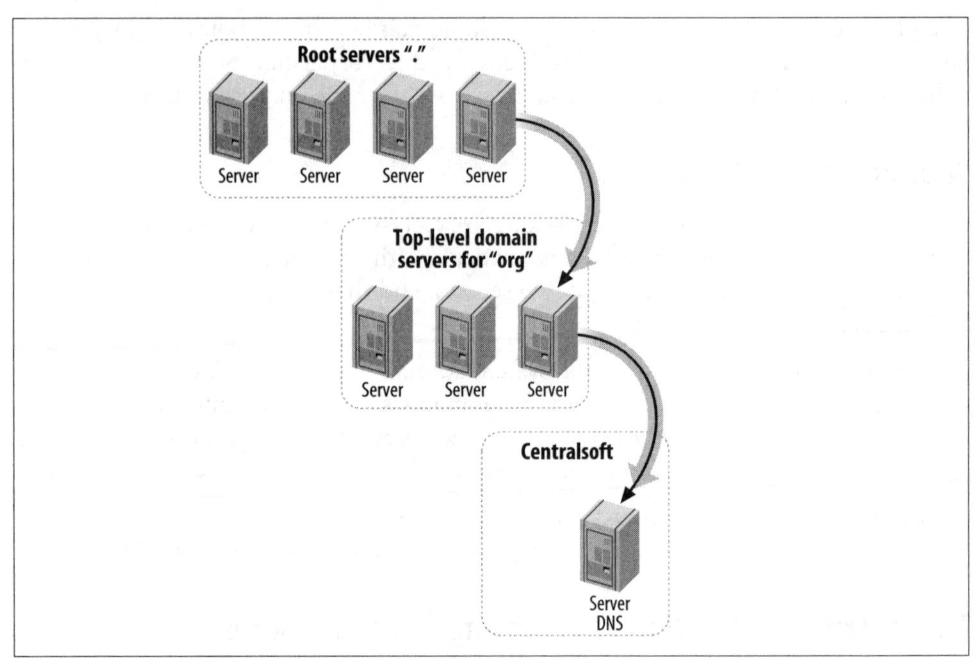

Figure 3-1. The DNS distributed directory structure

Finding a Domain

As mentioned earlier, besides providing the daemon to write the DNS entries into the distributed directory, BIND provides the mechanism for reading the directory. When your computer needs to find the address for a web site, it queries the DNS servers you specify (which are usually located on your local network or at your ISP).

Let's say your browser wants to find *www.google.com*. BIND's "client" executes a command that essentially asks its DNS server whether it knows the address of the web site. If the DNS server doesn't know the address, it asks a root server for the address.

The root server replies, "I don't know, but I do know where you can find the answer. Start with the TLD servers for *.com*." And it provides the IP address of a server that knows all the domains (quite a lot!) that are registered directly under *.com*.

On behalf of your browser, the resolver on the DNS server then queries a *.com* server for the address. The *.com* server says, "I don't have that information, but I know a nameserver that does. It has an address of 64.233.167.99 and its name is *ns1.google.com*."

Your friendly DNS server proceeds to the address, reads the directory information *ns1.google.com* provides, and comes back to tell your browser the address of *www.google.com*. The DNS server then places that information in its cache so it won't have to run around looking for Google's address again.

Basically, *resolv.conf* controls the queries that browsers and other clients make for domain names, while *named* answers the queries and makes sure information is kept up-to-date on all servers.

Answering Queries

Figure 3-2 depicts the process used to answer a query. Let's break it down.

In the upper-left corner of the figure is a drawing of a server tower (in our example this server is called *server1.centralsoft.org*; it performs the same function as *ns1.google.com*). Assume the server is running Linux and BIND. A server at a higher level directs resolvers to the system (in the case of *server1.centralsoft.org*, a TLD nameserver for the *.org* domain sends the requests).

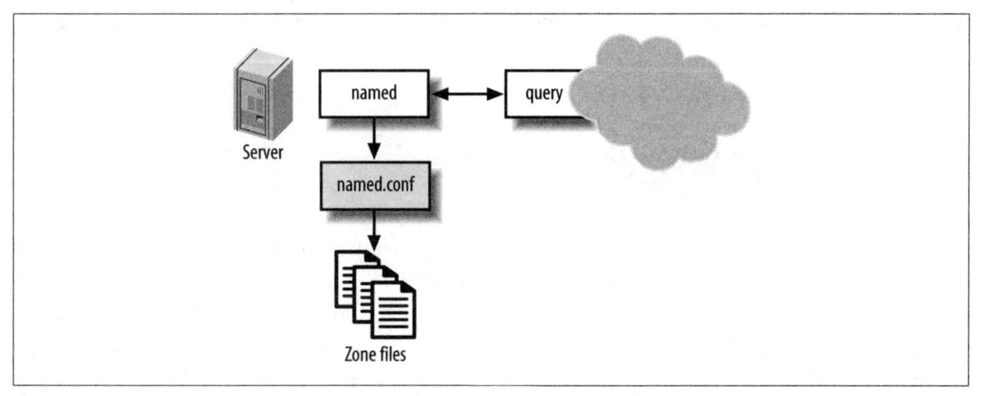

Figure 3-2. Answering a query

The *named* daemon listens on UDP port 53 for anyone making requests for names in the domain. When *named* receives a request, it consults its configuration file, */etc/named.conf*. If the server has information on the domain in question, it looks in the appropriate zone file. If the zone file has the information requested, the server hands it off to the system querying for the information.

Some people refer to configuration files as *rule files*. This makes some sense because correct DNS operation requires tight compliance with its rules and protocols. However, the zone files actually function as part of the DNS directory. Their primary function is to provide information, not to enforce rules.

Primary and Secondary DNS Servers

As we said earlier, you have to provide the names of at least two DNS servers when you register your domain. If you want, you can make an exact duplicate of the information you set up on the first DNS server you use and place it on the second server. Some providers do that, but a more common and maintainable practice is to consider one server the *primary* or *master* server (where you will make all manual updates) and the other server the *secondary* or *slave* server. BIND then allows the secondary server to contact the primary one and automatically replicate the directory—a practice called a *zone transfer*.

Secondary servers are authoritative, just as primary servers are. That is, secondary servers can respond to queries and give out information on all the zones for which they are responsible. The difference is that when you make changes, you should do so only on your primary server. The secondary servers will then obtain that information from the primary server.

The primary server does not push its new configuration to secondary servers immediately. Instead, each secondary server polls the primary server at regular intervals to find out whether any changes have been made. A secondary server knows it should poll its big brother because it is labeled with the term `slave` in its *named.conf* file, as shown here:

```
zone "centralsoft.org" {
     type slave;
     file "sec.centralsoft.org";
     masters { 70.253.158.42; };
};
```

We won't discuss the full syntax and role of this entry right now. The important things to notice are the `type slave;` line, which defines this server as secondary, and the `masters` line, which tells the server where to get its information. In this example, the master is at the IP address 70.253.158.42. This address matches what we put in the *resolv.conf* file earlier (see the section "Components of BIND"). The *resolv.conf* file helps a client connect to DNS, whereas the preceding entry in *named.conf* helps a secondary DNS server find the primary server.

Firewall Issues

If you have a firewall on your primary server, make sure you unblock UDP port 53. This port is used to receive and respond to queries. If the secondary servers lie on the other side of a firewall, you must also unblock TCP port 53. The secondary servers use both TCP and UDP to perform zone transfers, which are required to keep the servers up-to-date.

Designating the secondary server as a slave instructs it to periodically check in with the primary server to see whether any changes have been made in the domain directory files. The *named.conf* file on each server specifies how it does polling and zone transfers. The *refresh* value tells the secondary server how often it should check with the master. The *serial number* is a value you must increment on the primary server each time you change the information it offers; the secondary server compares the primary value to its own value to determine whether it should perform a zone transfer.

The primary configuration file also specifies a *retry* value, which the secondary server uses instead of the refresh value if it can't reach the primary server. This can happen if the master server or the network fails. In that case, the secondary server masquerades as the master for a little while.

A secondary server can't masquerade forever, though. Eventually, its information could become so outdated that it would be preferable for it to stop answering queries altogether. Hence, the configuration file also specifies an *expiry* time. If this time passes without a successful update, the secondary server continues trying to contact the primary server but refuses to answer queries.

There's one more value that you should be aware of before tackling the configuration files: the *minimum time to live* (TTL). When a remote DNS server receives an answer to a query from you, it caches that information and reuses it during the time specified in the TTL value. Caching is critical to the performance of DNS. Thanks to caching, if somebody spends an hour visiting various web pages at your site (each of which may involve multiple downloads), a server near the user will need to ask you for the domain name only once; thereafter, it will be able to satisfy each request out of its cache. To avoid the cached information becoming stale, however, the TTL ensures that eventually the server discards the cached value and returns to you, the authoritative server, to get the current value.

You will see all of these values in your zone file, not in the *named.conf* file. The *named.conf* file points to the location of your zone file.

Caching-Only Servers

In addition to primary and secondary servers, DNS offers caching-only servers. Administrators use these to reduce the load on authoritative servers. A caching server has no authority; it simply makes DNS work faster by storing the domain names it gets from authoritative servers and offering them to its clients.

The server you set up to host domains is usually tied up answering queries from other DNS servers on the Internet. That job alone puts a strain on its resources, so administrators often use caching servers to store information locally for user lookups. You'll see caching servers used by ISPs, for example, just to service their retail customers. They'll use another server to provide domain names to the Internet for the sites they host.

When you install BIND, it sets up a caching server by default. When you perform a query, the caching server keeps the results in its cache. The next time you attempt to find the same web site, you won't have to go through the entire search process again: you'll get the host-to-IP address information from the cache.

Editing the Configuration Files

So far, we have made a high-level exploration of the Domain Name System and explained the parts you have to maintain. We now need to get into the details of the configuration files so you can write them, change them, and fix them when the need arises.

When you install BIND on Linux, the package will provide configuration files for you; you won't have to write every file from scratch. Figure 3-3 illustrates the basic files. We'll start with the *named.conf* file, which coordinates the whole system on each BIND server and points to the rest.

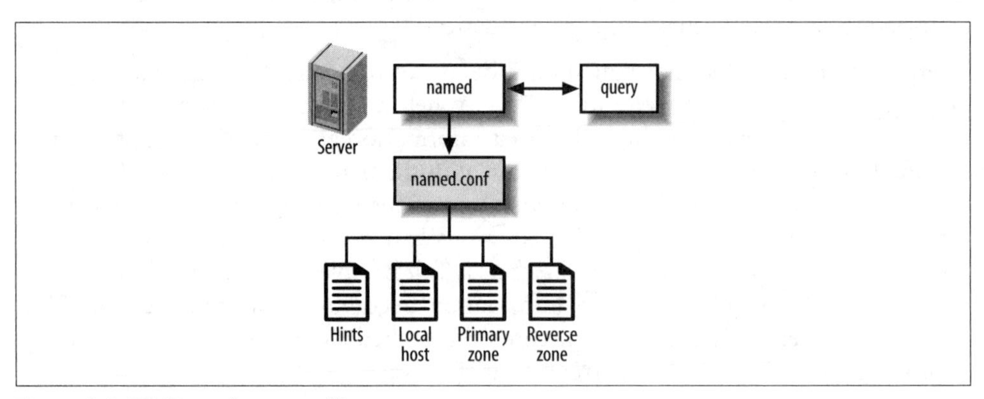

Figure 3-3. BIND configuration files

named.conf

Recall from the section "Answering Queries" that when *named* receives a request it consults its own small directory, the *named.conf* configuration file. This points *named* to the zone file for the requested domain.

Let's look at a simple *named.conf* file. If you can't understand it at this point, just familiarize yourself with the way it looks. We'll break it down into its components in a moment.

Remember, this file is typically already installed on your Linux server by default. Depending on the distribution, *named.conf* can live in different directories (it's located at */etc/bind/named.conf* for BIND 9 under Debian), and its appearance may vary slightly. Sometimes, for example, the file comes heavily commented.

Here's our sample *named.conf*. Comments follow double slash marks:

```
options {
     pid-file "/var/run/bind/run/named.pid";
     directory "/etc/bind";
     // query-source address * port 53; };
```

```
//
// a master nameserver config
//
zone "." {
     type hint;
     file "db.root";
};

zone "0.0.127.in-addr.arpa" {
     type master;
     file "db.local";
};

zone "158.253.70.in-addr.arpa" {
     type master;
     file "pri.158.253.70.in-addr.arpa";
};

zone "centralsoft.org" {
     type master;
     file "pri.centralsoft.org";
};
```

Basic Security in Data Transfers

In our current configuration, every nameserver is allowed to transfer our *centralsoft.org* zone from our primary nameserver. Because we want to allow only our secondary nameserver (70.253.158.45) to transfer the zone, we must add the following line to the *centralsoft.org* zone in the *named.conf file* on our primary nameserver, *server1.centralsoft.org*:

```
allow-transfer { 70.253.158.45; };
```

The zone should look like this:

```
zone "centralsoft.org" {
     type master;
     file "pri.centralsoft.org";
     allow-transfer { 70.253.158.45; };
};
```

The sample *named.conf* file refers to the four other configuration files. The third line down lists the directory containing them all, */etc/bind*.

The `options` statement contains two lines. The first shows the location of *named.pid*, which simply contains the process ID of the running *named* daemon. That may seem like an odd snippet of information to store, but it's very useful for utilities that have to kill or restart *named*. More significantly, the second line of the `options` statement defines the directory containing *named* and files related to how it runs.

The subsequent `zone` statements, an example of which we saw earlier, identify the locations of several files containing configuration information. In sum, *named.conf* will need to point to the following files in `zone` statements:

Hints file (for `zone "."`*)*
: This file contains the names and addresses of the root servers on the Internet. *named* must know the addresses of these servers so it can begin a query when none of the components of the requested domain are stored in *named*'s cache.

Local host file (for `zone "0.0.127.in-addr.arpa"`*)*
: This file represents your own system (IP address 127.0.0.1) to DNS. The point of creating local zone files for each aspect of your local host is to reduce traffic and allow software to operate the same way regardless of whether it is accessing your local system or a remote one.

Reverse zone file (for `zone "158.253.70.in-addr.arpa"`*)*
: This file maps IP addresses to hostnames. It's a mirror image of the primary zone file. You can recognize a reverse zone file because it has the extension *in-addr.arpa* and it uses `PTR` records (described later).

Primary zone file (for `zone "centralsoft.org"`*)*
: This file, sometimes called the *domain database*, defines most of the information needed to resolve queries about the domain you administer. It does not come preconfigured when you install BIND. Usually, you have to write this file from scratch or use one of the files accompanying BIND as a template.

  The primary zone file maps names to IP addresses and provides information about the services your computers offer to the Internet (including your web and FTP servers, email servers, nameservers, and so on).

The default configuration file will contain the first two `zone` statements (for the hints and local files—these files typically appear when you install BIND and do not need to be altered). You'll have to add the entries for the reverse and primary zone files.

Zone files use several record types, including:

- `SOA` (Start of Authority)
- `NS` (Name Server)
- `MX` (Mail eXchanger, which identifies a mail server in the domain)
- `A` (host name to Address mapping)
- `CNAME` (Canonical Name, which defines an alias for a hostname in an `A` record)
- `PTR` (Pointer, which maps addresses to names)

It's not necessary to try to memorize or understand these record types at this point. You will have ample opportunity to use them as we dig deeper into this subject.

Next, we'll look at a primary zone file and break it down.

The Primary Zone File

The primary zone file contains the bulk of the configuration information DNS needs. The format of the file is not standardized, but the elements it contains are specified by RFC 1035.

If you're using the set of files the Debian installation provides, you should name your own primary zone file after your domain. We've named the zone file for the *centralsoft.org* domain *pri.centralsoft.org*. (The *pri* prefix will help you recognize that it's primary.) We'll describe each part of the file here; to see it in its entirety, look ahead to the section "Putting it all together."

The first lines provide the information needed to sync with your secondary or slave server(s):

```
@ IN SOA server1.centralsoft.org. root.localhost. (
                        2006012103; serial-no
                        28800; refresh, seconds
                        7200; retry, seconds
                        604800; expiry, seconds
                        86400 ); minimum-TTL, seconds

;
```

This is an SOA record. SOA is the to Start of Authority, which distinguishes this as information for authoritative servers (both primary and secondary) as opposed to caching servers. By the time you write your part of the DNS distributed directory, the system has handed off authority for your part of the system to you. So your zone file has to indicate where your authority starts—that is, the domain you are serving.

A semicolon (;) does not mark the end of a line; it just marks the beginning of a comment. Thus, if you didn't want to include the "serial-no" comment, you could write the following line:

```
2006012103; serial-no
```

simply as:

```
2006012103
```

Let's look at the first line, the one beginning with the at sign (@). From left to right, the fields are:

Name
: The root name of the zone. The @ sign is a shorthand reference to the current zone in the */etc/named.conf* file. In other words, it's equivalent to using `server1.centralsoft.org` in our example. The @ sign is also known as the *origin* in DNS jargon.

Class
: The DNS class. A number of classes exist, but the vast majority of sites use the IN (Internet) class. The other classes exist for non-Internet protocols and functions.

Type
: The type of DNS resource record. In this case, this is an `SOA` resource record.

Nameserver
: The fully qualified name of the primary nameserver. One easy-to-miss detail is important: the name must end with a period (`.`), denoting the root of the DNS hierarchy, to indicate that the path is a full domain name.

Email address
: The email address of the person responsible for the domain. There is another important DNS-specific convention here: you can't use the `@` that appears in every Internet email address because, as we've seen, an `@` has another meaning in this file. Therefore, a period is substituted. Here we want to specify the *root* user on the local system, or *root@localhost*, but we have to specify that email address in the unusual format `root.localhost.`. Note that the email address must also end in a period.

The following lines in the `SOA` record contain fields for the slave server's benefit:

Serial-no
: The serial number for the current configuration. You increment this number each time you change your configuration so that slave servers will know that they have to update their information. This number is usually in a date format, YYYYMMDD, with a double-digit number tagged to the end (this allows you to do multiple edits each day). Thus, each serial number is higher than the previous one and documents the date on which the changes were made. Each slave periodically checks the serial number to see whether it has changed. If the current number on the server is higher than the one representing the slave's configuration information, the slave performs a zone transfer. `2006012103` is the starting serial number in our example zone file.

Refresh
: The interval at which a slave DNS server should check with the master to determine whether a zone transfer is required. The value is represented in seconds. In our example file we use the value `28800` (28,800 seconds = 8 hours).

Retry
: How often a slave should try to connect to the master in the event of a connection failure. The interval in our example is `7200` (7,200 seconds = 2 hours).

Expiry
: The length of time for which a slave should try to contact the master before expiring the data it contains. If the data expires and the slave is unable to contact the server for fresh information, it will direct future queries toward the root servers. The time specified here is also effectively the length of time that the slave server should continue to respond to queries even if it cannot update the zone file; it represents how long you can tolerate having outdated information handed out. In our example, we use `604800` (604,000 seconds = 7 days).

Minimum-TTL
: The default time-to-live for this domain in seconds. Any resource record that does not have a specified TTL uses the default value of 86400. Because 86,400 seconds is one day, the querying cache's record should die in one day.

That's it for the SOA record. It's followed by a list of hostnames of various types:

```
NS server1.centralsoft.org.;
NS server2.centralsoft.org.;
```

These NS records specify the nameservers for the domain (the ones you listed when you registered the domain). Once again, the semicolon is not necessary but is convenient in case you want to put a comment at the end of the line.

Next is an MX record, which identifies the mail server for the domain:

```
MX 10 server1.centralsoft.org.
```

We've used only one mail server in our example, but most production environments offer several (both to handle large loads and to provide a fallback if one fails). The second field in this record (10 in our example) can be used to indicate the order in which MX servers should be tried; it prioritizes servers.

The MX record in our sample primary zone file is followed by several A records:

```
centralsoft.org.    A 70.253.158.42
www                 A 70.253.158.42
server1             A 70.253.158.42
server2             A 70.253.158.45
```

An A record maps a name to an IP address. Because multiple names can be assigned to one computer, you can have multiple A records pointing to a single IP address. However, each hostname can have at most one A record. Our file has four A records, mapping three names to one address and one name to a different address.

Enhancements and advanced features

If you set up a file with the contents in the preceding section, just making sure to insert the proper hostnames and IP addresses for your environment, you'll have a working primary zone file. (Of course, you'll need other files too, as we'll explain later.) However, you should be aware of some other useful things you can do with the primary zone file.

MX records. As you've seen, a typical MX record looks like this:

```
MX 10 server1.centralsoft.org.
```

This record says that email addressed to the domain *centralsoft.org* should be delivered to *server1.centralsoft.org* (the mail server for the domain), which has a priority of 10.

Priorities come into play in more complex configurations, where more than one mail server is available. Lower numbers indicate higher priorities—think of `1` as being the highest priority. The priority system works as follows: the remote mail server tries to contact the server in your list with the highest priority first; if it does not respond, the server with the next-highest priority is tried, and so on down the list. Say you list more than one mail exchanger, as follows:

```
MX 10 server1.centralsoft.org.
MX 20 mail.someotherdomain.com.
```

Now if mail goes to *centralsoft.org*, the originating MTA first attempts to connect to *server1.centralsoft.org*, because it has the highest priority (`10`). If *server1.centralsoft.org* cannot be reached, the originating MTA will use the next server, *mail.someotherdomain.com*, which has a priority of `20`.

DNS doesn't specify how to treat multiple mail servers with the same priority. Many mailers choose one at random in order to implement a rough sort of load balancing.

Until now, we've defined `MX` records only for email addressed to *user@centralsoft.org*. What if you want to route email to different departments in a company or sections within a governmental agency? You can do that by adding subdomains to your `MX` records.

Thus, adding *accounting.centralsoft.org* would simply require another `MX` record:

```
accounting.centralsoft.org.   MX 10 server1.centralsoft.org.
```

Note the "." at the end of `accounting.centralsoft.org.`. If you do not add the period, the origin of the zone is appended to the name. For example, if you wrote:

```
accounting.centralsoft.org    MX 10 server1.centralsoft.org.
```

without a closing ".", this would transform to *accounting.centralsoft.org.centralsoft.org*, which of course is incorrect.

A records. `NS` and `MX` records use hostnames such as *centralsoft.org*, *server1.centralsoft.org*, and *server2.centralsoft.org*, but the primary zone file must also specify the IP addresses to which these names should map. `A` records accomplish this mapping. Many observers consider them the most important DNS records because you can use them to create host addresses such as *www.centralsoft.org*, where *www* is the host.

The following simple `A` record from our primary zone file indicates that *centralsoft.org* has the IP address 70.253.158.42:

```
centralsoft.org.        A 70.253.158.42
```

(Remember to add the period at the end of the hostname.)

In a browser, you're probably used to typing *www.centralsoft.org* instead of *centralsoft.org*. *www.centralsoft.org* is technically totally different from *centralsoft.org*, but most visitors expect to see the same web site regardless of whether they include the leading *www.* or not. Therefore, we've also created this record:

```
www                   A 70.253.158.42
```

The `www` is not followed by a period, so BIND appends the origin of the zone. The effect is the same as specifying:

```
www.centralsoft.org.  A 70.253.158.42
```

Specify the IP addresses for *server1.centralsoft.org* and *server2.centralsoft.org*:

```
server1               A 70.253.158.42
server2               A 70.253.158.45
```

The record for *server2.centralsoft.org* points to a different IP address, which makes sense because it is our secondary nameserver and therefore has to be on a different system in case our primary nameserver goes down.

The Bootstrapping Problem and Glue Records

You might wonder how *server1.centralsoft.org* and *server2.centralsoft.org* can be used to look up records for *centralsoft.org* if they are in the zone that is to be looked up. This is a classic bootstrapping problem: you can't use the same technique to start the lookup that you use for the bulk of the lookup.

The solution involves *glue records*. When the TLD servers for *.org* direct remote sites to the nameservers for *centralsoft.org*, they normally give out a name instead of an IP address (e.g., *server1.centralsoft.org* instead of 70.253.158.42). But for the authoritative DNS servers in the zone being looked up, a glue record exists on the TLD server that maps the name to an IP address (in our case, mapping *server1.centralsoft.org* to 70.253.158.42), and the TLD servers deliver the IP address instead of the name of the nameserver. This means you don't have to find it before you can ask where it is.

CNAME records. `CNAME` is short for *canonical name*; you can think of it as an alias to an `A` record. For example, this:

```
ftp              CNAME www
```

means that *ftp.centralsoft.org* is an alternative name for *www.centralsoft.org*, so *ftp.centralsoft.org* points to the same machine as *www.centralsoft.org*. You may encounter situations, especially when downloading Linux packages, where the repository looks like *http://ftp.mirrors.kernel.org*. In such cases it is almost certain that a `CNAME` record was used to assign the *ftp* part of the hostname to a system that has a different name in its `A` record.

A `CNAME` must always point to an `A` record, not to another `CNAME`. In addition, you must not use `CNAME` hostnames in `MX` or `SOA` records. This, for example, is not allowed:

```
MX 10 ftp
```

The use of CNAME records has pros and cons. Many DNS specialists advise against their use. Still, you might find that CNAME records have some value. For example, if your DNS directory contains many A records pointing to the same IP address and you move to another hosting service that assigns a different IP address, you'll have to update every A record. But if you have just one A record and all your other hostnames are in CNAME records, you'll only have to update one A record. So, we believe that CNAME records still have a place in the DNS pantheon.

TXT and SPF records. TXT records let you add text to a zone. People primarily use TXT records to embed SPF (Sender Policy Framework) records, which control whether mail exchangers should accept email addressed from their domains. The larger email providers, such as Yahoo! and Hotmail, now rely heavily on SPF records to prevent spammers from forging email addresses with the providers' domain names. If email arrives from a machine that is not listed in the SPF record, an MTA may classify it as spam.

A wizard for creating SPF records can be found at *http://www.openspf.org/wizard.html?mydomain=&x=26&y=8*. We used this wizard to create two SPF records for *centralsoft.org*, then embedded them in TXT records and added them to our zone file:

```
centralsoft.org.                  TXT "v=spf1 a mx ~all"
server1.centralsoft.org.          TXT "v=spf1 a -all"
```

Putting it all together

Now let's look at our zone file, *pri.centralsoft.org*. Note that we've added CNAME and TXT records to the pieces discussed earlier:

```
@ IN SOA server1.centralsoft.org. root.localhost. (
                       2006012103; serial-no
                       28800; refresh, seconds
                       7200; retry, seconds
                       604800; expiry, seconds
                       86400 ); minimum-TTL, seconds


;
                  NS server1.centralsoft.org.;
                  NS server2.centralsoft.org.;


;
                  MX 10 server1.centralsoft.org.


;

centralsoft.org.  A 70.253.158.42
www               A 70.253.158.42
server1           A 70.253.158.42
server2           A 70.253.158.45
ftp               CNAME www
centralsoft.org.                  TXT "v=spf1 a mx ~all"
server1.centralsoft.org.          TXT "v=spf1 a -all"
```

The Reverse Zone File

With our primary zone file completed, programs can look up the *centralsoft.org* domain and all its subdomains in DNS. But we still need a reverse zone file.

A reverse zone file maps IP addresses to names. It looks almost like a mirror of the primary zone file; instead of listing the names first, the reverse zone file lists the IP addresses first.

Why might someone use a reverse zone file? In the past, many organizations would refuse to allow you to use their services if they could not ping your domain name in reverse. Today, many Internet servers use reverse lookups to verify the origins of email to stop spammers; this is the purpose of the SPF records discussed earlier.

The system we've described here deals with a mail-relaying problem that will be explained further in Chapter 5. DNS indicates which MTA is responsible for mail from the domain listed in the email sender's address. Many spammers try to relay mail using different MTAs, but the receiving mail agent can do a reverse lookup, spot the irregularity, and refuse the unwanted email.

Since we don't want emails originating from the *centralsoft.org* domain to be classified as spam, we'll create a reverse zone file. First, to point to this file, we have to place this entry in our *named.conf* file:

```
zone "158.253.70.in-addr.arpa" {
     type master;
     file "pri.158.253.70.in-addr.arpa";
};
```

The numbers may look strange, but they follow a simple pattern. *centralsoft.org* is in the 70.253.158 net, so we reverse the elements of 70.253.158 to produce 158.253.70 and use that in the zone statement in *named.conf*. The domain *in-addr.arpa* is the top-level domain used by all reverse lookups.

We'll name our reverse zone file *pri.158.253.70.in-addr.arpa* and place the file in the same directory as our primary zone file, *pri.centralsoft.org*.

The beginning of *pri.158.253.70.in-addr.arpa* looks exactly like *pri.centralsoft.org*:

```
@ IN SOA server1.centralsoft.org. root.localhost. (
                        2006012103; serial-no
                        28800; refresh, seconds
                        7200; retry, seconds
                        604800; expiry, seconds
                        86400 ); minimum-TTL, seconds


;
                  NS server1.centralsoft.org.;
                  NS server2.centralsoft.org.;
```

But here, we do not add any A, MX, or CNAME records. Instead, we create PTR records.

PTR records

PTR is short for Pointer, and that's what it is: a pointer to a domain name. Let's create one by starting with the IP address of *centralsoft.org*, 70.253.158.42. The *named.conf* file has already indicated, through the zone statement we showed in the previous section, that this file defines hosts in the 70.253.158 domain. So all the PTR record has to specify is the final host part of the IP address, 42:

```
42                 PTR    centralsoft.org.
```

Create exactly one PTR record for each IP address in your domain. For our example, the only other IP address we use is 70.253.158.45 (for *server2.centralsoft.org*), so we add:

```
45                 PTR    server2.centralsoft.org.
```

That's all. Our reverse zone file looks now like this:

```
@ IN SOA server1.centralsoft.org. root.localhost. (
                        2006012103; serial-no
                        28800; refresh, seconds
                        7200; retry, seconds
                        604800; expiry, seconds
                        86400 ); minimum-TTL, seconds

;
                   NS server1.centralsoft.org.;
                   NS server2.centralsoft.org.;

42                 PTR    centralsoft.org.
45                 PTR    server2.centralsoft.org.
```

Testing Lookups

Once you've edited all the configuration and zone files, you need to let BIND know about your changes. You can stop and start *named* as follows:

```
# /etc/init.d/bind9 stop
# /etc/init.d/bind9 start
```

If you get any errors or if your BIND service does not act as expected, please see the upcoming troubleshooting section for details on the most common problems.

In the future, if the only change you perform is to update a zone file with a new DNS entry for the corresponding domain, it is enough tell BIND to just reload its information about this zone (rather than restarting the entire service):

```
# rndc reload centralsoft.org
```

The *rndc* command will be discussed in more detail shortly.

Now we can test our configuration by doing a lookup with the command-line tool *dig*. First, we'll look up the IP address of *centralsoft.org*:

```
# dig centralsoft.org

; <<>> DiG 9.2.1 <<>> centralsoft.org
;; global options:  printcmd
;; Got answer:
;; ->>HEADER<<- opcode: QUERY, status: NOERROR, id: 48489
;; flags: qr rd ra; QUERY: 1, ANSWER: 1, AUTHORITY: 0, ADDITIONAL: 0

;; QUESTION SECTION:
;centralsoft.org.               IN      A

;; ANSWER SECTION:
centralsoft.org.        86400   IN      A       70.253.158.42

;; Query time: 198 msec
;; SERVER: 81.169.163.104#53(81.169.163.104)
;; WHEN: Sat Mar 11 18:55:21 2006
;; MSG SIZE  rcvd: 49
```

As you see, this lookup returns the IP address 70.253.158.42.

Now we can do a reverse lookup:

```
# dig -x 70.253.158.42

; <<>> DiG 9.2.1 <<>> -x 70.253.158.42
;; global options:  printcmd
;; Got answer:
;; ->>HEADER<<- opcode: QUERY, status: NOERROR, id: 4096
;; flags: qr rd ra; QUERY: 1, ANSWER: 1, AUTHORITY: 0, ADDITIONAL: 0

;; QUESTION SECTION:
;42.158.253.70.in-addr.arpa.    IN      PTR

;; ANSWER SECTION:
42.158.253.70.in-addr.arpa. 5304 IN     PTR     centralsoft.org.

;; Query time: 2 msec
;; SERVER: 81.169.163.104#53(81.169.163.104)
;; WHEN: Sat Mar 11 18:57:54 2006
;; MSG SIZE  rcvd: 98
```

The forward and reverse lookups match each other. Our primary server setup is complete.

Configuring the Secondary Nameserver

Next, let's set up our secondary nameserver, *server2.centralsoft.org*. It will act as a backup nameserver in case the primary (*server1.centralsoft.org*) fails, so that people can still look up *centralsoft.org* and its subdomains.

server2.centralsoft.org's *named.conf* file resembles that of the primary nameserver, with a few differences:

```
options {
     pid-file "/var/run/bind/run/named.pid";
     directory "/etc/bind";
     // query-source address * port 53;
};


zone "." {
     type hint;
     file "db.root";
};

zone "0.0.127.in-addr.arpa" {
     type master;
     file "db.local";
};

zone "centralsoft.org" {
     type slave;
     file "sec.centralsoft.org";
     masters { 70.253.158.42; };
};
```

The most important difference is one we discussed earlier in this chapter. The `type slave;` line in the final zone statement indicates that this is a slave zone. In the `file` line we specify the filename where the slave zone should be stored, and in the `masters` line we specify the IP address of the primary nameserver.

That's all we have to do to set up the secondary nameserver.

Restart *named* on *server2.centralsoft.org*, and soon after you should find the file */etc/bind/sec.centralsoft.org* on your secondary nameserver. What has happened? The secondary nameserver has contacted the primary nameserver, which has transferred the zone to it.

Now whenever you update a zone on the primary nameserver, make sure the serial number increases. Otherwise, the updated zone will not transfer to the secondary nameserver.

BIND Tools

As we mentioned early in this chapter, BIND comes in three pieces: the *named* daemon, the *resolver* library, and some tools.

One tool you have already used is *dig*, which administrators use to interrogate DNS nameservers. *dig* does a DNS lookup and displays both the answers returned from the nameservers and statistics about the query.

Most DNS administrators use *dig* to troubleshoot DNS problems because of its flexibility, ease of use, and clarity. Other lookup tools tend to have less functionality. One alternative you should be aware of, however, is *nslookup*. We'll also take a look at *rndc*, a useful administration tool that's included with BIND.

nslookup

nslookup works similarly to *dig* but is deprecated in Linux. Using it requires more work, but you should be familiar with it because Microsoft Windows still uses it as its primary lookup tool.

nslookup queries Internet domain nameservers in two modes: interactive and noninteractive. The interactive mode allows you to query nameservers for information about various hosts and domains, or to print a list of hosts in a domain.

The noninteractive mode simply prints the name and requested information for a host or domain. For example, you could run the following lookup to find some information about Google's server:

```
# nslookup ns1.google.com
Server:         68.94.156.1
Address:        68.94.156.1#53

Non-authoritative answer:
Name:   ns1.google.com
Address: 216.239.32.10
```

In interactive mode, *nslookup* provides a prompt where you can execute commands. For example:

```
# nslookup
>
```

From the prompt you can do simple lookups, such as on an IP address:

```
> 70.253.158.42
Server:         172.30.1.2
Address:        172.30.1.2#53

Non-authoritative answer:
42.158.253.70.in-addr.arpa      name = adsl-70-253-158-42.dsl.rcsntx.swbell.net.

Authoritative answers can be found from:
158.253.70.in-addr.arpa nameserver = ns1.swbell.net.
158.253.70.in-addr.arpa nameserver = ns2.swbell.net.
>
```

You can also execute several commands, including *lserver* (which uses your local server to do a lookup), *server* (which uses another server to do a lookup), and *host*. The *lserver* command produces output like the following:

```
> lserver google.com
Default server: google.com
```

```
Address: 64.233.167.99#53
Default server: google.com
Address: 64.233.187.99#53
Default server: google.com
Address: 72.14.207.99#53
```

The *host* subcommmand provides a simple utility for performing lookups. When no arguments or options are given, *host* prints a short summary of its command-line arguments and options. People use it primarily to convert names to IP addresses and vice versa. Here's an example:

```
> host centralsoft.org
centralsoft.org has address 70.253.158.42
```

When you put *host* in verbose mode with the *-v* option, it provides information similar to the *dig* command:

```
> host -v centralsoft.org
Trying "centralsoft.org"
;; ->>HEADER<<- opcode: QUERY, status: NOERROR, id: 43756
;; flags: qr rd ra; QUERY: 1, ANSWER: 1, AUTHORITY: 1, ADDITIONAL: 0

;; QUESTION SECTION:
;centralsoft.org.               IN      A

;; ANSWER SECTION:
centralsoft.org.        86400   IN      A       70.253.158.42

;; AUTHORITY SECTION:
centralsoft.org.        29437   IN      NS      server1.centralsoft.org.

Received 71 bytes from 68.94.156.1#53 in 30 ms
```

This information came from the IP address 68.94.156.1, port number 53, which is the nameserver specified in the *resolv.conf* file of the desktop performing the lookup.

You can use *host* again to find out the name of that server:

```
> host 68.94.156.1
1.156.94.68.in-addr.arpa domain name pointer dnsr1.sbcglobal.net.
```

Type exit to quit an interactive *nslookup* session.

You can also use *named* to do troubleshooting in some instances. For example, to find out the version number of your BIND implementation, run the following command:

```
# named -v
named 8.4.6-REL-NOESW Tue Feb  1 10:10:48 UTC 2005
        buildd@rockhopper:/build/buildd/bind-8.4.6/src/bin/named
```

rndc

BIND provides the *rndc* command as part of the installation. *rndc* allows you to administer *named* using the command line. The utility sends the commands given on the command line to the running *named* server, which acts on them. *rndc* is also used by the BIND 9 system initialization script.

To prevent unauthorized users from accessing your nameserver, you should use a shared secret key to authenticate the access. In order for *rndc* to issue commands to any *named* server, even on a local machine, both must share the same key. This key is stored in the file */etc/bind/rndc.key*, and both *named* and *rndc* will read the key from this location. The *rndc.key* file should have been created during the installation of BIND.

The *rndc* command takes the following form:

```
# rndc rndc-options command command-options
```

The following are commonly useful `rndc-options` you might want to use (read the *rndc* manpage to see the full list):

-k key-file
: Use the specified *key-file* in place of the default */etc/bind/rndc.key* file.

-s server
: Send the command to the specified *server* instead of the local server.

-V
: Enable verbose logging for this command.

Here are some of the more commonly used commands that *rndc* can send to *named* (for a complete list of the commands, simply type the *rndc* command by itself):

halt
: Stop the nameserver immediately.

querylog
: Enable or disable logging of all queries made by clients to this nameserver. This is a toggling command: it switches logging on if it is currently off, and vice versa.

reload [zone]
: Reload the zone files, but keep all other previously cached responses. This allows you to make changes to zone files and have them take effect on your master and slave servers without losing all stored name resolutions. If your changes affected only a particular zone, you can tell *named* to reload only that zone.

retransfer zone
: Force the retransfer of the specified *zone* without checking the serial number.

stats
: Dump the current *named* statistics to the *named.stats* file.

status
: Show the current status of the nameserver.

stop
: Stop the server gracefully, saving any dynamic update data before exiting.

Troubleshooting BIND

At this point in the chapter, you should have a functional knowledge of DNS. You should also know how to configure your files and how to find syntax problems in them, such as typographical errors. In this section we will cover some basic, common problems that you may encounter when getting BIND and DNS working. This is not an exhaustive treatise, but it should help you get DNS running on your Linux server if you have problems getting your domain to resolve hostnames or do zone transfers.

The Domain Name System is designed very robustly, but strange errors can still occasionally happen. By strictly following the patterns for creating zone files described earlier in this chapter, you can avoid subtle problems that are beyond this book's scope.

Cannot Connect Using rndc

To begin, let's see a healthy indication of DNS resolution. Earlier, we discussed using the *rndc status* command to show the current running status of our DNS server. Let's try logging onto the server as *root* and running the command:

```
server1:~# rndc status
number of zones: 6
debug level: 0
xfers running: 0
xfers deferred: 0
soa queries in progress: 0
query logging is OFF
server is up and running
server1:~#
```

The *rndc* command depends on a shared key file at */etc/bind/rndc.key* for *named* to accept its commands. Problems with that file can prevent *rndc* from sending the commands. Here is an example of what we would see if the key file were missing:

```
server1:~# rndc status
rndc: neither /etc/bind/rndc.conf nor /etc/bind/rndc.key was found
server1:~#
```

We can verify that the file is indeed missing with this command:

```
server1:~# ls -l /etc/bind/rndc.key
ls: /etc/bind/rndc.key: No such file or directory
```

We can fix the problem by regenerating the file the same way the BIND initialization did:

```
server1:~# rndc-confgen -a
server1:~# ls -l /etc/bind/rndc.key
-rw-------  1 root bind 77 Jul 19 22:38 /etc/bind/rndc.key
server1:~#
```

Because *named* does not have this new key, we must now kill the *named* process and restart it. For this we make use of the system command *killall*, which takes the full pathname of the *named* program. To stop *named* as gracefully as possible, we do two *killall* commands with a few seconds pause in between, then restart *named*:

```
server1:~# killall -TERM /usr/sbin/named
server1:~# killall -KILL /usr/sbin/named
/usr/sbin/named: no process killed
server1:~# /etc/init.d/bind9 start
Starting domain name service: named.
server1:~# rndc status
number of zones: 6
debug level: 0
xfers running: 0
xfers deferred: 0
soa queries in progress: 0
query logging is OFF
server is up and running
server1:~#
```

named Starts but Does Not Resolve Names

Now, let's look at situations where *named* isn't running properly. Incorrectly located BIND files often cause problems, especially in chroot environments where the BIND files are placed in an isolated directory.

If *named* starts OK but does not load any zone files, they may not be present in the isolated directory. You'll need to look at the */var/log/syslog* file to see if that's the case. Here's an example from the log:

```
starting BIND 9.2.4 -u bind -t /var/lib/named
using 1 CPU
loading configuration from '/etc/bind/named.conf'
listening on IPv4 interface lo, 127.0.0.1#53
listening on IPv4 interface eth0, 70.253.158.42#53
command channel listening on 127.0.0.1#953
command channel listening on ::1#953
running
```

The log shows that BIND has started, but it includes no lines indicating that the zone files were loaded. Because *named* runs inside the chroot environment at */var/lib/named*, it will look for all files relative to that directory. So really, it's reading the file */var/lib/named/etc/bind/named.conf* for the list of zones to load. Each of those zone files must be placed relative to the */var/lib/named* directory.

Another common error is a connection failure involving *rndc* when reloading or restarting the nameserver:

```
# /etc/init.d/ bind9 reload
Stopping named: rndc: connect failed: connection refused
[OK]
Starting named: [OK]
#
```

This type of error can also happen as a result of running BIND in a chroot environment, when one or more files are missing from the isolation directory. You can check some of the essential files to be sure they are in the proper locations:

```
# ls -l /var/lib/named/etc/bind/named.conf
-rw-r--r-- 1 root bind 1611 2006-09-07 12:21 /var/lib/named/etc/bind/named.conf
# ls /var/lib/named/etc/bind/
db.0      db.local      named.conf.local              pri.centralsoft.org
db.127    db.root       named.conf.options            pri.opensourcetoday.org
db.255    named.conf    pri.156.18.67.in-addr.arpa    rndc.key
db.empty  named.conf~   pri.156.18.67.in-addr.arpa~   zones.rfc1918
#
...
```

If these files do not exist, the chroot environment is not set up properly or completely. Return to the section "Using a chroot Environment for Security" near the beginning of this chapter and follow its instructions carefully to ensure every file is in place.

Once you've fixed the problem, you'll need to stop and restart *named* to enable *rndc* to reach the running server. Use the *killall* command sequence described in the previous section:

```
server1:~# killall -TERM /usr/sbin/named
server1:~# killall -KILL /usr/sbin/named
/usr/sbin/named: no process killed
server1:~# /etc/init.d/bind9 start
Starting domain name service: named.
server1:~#
```

Next, check your */var/log/syslog* file to see whether the zone files loaded. You should see something like this:

```
starting BIND 9.2.4 -u bind -t /var/lib/named
using 1 CPU
loading configuration from '/etc/bind/named.conf'
listening on IPv4 interface lo, 127.0.0.1#53
listening on IPv4 interface eth0, 70.253.158.42#53
command channel listening on 127.0.0.1#953
command channel listening on ::1#953
zone 0.0.127.in-addr.arpa/IN: loaded serial 1
zone 158.253.70.in-addr.arpa/IN: loaded serial 2006070401
zone centralsoft.org/IN: loaded serial 2006070502
zone supportcall.org/IN: loaded serial 2006062704
running
```

Hosts Aren't Recognized

The next step in checking for correct DNS operation is to be sure queries for your hostnames are answered properly. First, you need to be sure the */etc/resolv.conf* file lists your nameservers with the correct addresses. Most programs use the addresses from this file to determine which nameservers to query, and in which order:

```
server1:~# cat /etc/resolv.conf
search centralsoft.org
nameserver 70.253.158.42
nameserver 70.253.158.45
server1:~#
```

The *host* command does a simple DNS lookup using the servers listed in the */etc/resolv.conf* file. It takes the host you want to look for as an argument, and an optional second argument makes the command query a specific nameserver. Here are two examples of the *host* command and its results:

```
server1:~# host www.centralsoft.org
www.centralsoft.org has address 70.253.158.42
server1:~# host www.centralsoft.org server2.centralsoft.org
Using domain server:
Name: server1.centralsoft.org
Address: 70.253.158.45#53
Aliases:

www.centralsoft.org has address 70.253.158.42
server1:~#
```

An alternative to *host* is the *dig* command, which is more complex but provides more detailed answers. It also has more options that enable you make very specific queries.

The output from *dig* is formatted in the syntax of a zone file. This is convenient, because once you've learned how records are formatted in a zone file you can easily understand all the details of those records in *dig*'s output. *dig* also provides some additional information about the results of the query in the form of zone-format comments beginning with the ";" character.

Let's take a look at the result of a *dig* command. Many lines of *dig*'s output are very long and do not fit this book's page layout. In the following printout, they are wrapped around to the next line. You'll likely see similar results when running this command in your shell session:

```
server1:~# dig www.centralsoft.org a

; <<>> DiG 9.2.4 <<>> www.centralsoft.org a
;; global options:  printcmd
;; Got answer:
;; ->>HEADER<<- opcode: QUERY, status: NOERROR, id: 1633
;; flags: qr aa rd ra; QUERY: 1, ANSWER: 1, AUTHORITY: 2, ADDITIONAL: 2

;; QUESTION SECTION:
;www.centralsoft.org.           IN      A

;; ANSWER SECTION:
www.centralsoft.org.    86400   IN      A       70.253.158.42

;; AUTHORITY SECTION:
centralsoft.org.        86400   IN      NS      server1.centralsoft.org.
centralsoft.org.        86400   IN      NS      server2.centralsoft.org.
```

```
;; ADDITIONAL SECTION:
server1.centralsoft.org. 86400  IN      A       70.253.158.42
server2.centralsoft.org. 86400  IN      A       70.253.158.45

;; Query time: 1 msec
;; SERVER: 70.253.158.42#53(70.253.158.42)
;; WHEN: Mon Jul 17 23:30:51 2006
;; MSG SIZE  rcvd: 129

server1:~#
```

The first part of the output indicates various status codes and flags. Pay particular attention to `status` value on the fourth line. In this example, the value is `NOERROR`. Any other value likely indicates a problem of some sort.

The actual zone data comes in four sections:

`QUESTION`
: This section actually details the query itself. It is displayed as a comment because it is not something that should be in a zone file.

`ANSWER`
: This section contains the actual results requested by the query. It will show the specific records requested, if available, or all records if the special query record type any is used.

`AUTHORITY`
: This section identifies the official nameservers for the zone for which the answer came.

`ADDITIONAL`
: This section provides the addresses of some or all of the names from the prior sections, to save you the trouble of doing more queries for that information.

Now let's take a look at what you would get if there was an error. The previous example used a valid hostname for the web server. This time we will query for the name of an FTP server that we have not configured into our zone file:

```
server1:~# dig ftp.centralsoft.org a

; <<>> DiG 9.2.4 <<>> ftp.centralsoft.org a
;; global options:  printcmd
;; Got answer:
;; ->>HEADER<<- opcode: QUERY, status: NXDOMAIN, id: 6531
;; flags: qr aa rd ra; QUERY: 1, ANSWER: 0, AUTHORITY: 1, ADDITIONAL: 0

;; QUESTION SECTION:
;ftp.centralsoft.org.           IN      A

;; AUTHORITY SECTION:
centralsoft.org.        86400   IN      SOA     server1.centralsoft.org. admin.
centralsoft.org. 2006070502 28800 7200 604800 86400
```

```
;; Query time: 1 msec
;; SERVER: 70.253.158.42#53(70.253.158.42)
;; WHEN: Mon Jul 17 23:30:59 2006
;; MSG SIZE  rcvd: 87

server1:~#
```

Notice that the status for this query is NXDOMAIN, which essentially means "no such domain name." If you leave out or misspell a hostname in the zone file, you'll get this error.

Another kind of error that you may see with *dig* is when a domain name is delegated to your nameserver, but that domain is not configured in the server or otherwise fails to load. This error returns a status of SERVFAIL. If you see this error for one of your domains, you need to add the domain to your *named.conf* file and ensure that there is a valid zone file for it. If the error recurs after you have done those steps, check the */var/log/syslog* file for any messages about why the zone was not loaded. We'll demonstrate the problem with a domain name that is registered, but not currently in use:

```
server1:~# dig linhelp.org a

; <<>> DiG 9.2.4 <<>> linhelp.org a
;; global options:  printcmd
;; Got answer:
;; ->>HEADER<<- opcode: QUERY, status: SERVFAIL, id: 29949
;; flags: qr rd ra; QUERY: 1, ANSWER: 0, AUTHORITY: 0, ADDITIONAL: 0

;; QUESTION SECTION:
;linhelp.org.            IN      A

;; Query time: 2 msec
;; SERVER: 70.253.158.42#53(70.253.158.42)
;; WHEN: Mon Jul 17 23:47:14 2006
;; MSG SIZE  rcvd: 37

server1:~#
```

What's Next

By now you should be familiar with the basics of DNS and BIND. Administrators in small-to-medium-size businesses may find that the information in this chapter is all they ever need, but enterprise system administrators are sure to encounter issues more complex than those that can be covered in a single chapter.

Several books exist that can provide much more detailed information for large enterprise and DNS administrators. These include *DNS and BIND* by Cricket Liu and Paul Albitz (O'Reilly), *DNS & BIND Cookbook* by Cricket Liu (O'Reilly), *Pro DNS and BIND* by Ron Aitchison (Apress), and *DNS in Action: A Detailed and Practical Guide to DNS Implementation, Configuration, and Administration* by L. Dostalek and A. Kableova (Packt).

Now that you have a working nameserver answering queries and being backed up by a slave or secondary server, in the next chapter you can move on to installing a web service application. The new application will utilize the services you set up in Chapter 2. Once the application, called ISPConfig, is set up and running, you'll have a working example of a fully operational web site. We can then begin exploring how to administer the complete suite of Linux services found on the Internet.

CHAPTER 4
An Initial Internet-Ready Environment

One of Linux's great traits is its flexibility. Commercial companies such as Cisco have hidden Linux under very simple interfaces to make its Linksys routers and other products user-friendly. We can do that, too.

ISPConfig (*http://ispconfig.org*), a user-friendly Linux project under a free software (BSD) license, allows us to build a multifunctional, working Internet server from a single downloadable application. Once we install it, we will have a tool that helps us to configure and easily maintain a server that allows us to manage web sites; provide domain name services; perform email and file transfers; and add users, administrators, and others who can access the system for various administrative tasks. Oh, and did we mention we can do all those administration tasks from a graphical interface?

We selected ISPConfig primarily because it allows us to deploy powerful server applications on Linux without sacrificing any power or flexibility. Furthermore:

- ISPConfig uses standard daemons that come with Linux distributions. We'll use Apache for serving web sites, Postfix for email, ProFTPD for FTP, BIND for DNS, and MySQL as the backend database.
- Installation of ISPConfig automatically configures the various server components.
- The packages included in ISPConfig work with most available distributions of Linux.
- Standard packages from the distributions can be used.
- Support for each bundled component can be found on the Internet.
- The ISPConfig team provides online support for the entire application.

As you progress through this chapter, you should gain a pretty good idea of what's involved in getting the various services a server provides up and running. You'll also learn how to decide whether your needs allow you to use a visual administrative panel instead of a command-line interface.

ISPConfig itself does not provide a command-line interface. Instead, it lets you manage servers though a web-based administrative interface, or panel, described later in this chapter. You'll have to do some command-line work at the beginning of the chapter, when setting up ISPConfig so it can install everything else subsequently, but in later sections we'll focus entirely on this visual interface.

ISPConfig's web application panel simplifies the execution of many Linux administrative tasks, but it's important to know how to use standard command-line utilities to accomplish the same results. We'll cover those topics in later chapters. You won't be tied to ISPConfig; if you choose to do without it, you will have the knowledge to do so.

Installing ISPConfig

ISPConfig comes from Projektfarm GmbH. Till Brehm and Falko Timme developed the application, which they originally sold as a proprietary system marketed on *http://42go.de*. Now you can download it from *http://sourceforge.net/projects/ispconfig*.

The project configures these services:

- *httpd* (virtual hosts, domain-based and IP-based)
- FTP
- BIND
- POP3 autoresponder
- MySQL client databases
- Webalizer statistics
- Hard disk quotas
- Mail quotas
- Traffic limits
- IP addresses
- SSL
- SSI
- Shell access
- Mailscanner (antivirus)
- Firewall

Requirements

At the time of this writing, system requirements include:

Operating system

Linux (2.4 kernel or later with the *glibc6* library). The following distributions are supported:

- CentOS 4.1, 4.2, 4.3, and 4.4
- Debian Version 3.0 or later
- Fedora Core 1 through 6
- Mandrake Linux Version 8.1 or later
- Mandriva 2006 and 2007
- Red Hat Linux Version 7.3 or later
- SUSE Linux Version 7.2 or later
- Ubuntu 5.04 through 6.10

Linux packages

The project maintainers list the specific Linux distribution components that need to be installed on your system before you can install ISPConfig. These include:

- Apache web server Version 1.3.12 or later, or 2.0.40 or later
- BIND 8 or 9
- *iptables* or *ipchains*
- MySQL database
- OpenSSL and *mod_ssl* for the creation of SSL virtual hosts
- PHP 4.0.5 or later as an Apache module
- POP3/IMAP daemon that supports either the traditional Unix mailbox format (e.g., *gnu-pop3d*, *qpopper*, *ipop3d*, *popa3d*, or *vm-pop3d*) or the *maildir* format (e.g., Courier-Imap, Dovecot)
- Procmail
- ProFTP as standalone version or *vsftpd* as *inetd*/*xinetd*/standalone version
- *quota* package
- Sendmail or Postfix

It is important to understand that that these servers and packages must already be installed on your system, as described in Chapter 2, before you install ISPConfig. ISPConfig does not come with these services, but requires that they already exist on your system. The advantage of this approach is that you can use your distribution's default packages and can later update them as you would normally update packages on your system using your distribution's tools. You don't have to compile these services from the sources with specific options for use with ISPConfig—the default packages will do.

ISPConfig sets up two directories containing the files and subdirectories that make up the application panel: */root/ispconfig* and */home/admispconfig*. You can uninstall ISPConfig and go back to a standard text-based server by running */root/ispconfig/uninstall*; some readers may choose to do that after working for a while with this book.

> ### Special ISPConfig Daemons
>
> In addition to managing the applications you already have installed on your system, ISPConfig maintains its own versions of a few applications for its own use. You can find sources for these in the *install_ispconfig/compile_aps* directory of the package. These redundant services exist so that you can continue to manage ISPConfig even if the regular services (such as your public Apache web server) go down.
>
> ISPConfig allows both the public and internal servers to run by using a nonstandard port for the internal server. For instance, ISPConfig's internal Apache server listens on port 81 instead of port 80, which is typically used by the distribution's web server that hosts the publicly available web sites.

Getting Started

Like many Linux and Unix packages, ISPConfig is provided as a set of files combined with the *tar* utility, the result of which is often called a *tarball*. When you click on the Download link at *http://sourceforge.net/projects/ispconfig*, it will lead you to one of the SourceForge site's mirrors. A typical site containing ISPConfig is *http://superb-west.dl.sourceforge.net/sourceforge/ispconfig/ISPConfig-2.2.6.tar.gz*.

You can just click the Download link to download the file, but because the file is quite large, you may find it useful to copy the URL and paste it into a *wget* command in your terminal window. The advantage of using *wget* is that you can recover easily if something disrupts your download. If you issue the command with the *-c* option, you can resume the download rather than starting again from scratch: if the download gets aborted, simply rerun the *wget* command as before and it will resume where it left off.

In this chapter we'll assume you start in a directory called */root* on your system. You can download the ISPConfig tarball with this command (on one line, substituting the URL for the most recent version on the SourceForge site):

```
# wget -c http://superb-west.dl.sourceforge.net/sourceforge/ispconfig/ISPConfig-2.2.
6.tar.gz
```

Your terminal will display messages similar to the following:

```
--16:20:48--  http://superb-west.dl.sourceforge.net/sourceforge/ispconfig/ISPConfig-
2.2.1.tar.gz
           => `ISPConfig-2.2.1.tar.gz'
```

```
Resolving superb-west.dl.sourceforge.net... 209.160.59.253
Connecting to superb-west.dl.sourceforge.net|209.160.59.253|:80... connected.
HTTP request sent, awaiting response... 200 OK
Length: 26,633,490 (25M) [application/x-gzip]
24% [========>                           ] 6,533,049    252.80K/s    ETA 01:32
```

Unpack the *ISPConfig-archive* with the command:

```
# tar xvfz ISPConfig*.tar.gz
```

which creates a subdirectory called *install_ispconfig*. Change into the directory */root/install_ispconfig*. Check the file *dist.txt* and see whether the values given there suit your Linux server.

For Debian 3.1, the values in *dist.txt* look something like this:

```
dist_init_scripts=/etc/init.d ##       # debian31
dist_runlevel=/etc ##                  # debian31
```

The file contains 19 additional values for Debian that we will not list here. Unless you have significant proficiency with Linux administration and familiarity with ISPConfig, stick to the default values. They should work so long as you are using one of the supported distributions listed earlier in this chapter. Knowledgeable administrators can change values, so long as the format of the file is preserved.

Now start the installation. Run the installation command *./setup* from the root prompt. The installer script will begin by compiling Apache with PHP 5 running on port 81. First, you will be asked to choose your language:

```
server2:~/install_ispconfig # ./setup
SuSE 10.0
Neuinstallation eines ISPConfig-Systems. / Installation of a new ISPConfig system. /
Installation d'ISPConfig sur un nouveau systeme.
Whlen Sie Ihre Sprache (deutsch/englisch/spanisch/franzsisch/italienisch/
niederlndisch/polnisch/
schwedisch): / Please choose your language (German/English/Spanish/French/Italian/
Dutch/Polish/Swedish): / Merci de choisir votre langue (Allemand/Anglais/Espagnol/
Francais/Italien/Nerlandais/Polonais/Sudois):
1) de
2) en
3) es
4) fr
5) it
6) nl
7) pl
8) se
Ihre Wahl: / Your Choice: / Votre Choix:
```

You will see a warning screen:

```
With the system installation, some system files are replaced where adjustments were
made. This can lead to loss of entries in httpd.conf, named.conf as well as in the
Sendmail configuration.
Do you want to continue with the installation? [y/n] y
```

The system will display a license, which you should read and then accept:

```
Do you accept the license? [y/n] y
```

The installation program will proceed to ask you questions about your system setup (e.g., which MTA, FTP server, web server, logs, etc. to use). Because you have already installed these packages on your system, you should be able to answer all of the questions.

During the early part of the installation, the script will ask you in which mode you want to run the installation. Select expert mode:

```
1) standard
2) expert
Your Choice: 2
```

In expert mode, you will be given additional choices for which ISPConfig assigns defaults in standard mode.

```
When prompted for a default directory, you can choose any directory you like, but
make sure it is on a partition with enough disk space for the web sites you plan to
host. Furthermore, if you want to configure quotas with ISPConfig, make sure you
enabled quotas for that partition as described in Chapter 2. If you want to enable
suExec for web sites that are allowed to run Perl/CGI scripts, the directory should
be within suExec's document root. On Debian and Fedora/Red Hat, suExec's default
document root is /var/www, while on SUSE it's /srv/www. If you're enabling suExec,
the document root is a good choice for the directory in which to put ISPConfig:
########## WEB SERVER ##########
Checking for program httpd...
/usr/sbin/httpd
OK
Checking the syntax of the httpd.conf...
Syntax OK
The syntax is ok!
Web-Root: /home/www
Is this correct? [y/n] n
Web-Root: /var/www
```

suExec is a security enhancement on a web server that requires CGI scripts to be owned and run by certain users.

At this point, the installation begins by compiling the Apache server that will be used for presenting the ISPConfig web interface on port 81. When the ISPConfig Apache build completes, you will see a custom SSL certificate compiled. The installation program will ask you to provide several values. You can accept the default values or enter your own. The screen will look similar to the following:

```
SSL Certificate Generation Utility (mkcert.sh)
Copyright (c) 1998-2000 Ralf S. Engelschall, All Rights Reserved.
Generating custom certificate signed by own CA [CUSTOM]
______________________________________________________________________
```

```
STEP 0: Decide the signature algorithm used for certificates
The generated X.509 certificates can contain either
RSA or DSA based ingredients. Select the one you want to use.
Signature Algorithm ((R)SA or (D)SA) [R]:
______________________________________________________________________
STEP 1: Generating RSA private key for CA (1024 bit) [ca.key]
1698765 semi-random bytes loaded
Generating RSA private key, 1024 bit long modulus
............++++++
.........++++++
e is 65537 (0x10001)
______________________________________________________________________
STEP 2: Generating X.509 certificate signing request for CA [ca.csr]
You are about to be asked to enter information that will be incorporated
into your certificate request.
What you are about to enter is what is called a Distinguished Name or a DN.
There are quite a few fields but you can leave some blank
For some fields there will be a default value,
If you enter '.', the field will be left blank.
1. Country Name             (2 letter code) [XY]:
2. State or Province Name   (full name)     [Snake Desert]:
3. Locality Name            (e.g, city)     [Snake Town]:
4. Organization Name        (e.g, company)  [Snake Oil, Ltd]:
5. Organizational Unit Name (e.g, section)  [Certificate Authority]:
6. Common Name              (eg, CA name)   [Snake Oil CA]:
7. Email Address            (e.g, name@FQDN) [ca@snakeoil.dom]:
8. Certificate Validity     (days)          [365]:
______________________________________________________________________
STEP 3: Generating X.509 certificate for CA signed by itself [ca.crt]
Certificate Version (1 or 3) [3]:
Signature ok
subject=/C=XY/ST=Snake Desert/L=Snake Town/O=Snake Oil, Ltd/OU=Certificate Authority/
CN=Snake Oil CA/emailAddress=ca@snakeoil.dom
Getting Private key
Verify: matching certificate & key modulus
Verify: matching certificate signature
../conf/ssl.crt/ca.crt: /C=XY/ST=Snake Desert/L=Snake Town/O=Snake Oil, Ltd/
OU=Certificate Authority/CN=Snake Oil CA/emailAddress=ca@snakeoil.dom
error 18 at 0 depth lookup:self signed certificate
OK
______________________________________________________________________
STEP 4: Generating RSA private key for SERVER (1024 bit) [server.key]
1698765 semi-random bytes loaded
Generating RSA private key, 1024 bit long modulus
...........................++++++
.............++++++
e is 65537 (0x10001)
______________________________________________________________________
STEP 5: Generating X.509 certificate signing request for SERVER [server.csr]
You are about to be asked to enter information that will be incorporated
into your certificate request.
What you are about to enter is what is called a Distinguished Name or a DN.
There are quite a few fields but you can leave some blank
For some fields there will be a default value,
```

```
If you enter '.', the field will be left blank.
1. Country Name             (2 letter code) [XY]:
2. State or Province Name   (full name)     [Snake Desert]:
3. Locality Name            (eg, city)      [Snake Town]:
4. Organization Name        (eg, company)   [Snake Oil, Ltd]:
5. Organizational Unit Name (eg, section)   [Webserver Team]:
6. Common Name              (eg, FQDN)      [www.snakeoil.dom]:
7. Email Address            (eg, name@fqdn) [www@snakeoil.dom]:
8. Certificate Validity     (days)          [365]:
______________________________________________________________________
STEP 6: Generating X.509 certificate signed by own CA [server.crt]
Certificate Version (1 or 3) [3]:
Signature ok
subject=/C=XY/ST=Snake Desert/L=Snake Town/O=Snake Oil, Ltd/OU=Webserver Team/CN=www.
snakeoil.dom/emailAddress=www@snakeoil.dom
Getting CA Private Key
Verify: matching certificate signature
../conf/ssl.crt/server.crt: OK
```

In steps 7 and 8 of the certificate creation process, you will be asked whether you want to encrypt the respective keys now:

```
______________________________________________________________________
STEP 7: Enrypting RSA private key of CA with a pass phrase for security [ca.key]
The contents of the ca.key file (the generated private key) has to be
kept secret. So we strongly recommend you to encrypt the server.key file
with a Triple-DES cipher and a Pass Phrase.
Encrypt the private key now? [Y/n]: n
writing RSA key
Enter PEM pass phrase:
Verifying - Enter PEM pass phrase:
Fine, you're using an encrypted private key.
______________________________________________________________________
STEP 8: Enrypting RSA private key of SERVER with a pass phrase for security [server.
key]
The contents of the server.key file (the generated private key) has to be
kept secret. So we strongly recommend you to encrypt the server.key file
with a Triple-DES cipher and a Pass Phrase.
Encrypt the private key now? (Y/n): n
What email address or URL should be used in the suspected-spam report text for users
who want more information on your filter installation?
(In particular, ISPs should change this to a local Postmaster contact)
default text: [the administrator of that system]
```

Choose n in response to these questions. Otherwise, you will always be asked for a password whenever you want to restart the ISPConfig system, which means it cannot be restarted without human interaction.

If the compilation fails, the setup is stopped and all compiled files are removed. The error message you get should indicate the reason for the failure. In most cases, header files for a package are missing.

Whatever the reason, look back at your server setup and solve the problem. If the *install_ispconfig* directory has not been deleted despite the error, delete it manually.

Then unpack the ISPConfig sources again, go to the new *install_ispconfig* directory, and run *./setup*. You cannot install ISPConfig twice from the same *install_ispconfig* directory after any errors have occurred.

Similarly, if any of the required packages are not present, the installation routine will be stopped. Install the missing package, delete the directory *install_ispconfig*, unpack ISPConfig again, and start over.

The installation script verifies the syntax of your existing Apache configuration files. An error will cause ISPConfig's installation to stop.

If all conditions are fulfilled, you will need to supply values during installation. These include:

```
Please enter your MySQL server: localhost
Please enter your MySQL user: root
Please enter your MySQL password: Your MySQL password
Please enter a name for the ISPConfig database: ispconfigdb
Please enter the IP address of the ISPConfig web: 192.168.0.1
Please enter the host name: www
Please enter the domain: xyz.de
```

Next, the configuration program asks which protocol you wish to use. Select item 2, `HTTP`:

```
Please select the protocol (http or https (SSL encryption)) to use to access the
ISPConfig system:
1) HTTPS
2) HTTP
Your Choice: 2
```

You will see the system run the final scripts and restart some services:

```
Connected successfully to MySQL server
ls: /etc/apache2/vhosts.d/*.conf: No such file or directory
Restarting some services...
which: no apachectl in (/sbin:/usr/sbin:/usr/local/sbin:/root/bin:/usr/local/bin:/
bin:/usr/bin:/usr/X11R6/bin:/usr/local/libexec)
Shutting down mail service (Postfix)                                 done
Starting mail service (Postfix)                                      done
Shutting down mail service (Postfix)                                 done
Starting mail service (Postfix)                                      done
Shutting down ProFTPD Server:                                        done
Starting ProFTPD Server:  - warning: "ProFTPD" address/port (70.253.158.45:21)
already in use by "ProFTPD Default Installation"
done
Shutting down ProFTPD Server:                                        done
Starting ProFTPD Server:  - warning: "ProFTPD" address/port (70.253.158.45:21)
already in use by "ProFTPD Default Installation"
                                                                     done
Starting ISPConfig system...
/root/ispconfig/httpd/bin/apachectl startssl: httpd started
ISPConfig system is now up and running!
```

The developers end the installation script with:

```
Congratulations! Your ISPConfig system is now installed. If you had to install quota,
please take the steps described in the installation manual. Otherwise your system is
now available without reboot.
```

At this point, you can enter your server's IP address or domain name followed by *:81* in your browser to access the ISPConfig login screen.

ISPConfig Directory Structure

As mentioned previously, the main directory set up by ISPConfig is called *ispconfig*, and it's located under the directory where you did the build (*/root* in this chapter's build). You will also find another directory in */home* called *admispconfig*. Each directory contains the files required to run ISPConfig independently.

Let's take a look at the */root/ispconfig* directory first:

```
-rwxr-xr-x   1 root root 33660 2006-04-26 12:28 cronolog
-rwxr-xr-x   1 root root  9673 2006-04-26 12:28 cronosplit
drwxr-xr-x  12 root root  4096 2006-04-26 09:55 httpd
drwxr-xr-x  12 root root  4096 2006-04-26 12:28 isp
-rw-r--r--   1 root root     8 2006-04-26 13:54 .old_path_httpd_root
drwxr-xr-x   6 root root  4096 2006-04-26 09:50 openssl
drwxr-xr-x   6 root root  4096 2006-04-26 10:00 php
drwxr-xr-x   4 root root  4096 2006-04-26 12:28 scripts
drwxr-xr-x   4 root root  4096 2006-04-26 12:28 standard_cgis
drwxr-xr-x   2 root root  4096 2006-04-26 12:28 sv
-rwx------   1 root root  9389 2006-04-26 12:28 uninstall
```

It contains ISPConfig's Apache, PHP, and OpenSSL configuration files, as well as templates for all kinds of configuration files (for Apache, Postfix, Sendmail, BIND, *procmail* recipes, etc.). ISPConfig uses these templates to write the configuration files for the services it configures.

You will also find a lot of PHP classes here that provide the functions to write the system's configuration files. In short, */root/ispconfig* contains ISPConfig's backend.

Under the */home/admispconfig* directory, you will see another set of directories:

```
-rwxr-xr-x  1 admispconfig admispconfig   24 2006-04-26 12:28 .forward
drwxr-xr-x  8 admispconfig admispconfig 4096 2006-04-26 13:53 ispconfig
drwxr-xr-x  2 admispconfig admispconfig 4096 2006-04-26 12:28 mailstats
-rwxr-xr-x  1 admispconfig admispconfig  176 2006-04-26 12:28 .procmailrc
```

They contain the ISPConfig frontend—i.e., its web interface—as well as some tools, such as SpamAssassin (*http://spamassassin.apache.org*) and ClamAV (*http://clamav.elektrapro.com*). You can configure these through ISPConfig to protect against spam and viruses.

Setting Up a Server and Users with ISPConfig

Setting up a web site is one of the first moves toward having a fully functional Internet server. This section will walk you through all the necessary steps.

If you're wondering why we don't just ask you to navigate over to the ISPConfig web site and read the manuals, consider the following: ISPConfig's developers wrote their users' documentation for ISPs hosting customer web sites. If that's your intended use, we recommend reading the manuals at *http://ispconfig.org*. Otherwise, we will assume you plan on using your server with a single system administrator who manages her own secure web sites, mail, and FTP services.

ISPConfig requires you to set up a *client* who will own one or more Internet domains. In our example, we will set up a single client (one of the authors of this book) who will own four domains:

- *centralsoft.org*
- *linuxnewswire.org*
- *opensourcetoday.org*
- *tadelstein.com*

When you look at the directory contents in */var/www*, you will see how ISPConfig sets up domains:

```
$ ls -a
apache2-default  sharedip  web2  web4  webalizer    www.opensourcetoday.org
localhost        web1      web3    www.centralsoft.org  www.linuxnewswire.org
www.tadelstein.com
```

Compare this directory listing with the list of web sites in Figure 4-1. Each web site contains a directory. The *www* directories whose names show the domains (such as *www.opensourcetoday.org*) are symbolic links to what the system knows as *web1*, *web2*, and so on.

Figure 4-2 gives you a better look at the list of domains. Note in Figure 4-2 that a domain appears for each directory in the command-line listing.

Adding Clients and Web Sites

To configure the client and the domains, you must first log into the ISPConfig interface. In your web browser, enter the IP address of your server followed by the port for ISPConfig, *:81*—in our case, *http://70.253.158.45:81* (use *https://* if you selected HTTPS as the ISPConfig protocol during installation). At the login screen (Figure 4-3), enter the user ID *admin* and the password *admin*.

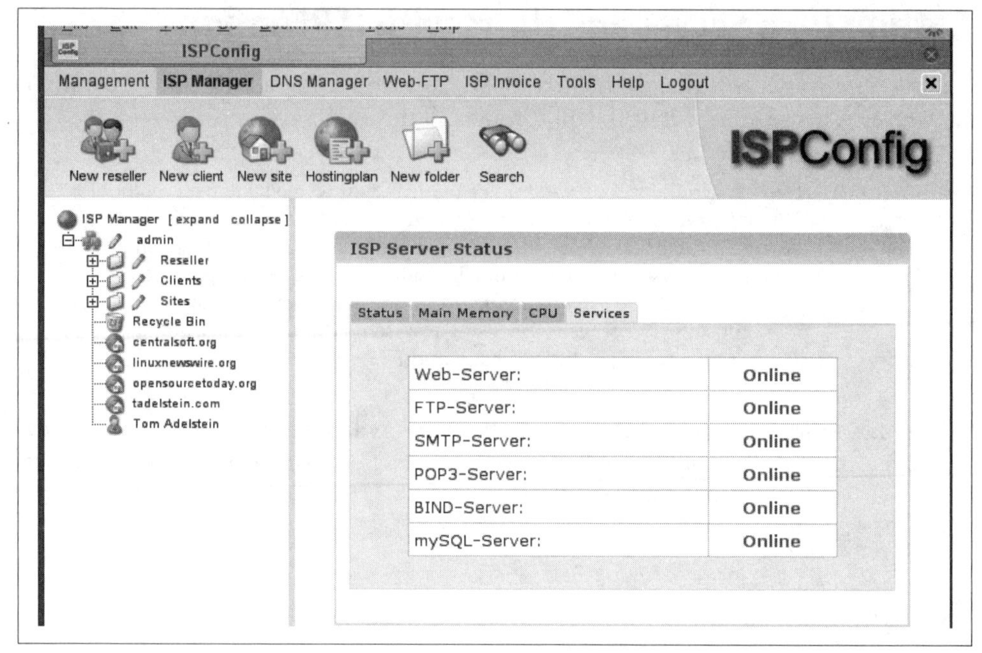

Figure 4-1. The ISP Manager interface

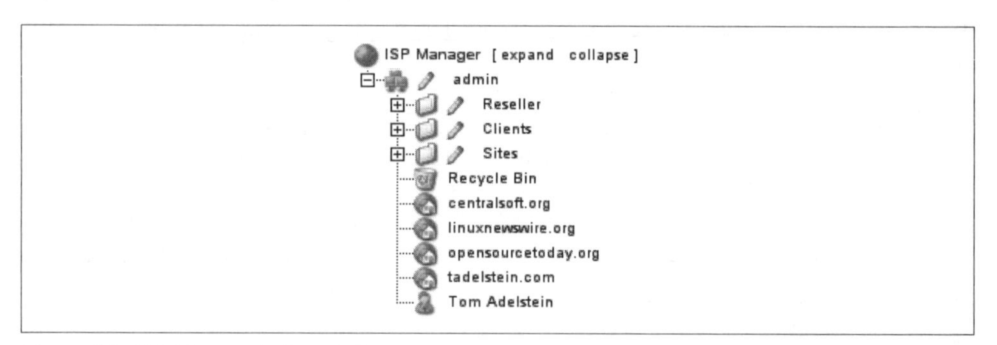

Figure 4-2. ISP Manager's domain list

Then, immediately change the password to one that only you will know. To change the password, select Tools from the toolbar and then click on the symbol for the password (Figure 4-4).

The Change Password dialog shown in Figure 4-5 will appear, and you can fill out the form.

Log out and log in again with the new password.

Figure 4-3. ISPConfig login screen

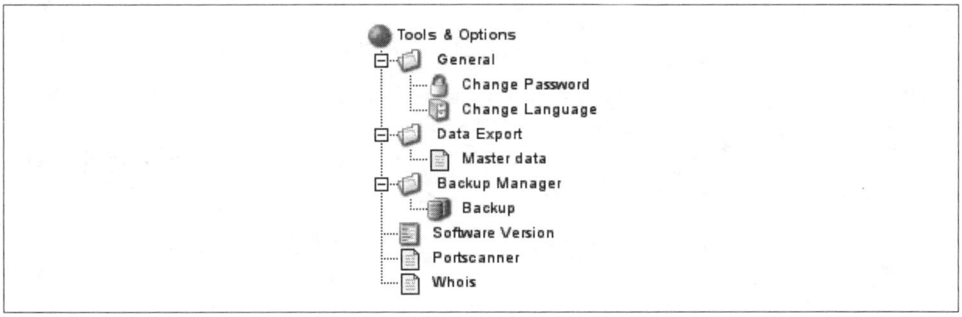

Figure 4-4. The Tools menu

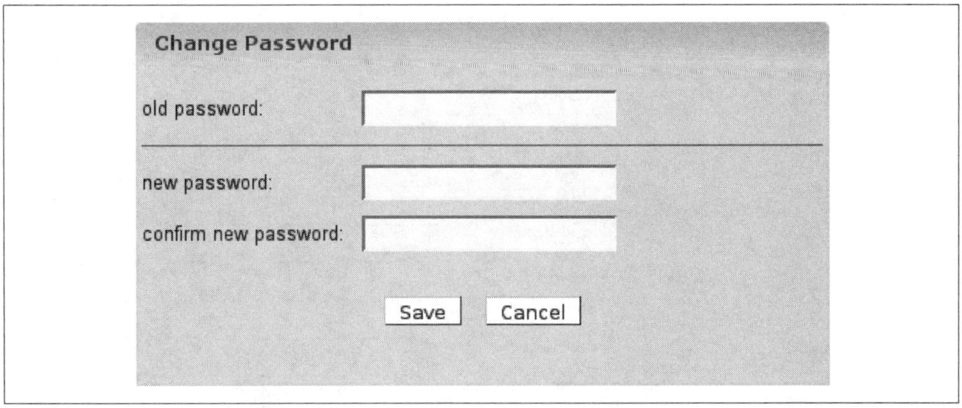

Figure 4-5. ISPConfig form for changing passwords

Before you can set up a web site, you'll have to create an owner for the site. Select ISP Manager in the top toolbar. You will see a navigation menu similar to the one shown in Figure 4-6.

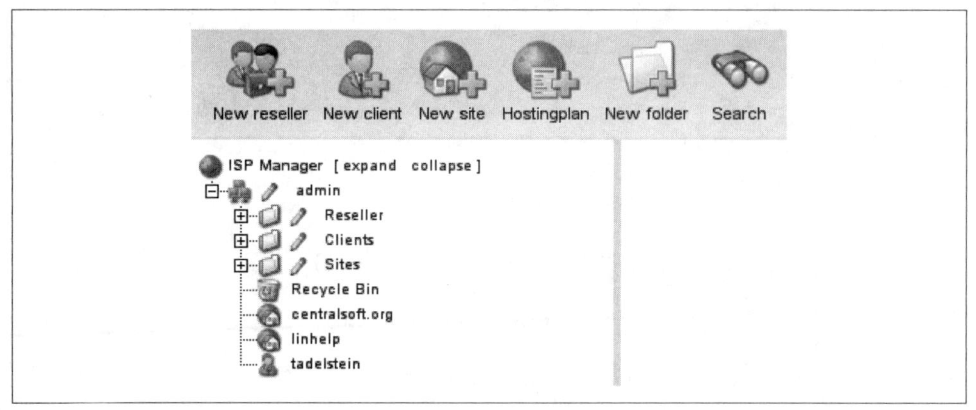

Figure 4-6. The ISP Manager menu with a client and a domain added

Now let's look at how we created the client *tadelstein* and the web site *linhelp*. Click on "New client" in the ISP Manager menu. You will see a dialog similar to the one in Figure 4-7.

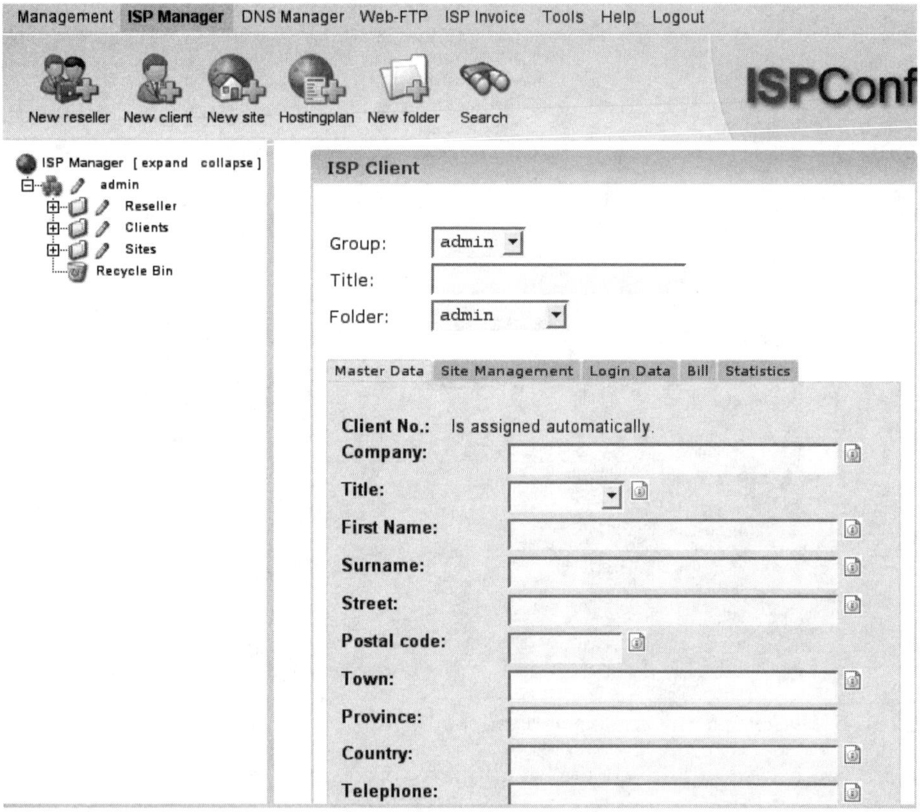

Management ISP Manager DNS Manager Web-FTP ISP Invoice Tools Help Logout
New reseller New client New site Hostingplan New folder Search
ISPConf
ISP Manager [expand collapse]
admin
Reseller
Clients
Sites
Recycle Bin
ISP Client
Group: admin
Title:
Folder: admin
Master Data | Site Management | Login Data | Bill | Statistics
Client No.: Is assigned automatically.
Company:
Title:
First Name:
Surname:
Street:
Postal code:
Town:
Province:
Country:
Telephone:

Figure 4-7. The client information form

Enter the relevant information for the client. Figure 4-8 shows how we filled out the form. Notice that we used *Linhelp.org* as the company name.

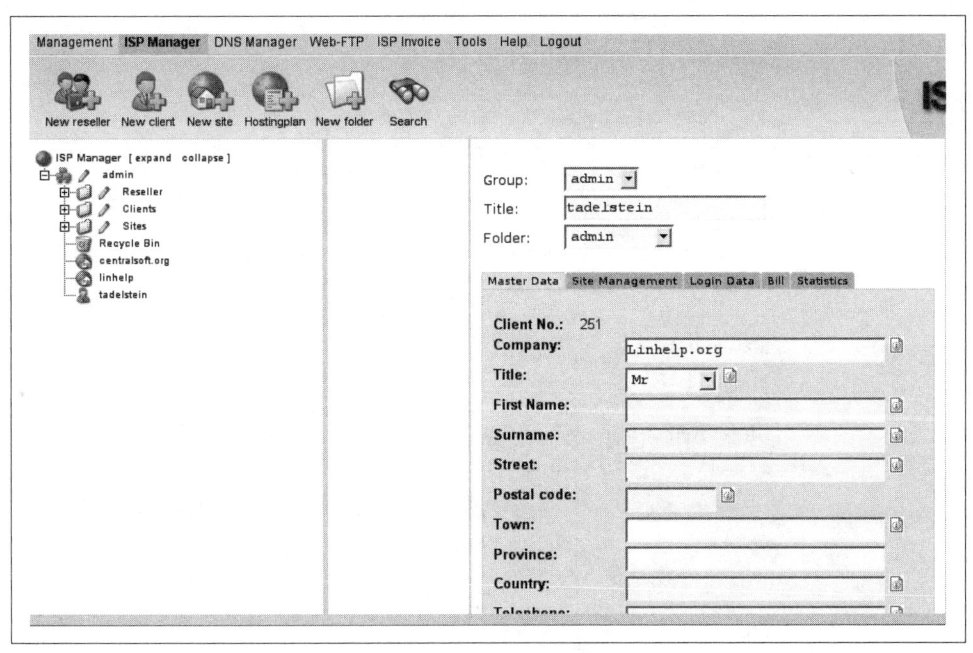

Figure 4-8. The completed form for the administrative client

On the lefthand side of the navigation menu, you'll now see a new icon representing a person, accompanied by the client's name. Now you can set up a web site. Simply select "New site" from the toolbar, and you will see the dialog in Figure 4-9.

Give the web site a name and an IP address, and create a DNS record. Also notice the tabs within the form, across the top of the area where you enter the site name:

- Basis
- User & Email
- Co-Domains
- Statistics
- Options
- Invoice

Each of these tabs provides various configuration and management functions.

Figure 4-9 does not show all of the options on the Basis tab. You will also find several other options that you can give the administrator of the site. For our site, we will provide shell access, database creation, FTP, and login options, as shown in Figure 4-10.

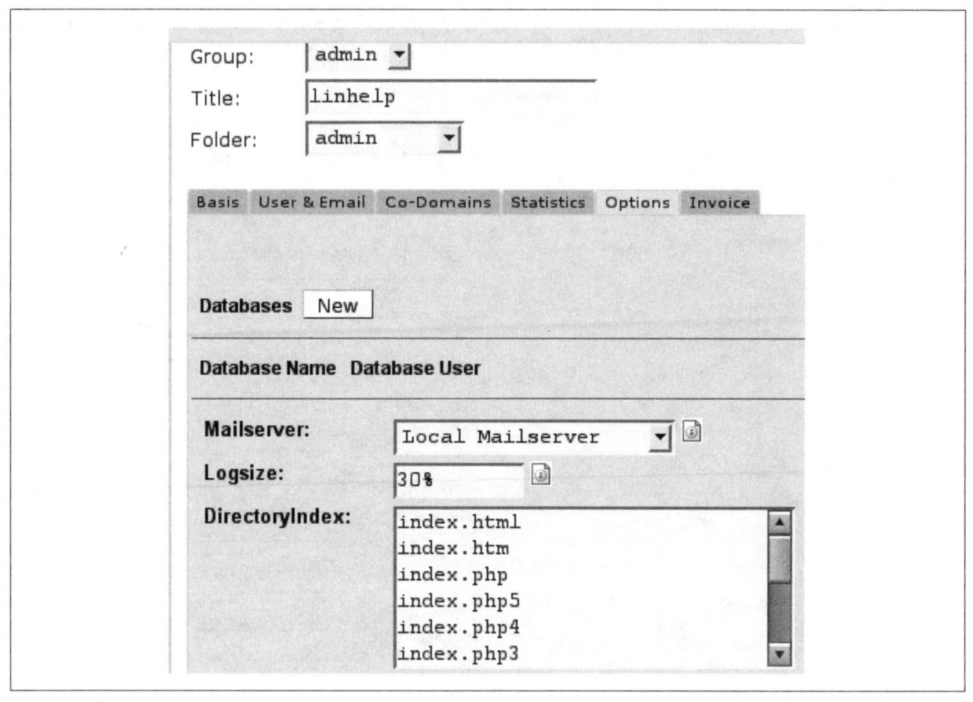

Figure 4-9. The form used to create the web site linhelp.org

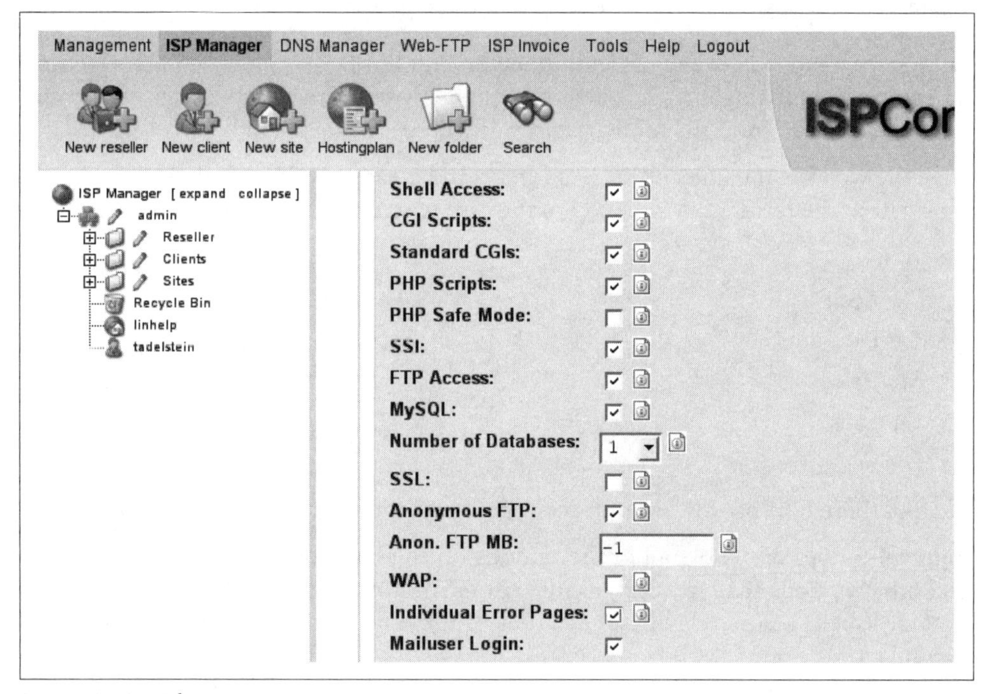

Figure 4-10. Web site options

Notice also in Figure 4-10, under Anon. FTP MB, that the system defaults to –1. That allows the site to provide unlimited FTP disk space. You might want to provide such access if you mirror a download site; otherwise, you might prefer to set a limit so no one can upload enough data to squeeze the disk space used by other services.

By this point you have a usable web site. An easy way to add pages is to use an FTP client such as the graphical *gftp* to transfer a site you have already built from a folder on your desktop, as shown in Figure 4-11.

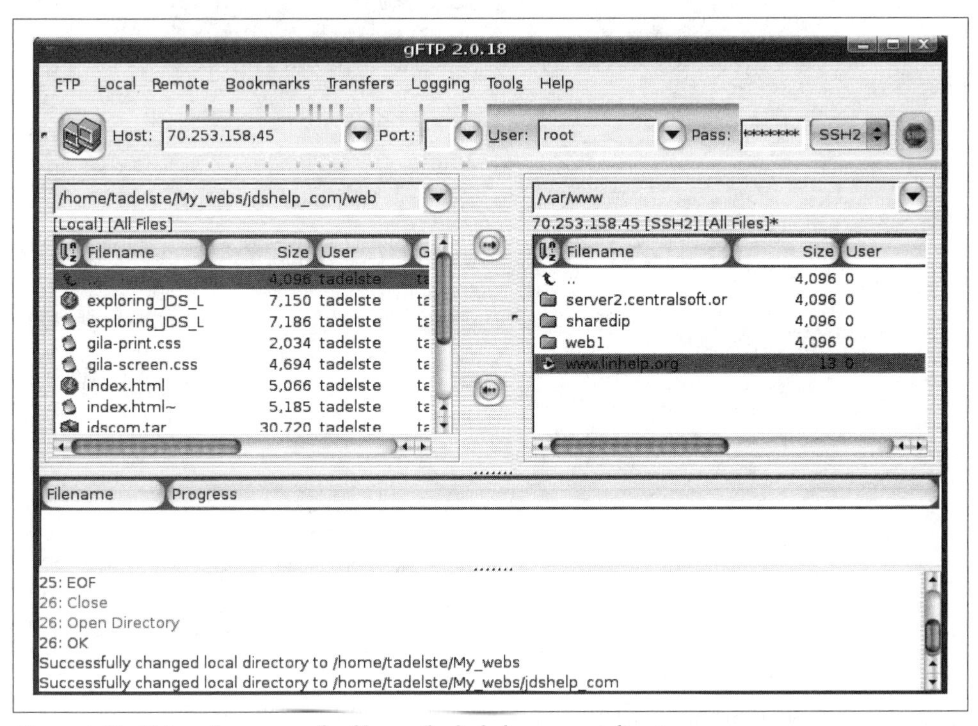

Figure 4-11. Using gftp to transfer files to the linhelp.org root directory

Aiming a browser at *http://linhelp.org* now displays our *index.html* page. You can see the rendering of the page in Figure 4-12.

We now have a simple but functional web site in place. Take a look at Figure 4-13 to gain an understanding of what we've set up.

ISPConfig uses a hierarchical model with */var/www/web1/web* as the root for port 80. In each directory you create under this path, Apache creates another branch where you can put pages. By default, when a browser requests the directory, Apache looks for an HTML file named *index.html* to display. If you don't provide an *index.html* file, the names of the files and directories under the root will be displayed.

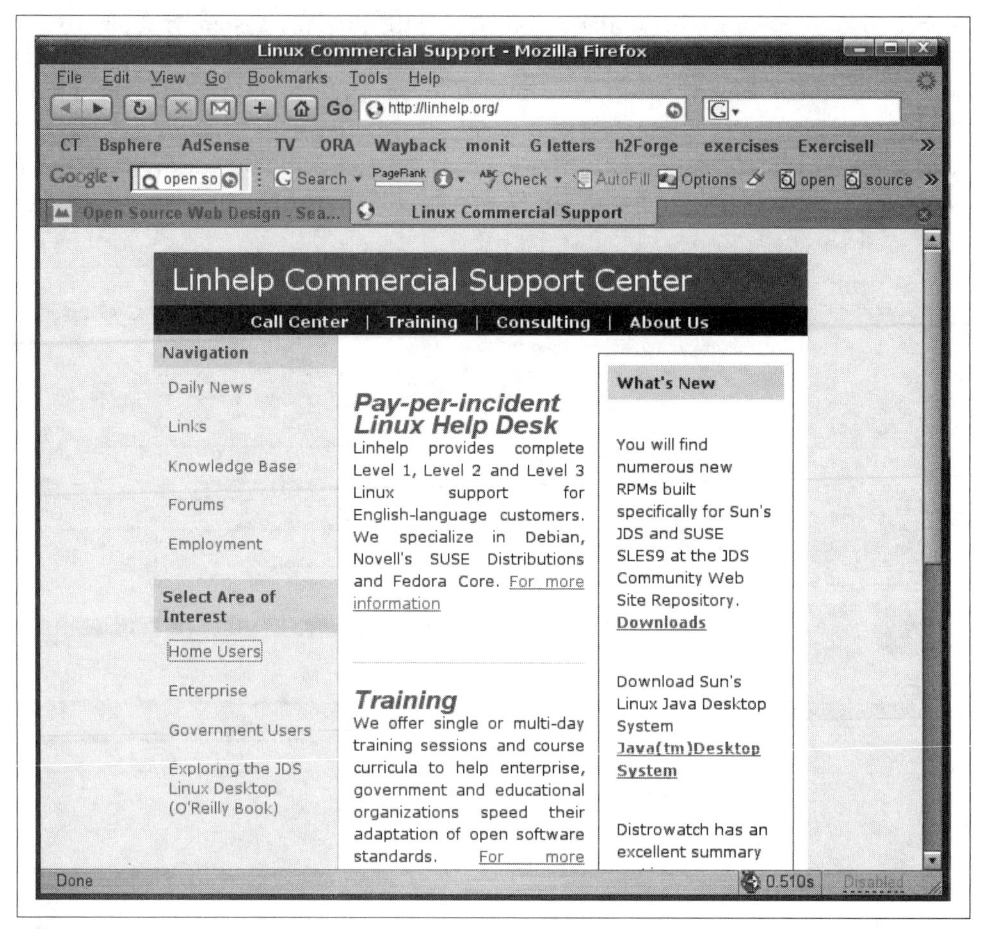

Figure 4-12. The Linhelp.org web site in the Firefox browser

Figure 4-13 provides an example of the root directory of a web site. The home page is displayed whenever a browser specifies the directory name, because it has the default title. The home page contains links to other pages in the site.

The example diagram in Figure 4-13 could be treated like a flow chart. The actual code within the home page would look something like this:

```
<a href="./about_us.html">About Us </a><br><br>
<a href="./products.html">Products </a><br><br>
<a href="./services.html">Services </a><br><br>
<a href="./support.html">Support </a><br><br>
```

Usually, the web team you're supporting will create the directory structure and web pages. You will probably need to offer them a database, too, but that's a topic for another chapter. For now, you just need to know how to establish a web site and Internet domain presence.

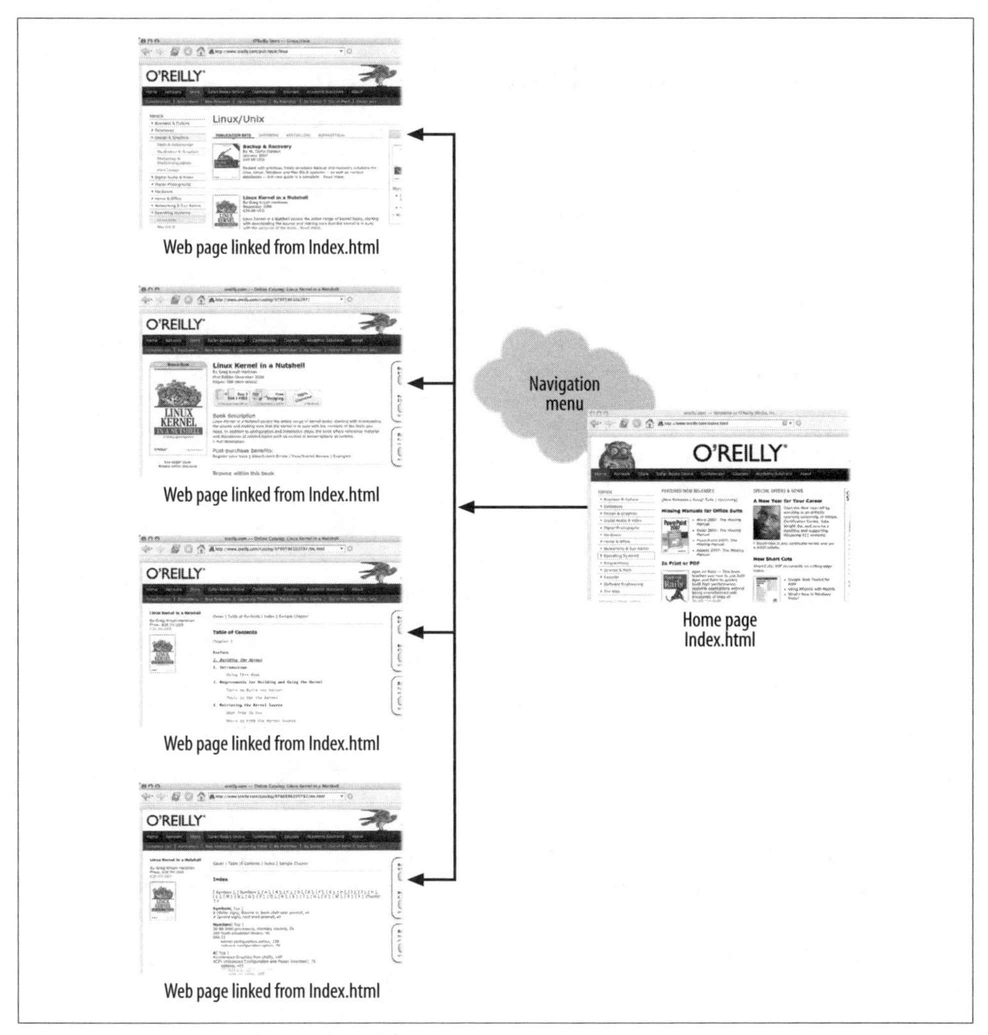

Figure 4-13. Structure of a simple web site

Managing Users and Email

One of the primary Linux system administration tasks is the management of users and their accounts. You can do this using ISPConfig's graphic panel.

Once you've set up your domains, selecting one of them from the ISP Manager section of the toolbar will pull up the ISP Site screen shown previously in Figure 4-9. Let's go back and take another look at it.

The form has six tabs. The second tab from the left is called User & Email. From this tab, you can add new users and manage existing users. When you select New, you will see another form like the one in Figure 4-14.

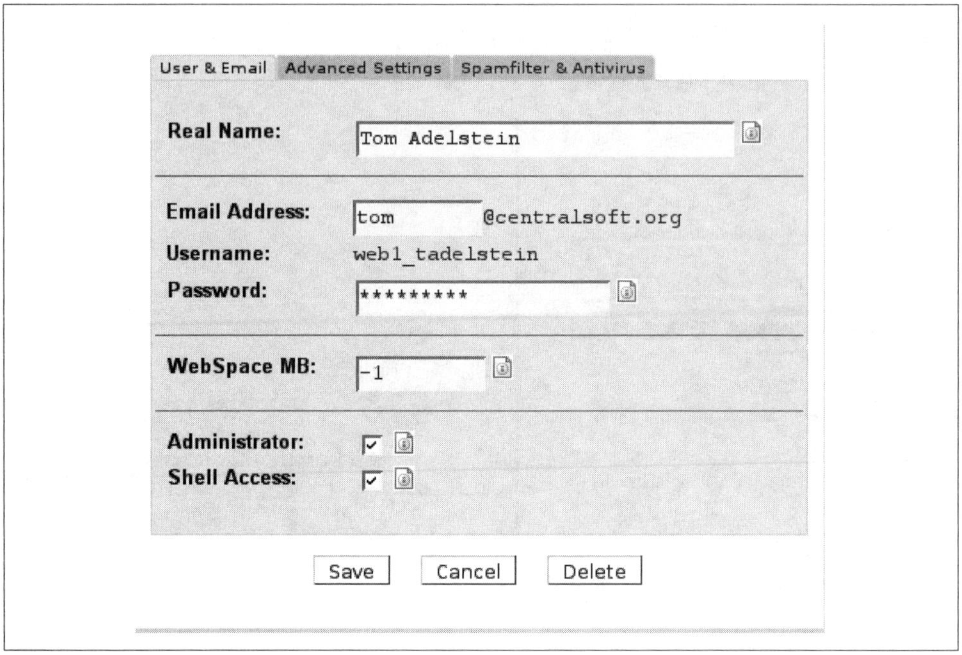

Figure 4-14. The ISP User form

On this form, you can enter the new user's details and set storage space limits. A value of –1 provides unlimited space, but you can manage the quotas in any way you prefer.

On the Advanced Settings tab (Figure 4-15), you can use the forwarding option to allow email sent to the user to be forwarded on to another address. In other words, if the user already has a primary email address that he wishes to use, you can use the forwarding options to send his mail to that account.

Other options on this tab include:

Keep Copy
: Selecting this option when you have email forwarding set up preserves copies of all incoming messages in the user's local mailbox. This is useful in case the forwarded messages don't make it to the destination email address (due to spam filtering or some other problem).

Email Alias
: If you don't want to expose the user's mailbox publicly, visitors to the site can send mail to a generic name such as *info@centralsoft.org* or *webmaster@centralsoft.org*. You can do this by providing an alias account.

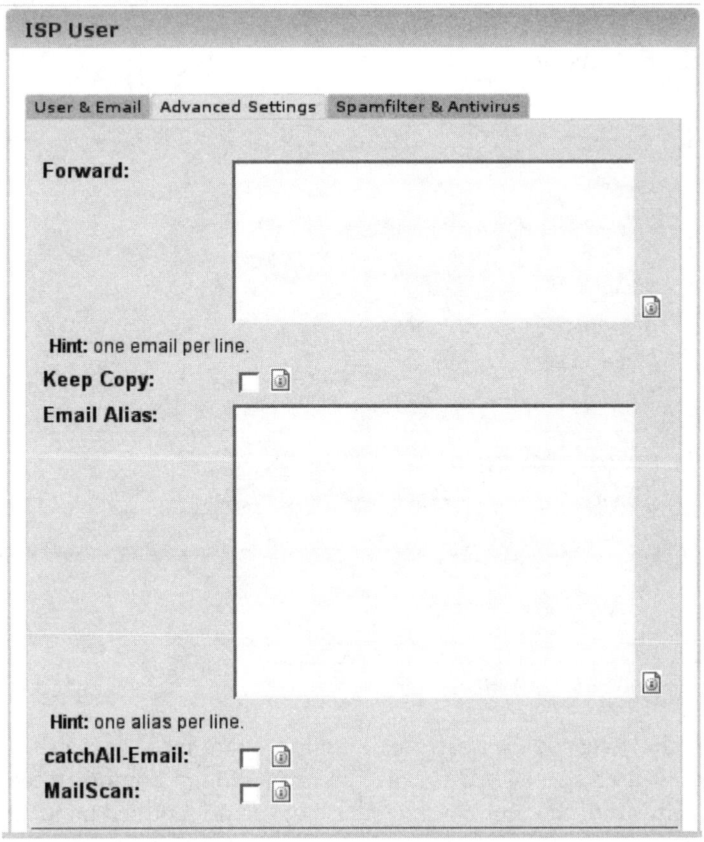

Figure 4-15. Advanced mail options

catchAll-Email

This option redirects to the specified mailbox any emails that are addressed to nonexisting user accounts. People sometimes write to commonly used addresses such as *editor@centralsoft.org* or *advertising@centralsoft.org* without verifying that those addresses are valid. You can collect any such messages at one user account per domain site.

MailScan

If you want emails scanned for viruses or JavaScript code on the server, use this option.

Autoresponder

This option allows you to send an automatic reply to incoming emails addressed to a specific user, for times when the user is out of the office for some extended period.

Moving on to the Spamfilter & Antivirus tab, shown in Figure 4-16, you can consider what spam strategy to use. Activate Spamfilter for an account; you can then specify the filter's behavior.

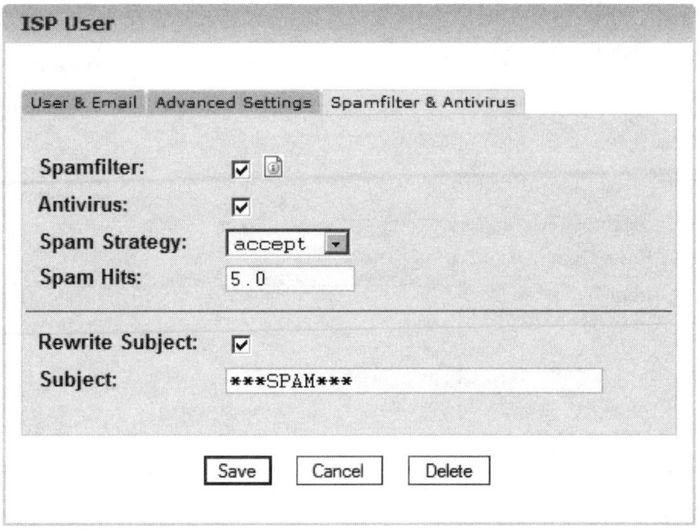

Figure 4-16. The Spamfilter & Antivirus tab

If you select the *accept* spam strategy, you allow spam into the user's inbox and let the user's mail user agent (MUA) sort the spam. Many administrators prefer this strategy initially, until the user has a database of spam-identified mail. Afterward, the user can switch to the *discard* mode, where all emails identified as spam get deleted at the server.

Now let's look at the other spam options:

Spam Hits
: The spam filter runs a number of tests on incoming emails and assigns points for each test. If the sum of points for these tests reaches or surpasses the value specified in the Spam Hits field, the email is categorized as spam and handled according to the user's spam strategy.

Rewrite Subject
: In *accept* mode, choosing this option indicates that the subject line of each email identified as spam should get an identifying prefix (by default, `***SPAM***`). This allows the user to sort emails by subject line.

To enable a user to make changes to her email account herself (including password, spam filter, and antivirus settings), you must select the Mailuser option for that user on the Basis tab of the ISP Site form (see Figure 4-10). To make changes, the mail user can then simply log into a site with a name such as *http://centralsoft.org:81/mailuser*.

User, email, home, and public web directories

Every user of a domain under ISPConfig has his own home directory under the folder *users*. If FTP access is allowed for a domain, users are placed in their home directories when they log in via FTP. Every home directory also contains a folder called *web* that a user can access by visiting a URL like *http://www.centralsoft.org/~user* or *http://www.centralsoft.org/users/user*.

Figure 4-17 shows the structure of the home directory for the user we created for *centralsoft.org*.

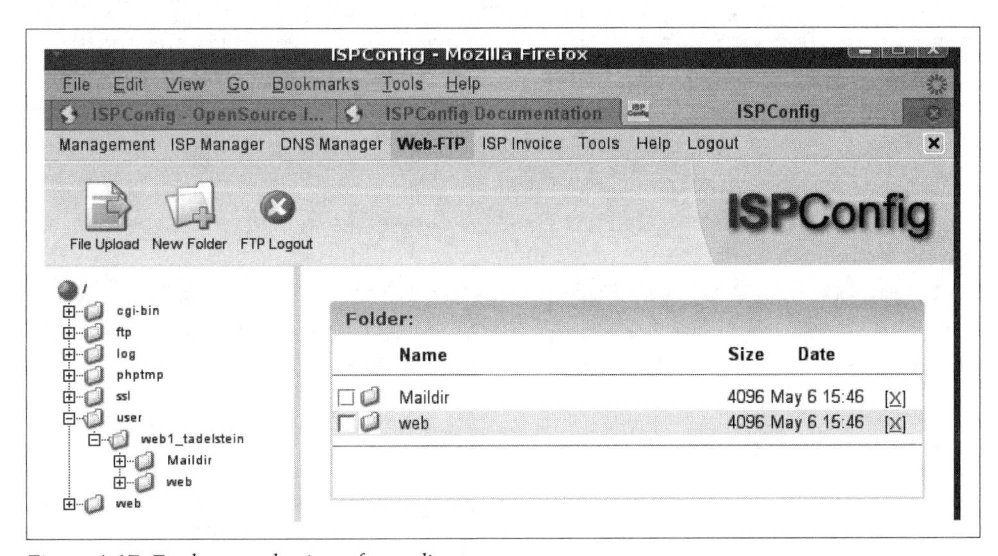

Figure 4-17. Explorer-style view of user directory

Email Client Configuration

At this point, you should understand the basics of setting up a web site, creating a user, and handling mail. But you will probably have to help your users configure their email clients, specifying the outgoing and incoming mail servers. On our system, ISPConfig uses *server1.centralsoft.org* as both the outgoing SMTP server and the incoming POP3/IMAP server.

With most modern email clients, you have the option of choosing Transport Layer Security (TLS). Select TLS when possible when configuring the outgoing server. Because most email clients use their ISP's outgoing server for SMTP, you can select TLS if your ISP uses it. In the vast majority of cases, your user ID and password will travel over your ISP's lines in clear text.

For receiving mail, set up the incoming server (we used *server1.centralsoft.org*), and select either POP3 or IMAP. Use your system name (e.g., *web1_adelstein*) and specify your email address as the alias (e.g., *tom@centralsoft.org*).

If you get an "-ERR Unknown AUTHORIZATION state command" error message when trying to fetch your mail via POP3, you have probably forgotten to activate SSL/TLS encryption. Reconfigure your email client, activate POP3-over-SSL, and try again.

Safeguarding a Linux Web Server

In today's business environment, unexpected events often occur. Ill-intentioned individuals scan IP addresses looking for exploits. They use sophisticated password dictionaries to attempt to gain root access to servers so they can relay spam, viruses, and worms. The situations system administrators face arise from a unique combination of shifting factors that cannot be controlled with precision or certainty. Consequently, administrators need to learn to adapt quickly to new (often hostile) situations.

There are two ways to adapt. First, if you have enough awareness to understand a situation in advance, you can take precautions. We'll call this *anticipation*.

At other times, however, you'll have to adapt to the situation on the spur of the moment, without time for preparation. This involves *improvisation*. To be fully adaptable, you must be able to both anticipate and improvise.

The Role of a Daemon-Monitoring Daemon

No matter how rigorously you work at safeguarding your Internet server, for some unknown combination of reasons, something on your system could fail. In a perfect world, you could monitor every service and the system would immediately alert you of any failures. But then, we don't live in a world where our expectations are always borne out.

Imagine you cohosted your server at an ISP 250 miles from your base of operations. If that server went down, someone would have to call the ISP and get one of their service personnel to run down to the server rack and power it back to a working state. The tech support person at the ISP wouldn't necessarily be immediately available, though, so you might have to wait while a critical application sat idle.

In a large enterprise, you might feel as isolated as if your server was 250 miles away. Data center operators rarely grant access to the server room even to system administrators, so regardless of their locations, it's important for administrators to know how to manage their systems remotely.

A *daemon-monitoring daemon* (DMD) is a utility that watches your services for you and automatically attempts to restart them when they fail. If a service fails, normally you have to log into your server and open a console to execute a command such as */etc/init.d/mysql restart*. A DMD, however, can execute that command for you without any intervention on your part.

If the service restarts, that's the end of the issue. If it doesn't restart successfully, the DMD will make a set number of attempts (say, five) and then contact you via a text message, email, or some other form of communication to alert you of the problem. At that point, you will have to intervene and find out why your service has failed.

The DMD runs like any other service on your system. It has a configuration file that allows you to choose the options that best suit your needs. You can have it start at boot time or start it manually.

In the next section we'll set up a DMD called *monit*, which has the simple web interface shown in Figure 4-18.

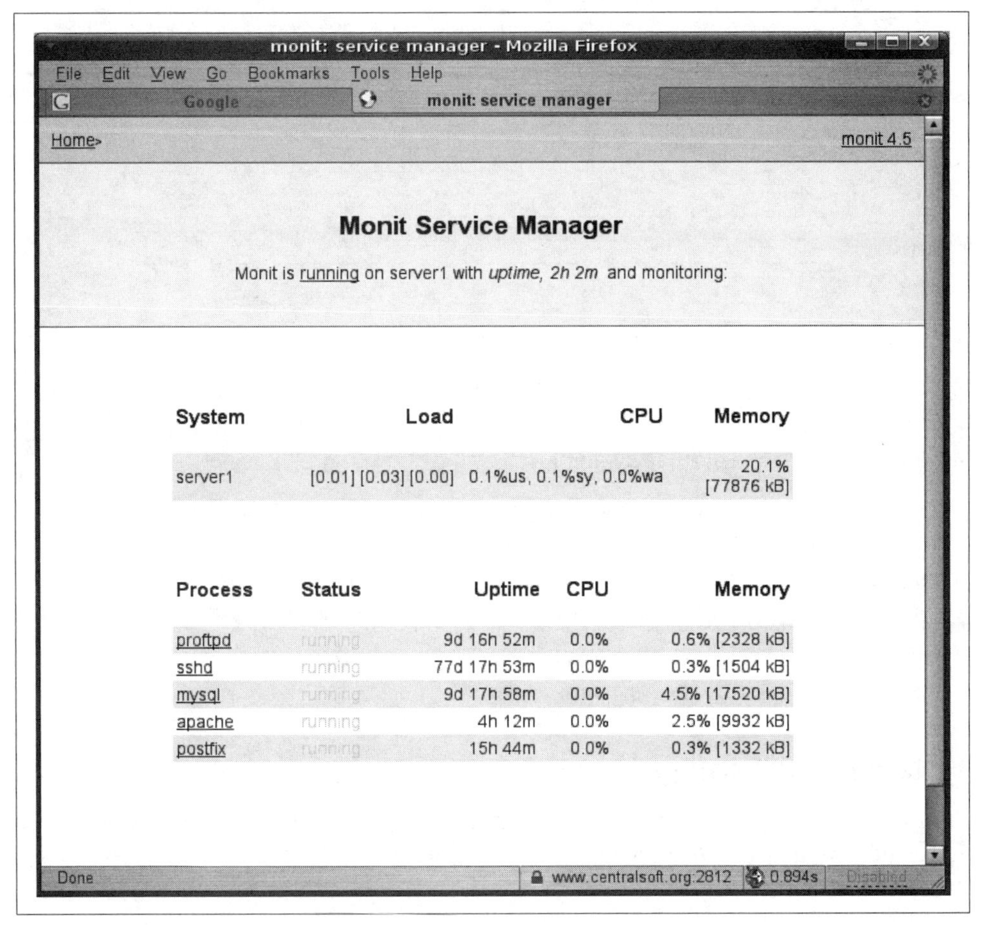

Figure 4-18. Web interface for monit running on centralsoft.org

Notice the five services under surveillance. In Figure 4-19, we drill down to show how the system handles each process. In this case, we're displaying *sshd*.

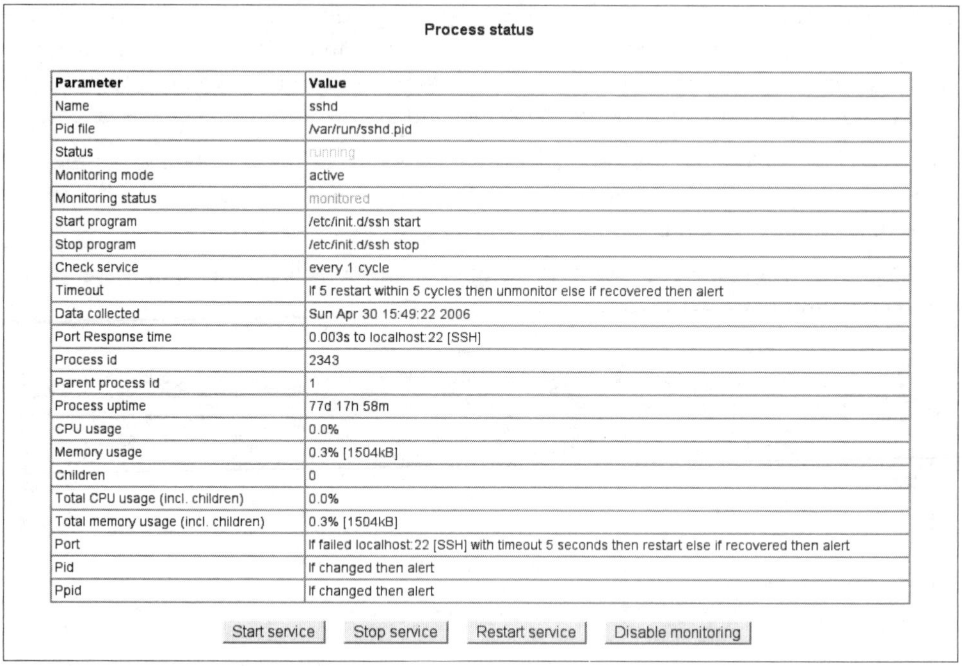

Process status

Parameter	Value
Name	sshd
Pid file	/var/run/sshd.pid
Status	running
Monitoring mode	active
Monitoring status	monitored
Start program	/etc/init.d/ssh start
Stop program	/etc/init.d/ssh stop
Check service	every 1 cycle
Timeout	If 5 restart within 5 cycles then unmonitor else if recovered then alert
Data collected	Sun Apr 30 15:49:22 2006
Port Response time	0.003s to localhost:22 [SSH]
Process id	2343
Parent process id	1
Process uptime	77d 17h 58m
CPU usage	0.0%
Memory usage	0.3% [1504kB]
Children	0
Total CPU usage (incl. children)	0.0%
Total memory usage (incl. children)	0.3% [1504kB]
Port	If failed localhost:22 [SSH] with timeout 5 seconds then restart else if recovered then alert
Pid	If changed then alert
Ppid	If changed then alert

Start service | Stop service | Restart service | Disable monitoring

Figure 4-19. Drilling down to sshd

Notice in Figure 4-19 that the status of *sshd* shows that it is running and that the system is monitoring it. Three lines from the bottom of the screen, you can see the instructions on what to do if *sshd* fails:

```
If failed localhost:22 [SSH] with timeout 5 seconds then restart else if recovered
then alert
```

This policy simply restarts a failed service and sends a message when it successfully restarts.

Finally, *monit* provides four buttons at the bottom of the page for manual intervention. Now, let's see how this system works.

Installing and Configuring monit

To install *monit*, you can either use your Linux system package manager or download the tarball from *http://www.tildeslash.com/monit*. If you're using the Debian setup from Chapter 2, simply enter:

```
# apt-get install monit
```

After you've installed *monit*, edit */etc/monit/monitrc*. The file created during installation contains lots of examples, and you can find more configuration examples at *http://www.tildeslash.com/monit/doc/examples.php*. In our case, we want to:

- Enable the *monit* web interface on port 2812.
- Monitor the *proftpd*, *sshd*, *mysql*, *apache*, and *postfix* services.
- Create a Secure Sockets Layer (*https*) web interface where we can log in with the username *admin*.
- Tell *monit* to send email alerts to *root@localhost*.

Our */etc/monit/monitrc* configuration file looks like this:

```
set daemon  60
set log file syslog facility log_daemon
set mailserver localhost
set mail-format { from: monit@server1.centralsoft.org }
set alert root@localhost
set httpd port 2812 and
     SSL ENABLE
     PEMFILE  /var/certs/monit.pem
     allow admin: test
check process proftpd with pidfile /var/run/proftpd.pid
   start program = "/etc/init.d/proftpd start"
   stop program  = "/etc/init.d/proftpd stop"
   if failed port 21 protocol ftp then restart
   if 5 restarts within 5 cycles then timeout
check process sshd with pidfile /var/run/sshd.pid
   start program  "/etc/init.d/ssh start"
   stop program  "/etc/init.d/ssh stop"
   if failed port 22 protocol ssh then restart
   if 5 restarts within 5 cycles then timeout
check process mysql with pidfile /var/run/mysqld/mysqld.pid
   group database
   start program = "/etc/init.d/mysql start"
   stop program = "/etc/init.d/mysql stop"
   if failed host 127.0.0.1 port 3306 then restart
   if 5 restarts within 5 cycles then timeout
check process apache with pidfile /var/run/apache2.pid
   group www
   start program = "/etc/init.d/apache2 start"
   stop program  = "/etc/init.d/apache2 stop"
   if failed host www.centralsoft.org port 80 protocol http
      and request "/monit/token" then restart
   if cpu is greater than 60% for 2 cycles then alert
   if cpu > 80% for 5 cycles then restart
   if totalmem > 500 MB for 5 cycles then restart
   if children > 250 then restart
   if loadavg(5min) greater than 10 for 8 cycles then stop
   if 3 restarts within 5 cycles then timeout
check process postfix with pidfile /var/spool/postfix/pid/master.pid
   group mail
   start program = "/etc/init.d/postfix start"
   stop  program = "/etc/init.d/postfix stop"
   if failed port 25 protocol smtp then restart
   if 5 restarts within 5 cycles then timeout
```

Statements and options are described in the *monit* documentation at *http://www.tildeslash.com/monit/doc/manual.php*.

In the *apache* section of the *monit* configuration, you'll see this statement:

```
if failed host www.centralsoft.org port 80 protocol http
     and request "/monit/token" then restart
```

This means that *monit* tries to connect to *www.centralsoft.org* on port 80 and tries to access the file */monit/token*. Because our web site's document root is */var/www/www.centralsoft.org/web*, the filename expands to */var/www/www.centralsoft.org/web/monit/token*. If *monit* doesn't succeed, this means Apache isn't running, so *monit* tries to restart it.

Now we must create the file */var/www/www.centralsoft.org/web/monit/token* and write some arbitrary string into it:

```
# mkdir /var/www/www.centralsoft.org/web/monit
# echo "hello" > /var/www/www.centralsoft.org/web/monit/token
```

You can follow a similar procedure on your own system.

Next, create a directory to hold the pem cert file (*/var/certs/monit.pem*) required for the SSL-encrypted *monit* web interface:

```
# mkdir /var/certs
# cd /var/certs
```

You'll need an OpenSSL configuration file to create the certificate. The resulting */var/certs/monit.pem* file should look like this:

```
# create RSA certs - Server
RANDFILE = ./openssl.rnd
[ req ]
default_bits = 1024
encrypt_key = yes
distinguished_name = req_dn
x509_extensions = cert_type
[ req_dn ]
countryName = Country Name (2 letter code)
countryName_default = MO
stateOrProvinceName             = State or Province Name (full name)
stateOrProvinceName_default     = Monitoria
localityName                    = Locality Name (eg, city)
localityName_default            = Monittown
organizationName                = Organization Name (eg, company)
organizationName_default        = Monit Inc.
organizationalUnitName          = Organizational Unit Name (eg, section)
organizationalUnitName_default  = Dept. of Monitoring Technologies
commonName                      = Common Name (FQDN of your server)
commonName_default              = server.monit.mo
emailAddress                    = Email Address
emailAddress_default            = root@monit.mo
[ cert_type ]
nsCertType = server
```

Now create the certificate:

```
# openssl req -new -x509 -days 365 -nodes -config ./monit.cnf -out \
/var/certs/monit.pem -keyout /var/certs/monit.pem
# openssl gendh 512 >> /var/certs/monit.pem
# openssl x509 -subject -dates -fingerprint -noout -in /var/certs/monit.pem
# chmod 700 /var/certs/monit.pem
```

Then edit */etc/default/monit* to enable the *monit* daemon. Change `startup` to `1` and set `CHECK_INTERVALS` to the interval in seconds at which you would like to check your system. We chose `60`. The file should now look like this:

```
# Defaults for monit initscript
# sourced by /etc/init.d/monit
# installed at /etc/default/monit by maintainer scripts
# Fredrik Steen <stone@debian.org>
# You must set this variable to for monit to start
startup=1
# To change the intervals which monit should run uncomment
# and change this variable.
CHECK_INTERVALS=60
```

Finally, start *monit*:

```
# /etc/init.d/monit start
```

Now point your browser to *https://your_domain:2812/* (make sure port 2812 isn't blocked by your firewall) and log in with the username *admin* and password *test*. You should see the *monit* web interface, shown earlier in Figure 4-18.

What's Next

We started out by getting your server up and running so you could use it as an Internet platform. We installed a text-based server without the X Window System (for security and performance reasons) and then set up web-based interfaces to allow you to securely manage and monitor your web services platform.

In the remaining chapters, we will deepen our exploration of Linux system administration. Starting with Chapter 5, you will lose your dependence on self-installing administrative software. We will configure the major Linux applications people use in everyday life in the enterprise and in small-to-medium size businesses.

CHAPTER 5
Mail

This chapter shows how to build an email service for a small- to medium-size site. The elements of the service include:

- The Postfix server as the SMTP mail transfer agent (MTA), which accepts mail from your users and interacts with other sites across the Internet to affect the delivery of mail.
- Post Office Protocol (POP) and Interactive Mail Access Protocol (IMAP) servers, to deliver mail at your site to your users.
- Simple Authentication and Security Layer (SASL) for authenticating mail, to prevent spoofing.

We'll configure Postfix to use traditional file-based authentication, which will scale to thousands of users. Larger email installations might store email account names and passwords in a relational database or an LDAP directory. For an example of an extremely scalable email server based on Postfix with LDAP authentication, see Zimbra (*http://www.zimbra.com*).

The solutions in this chapter bring diverse components together to make a robust, secure, and efficient mail delivery system. Today, people like Wietse Venema (the inventor of Postfix) have reduced much of the complexity and uncertainty involved in configuring email systems. Instead of sweating over complex MTA configuration of an email server, Linux system administrators have other interesting problems to solve:

- How to secure email, a medium not designed with security in mind, against spoofing attempts and other attacks by malicious attackers
- How to protect sensitive company data
- How to give email access to remote users outside a company's network

Key Mail Service Terms

Mail transfer agents do the heavy lifting of Internet communication, moving mail from site to site on the Internet. To send mail, an email sender attaches his system to an MTA, which then uses SMTP to transfer the mail to the MTA responsible for delivering mail to the recipient.

The recipient has several ways to retrieve mail from the MTA, none of them using SMTP: she can log in as a user on the system that runs the MTA, attach to the MTA through a direct connection (such as a dial-up line to an ISP), or tunnel though the Internet to a remote MTA. (We're ignoring methods that are further removed, such as retrieving email through a web interface such as Gmail or using a cell phone.)

Regardless of which of these methods the recipient uses, she retrieves her mail through a *mail delivery agent* (MDA) such as Courier IMAP. The MDA talks to the MTA to get the mail and provides an inbox so she can collect her mail. Mail can then be displayed on the user's system through a *mail user agent* (MUA), such as Outlook, Evolution, or Thunderbird.

Users typically retrieve email using either POP3 or IMAP4 over TCP/IP. Virtually all modern MUAs support both POP3 and IMAP4. MUAs send mail by attaching to MTAs and transferring the mail over SMTP.

Most people keep address books listing their contacts so their MUAs can look up people's email addresses. In enterprise environments, those contact lists are often stored in LDAP directory servers. A lot of users don't even know that their contact lists have LDAP backends.

Postfix, Sendmail, and Other MTAs

You may be wondering why we've chosen to use Postfix as our MTA rather than Sendmail, the original Internet mail server developed in the early 1980s by Eric Allman at UC Berkeley. Sendmail has long had the largest base of MTA installations on the Internet, although we're not sure that's still the case today. Many surveys indicate that Sendmail's popularity has faded rapidly; has less than a 40 percent share of the servers on the Internet. While some hardened supporters of Sendmail say it's flexible and scalable, many system administrators consider Sendmail extremely complex and hard to set up and maintain.

Sendmail was developed before spam and malware evolved, and consequently it has several security flaws. One of the most serious problems with Sendmail is that, by default, it allows *open relaying*—that is, it will relay mail that originates from anywhere outside the server's local network. This security problem is illustrated in Figure 5-1.

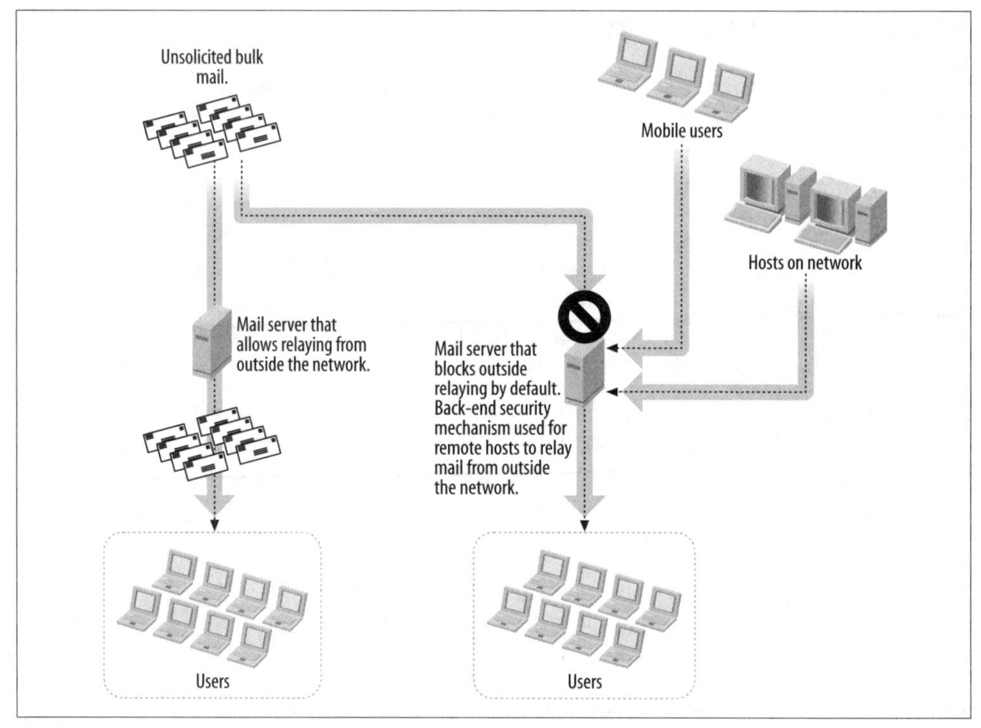

Figure 5-1. Security issues in email's hostile environment

Unsolicited bulk emailers (UBEs), also known as *spammers* or unsolicited commercial emailers (UCEs), are currently responsible for more than 50 percent of the email traffic on the Internet. This severely ties up mail queues, DNS servers, CPU and storage capacity, and infrastructure resources. UBEs use a variety of techniques to hide their real identities, including spoofing IP addresses, forging mail envelopes, and relaying through open SMTP servers.

Well-configured MTAs accept (relay) outgoing mail only from network addresses belonging to legitimate users, normally limited to a particular subnet. But, by default, Sendmail will relay mail sent by anyone. If you use Sendmail and don't take care to turn off open relaying, UBEs can take advantage of your MTA to hide their origins. Your mail server could then be blacklisted as an open relay, which would cause all the legitimate email flowing through it to be treated as spam. In theory, you can even get into legal trouble if illicit material is sent through your relay.

Sendmail's large and entrenched user base, often operating with unpatched, undocumented, and old versions of the application, help UBEs along. Sendmail's developers are aware of the problem* and are working hard to make it more secure, but the best

* See *BusinessWire*, May 25, 2006, "One in Three Companies Operate Without Email Usage Policies, Risking Damage to Their Systems and Reputations, Sendmail Finds" (*http://goliath.ecnext.com/coms2/summary_0199-5568576_ITM*).

security advances have been made in the fee-based version of the product. Aaron Weiss helps clear up some of the confusion about the free and fee-based Sendmail versions in his article, "The Fee vs. Free Divide" (*http://www.serverwatch.com/tutorials/article.php/3580006*):

> To commercialize Sendmail and offer value-added products that significantly enhance its deployment, Sendmail, Inc. was formed. The leading product, Sendmail Switch, is built on the free Sendmail. It sits on top of the Sendmail core and adds a centralized, graphical management console; ongoing security maintenance; round-the-clock support; content management filters (including anti-spam and anti-virus defenses); support for SSL, SASL, and LDAP directories; and auditing, clustering, and remote management capabilities. All of this is wrapped up with a graphical installer and task-based wizards.

In sum, the Sendmail Consortium (responsible for the free, open source Sendmail MTA) is sponsored by Sendmail, Inc., which provides anti-spam, anti-virus, and policy management add-ons for that MTA. Following is a description of Sendmail, Inc.'s business model (from *http://www.sendmail.com/company*):

> Sendmail provides enterprise solutions for secure, dependable, compliant messaging including email, voice, and instant messaging. Sendmail solutions control inbound, outbound and intra-bound email security and compliance. Sendmail is deployment agnostic, deployable in software or appliances. Sendmail products work within the heterogeneous email infrastructure supporting Exchange, Notes, Groupwise, and other email solutions.

Postfix was designed from the ground up as a secure and robust replacement for Sendmail. Debian's default MTA is Exim 4, but we prefer Postfix because Exim has some problems with scalability. It lacks a central queue manager and centralized load balancing. Additionally, there is some indication that the developers of the Debian distributions may make Postfix their default MTA in the near future. In the meantime, you can easily swap Exim for Postfix yourself, as you'll see in the next section.

The Postfix SMTP Mail Server on Debian

To build our server, we're going to use a fresh installation of Debian. If you choose to use another distribution, you can apply procedures similar to those outlined in this chapter to achieve the same results.

Debian Postfix-Related Packages

Use the latest stable version of Debian and configure it with the minimum number of packages. If you don't already have a Debian net installation disk, download one from *http://www.us.debian.org/CD/netinst*. Then do a netinstall, and make sure to provide a fully qualified domain name. Configure Debian as we suggest in this section.

The Debian installer takes you through a standard script before configuration. Follow the standard setup routine until you see a graphic screen asking you to choose the type of installation you want. The screen will look like this:

```
( ) Desktop Environment
( ) Web Server
( ) Print Server
( ) DNS Server
( ) File Server
( ) Mail Server
( ) SQL database
( ) manual package selection
```

Don't select any of the options; you're not going to use the default Debian mail server (Exim) because you'll install Postfix instead. Just press the Tab key and click the OK button that comes up. Debian's installer will then proceed to download and install packages. During the downloads, it will present one more graphical screen asking if you want you to configure Exim (*Exim-config*). Choose "no configuration." Then answer yes when it asks you, "Really leave the mail system unconfigured?"

The Debian installer will continue downloading and configuring packages. When Debian finishes its job, you'll see a screen thanking you for using Debian.

At this point you should remove some unnecessary programs using Debian's *apt-get* utility. If you decided to use another distribution, you can delete the packages according to its procedures. Under Debian, run:

```
# apt-get remove lpr nfs-common portmap pidentd pcmcia-cs pppoe \
pppoeconf ppp pppconfig
```

Now, disable some service scripts:

```
# update-inetd --remove daytime
# update-inetd --remove telnet
# update-inetd --remove time
# update-inetd --remove finger
# update-inetd --remove talk
# update-inetd --remove ntalk
# update-inetd --remove ftp
# update-inetd --remove discard
```

and restart the *inetd* superserver:

```
# /etc/init.d/inetd reload
```

Installing Postfix on Debian

The following command installs the packages necessary to run Postfix, along with TLS and SASL security, which allows you to authenticate users:

```
# apt-get install postfix postfix-doc postfix-tls libsasl2 \
sasl2-bin libsasl2-modules
```

When you install these packages, Debian may choose to install *libldap2* at the same time. *libsasl2* may already be installed on your system.

At this point, Debian's installation utility will begin downloading and configuring several files. You'll notice a long dialog during this process that begins with the following lines:

```
Reading Package Lists... Done
Building Dependency Tree... Done
```

Next, you will see a verbose screen that starts with:

```
You have several choices for general configuration at this point...
```

At the bottom of the screen you'll find the question of interest to us:

```
General type of configuration?

    No configuration
    Internet Site
    Internet with smarthost
    Satellite system
    Local only

     <Ok>          <Cancel>
```

Choose "Internet Site" even if you plan to use Postfix only for local delivery.

Next, an informational dialog will tell you the installation is writing Postfix's configuration file. If you already have a server in production using Sendmail, you will have an existing *aliases* file. In this chapter we assume you're starting from scratch, so enter `NONE` at the following screen:

```
The user root (and any other users with a uid of 0) must have mail
redirected via an alias, or their mail may be delivered to /var/mail/nobody.
This is by design: mail is not delivered to external delivery agents as
root.
If you already have a /etc/aliases file, then you possibly need to add this
entry.  (I will only add it if I am creating a new /etc/aliases.)
What address should I add to /etc/aliases, if I create the file? (Enter NONE
to not add one.)
Where should mail for root go
NONE_____________________________________________
                 <Ok>                          <Cancel>
```

The next question during the installation concerns your FQDN. Postfix requires that the *hostname* command return an FQDN like *mail.centralsoft.org*. But by default, on Debian the *hostname* command yields only *mail*. To let you configure the FQDN, the installation script offers the following dialog:

```
Your 'mail name' is the hostname portion of the address to be shown on
outgoing news and mail messages (following the username and @ sign).
This name will be used by other programs besides Postfix; it should be the
single, full domain name (FQDN) from which mail will appear to originate.
Mail name?
mail.centralsoft.org______________________________
                 <Ok>                         <Cancel>
```

Answer <Ok> to accept the default value that appears in the blue text box.

The next dialog lists default values for the domains your server should answer:

```
Give a comma-separated list of domains that this machine should consider itself the
final destination for. If this is a mail domain gateway, you probably want to include
the top-level domain.
Other destinations to accept mail for? (blank for none)
server2.centralsoft.org, localhost.centralsoft.org, , localhost
                <Ok>                          <Cancel>
```

The listed domains will appear in your *main.cf* configuration file.

The final question is relevant to systems with non-journaled filesystems:

```
If synchronous updates are forced, then mail is processed more slowly.
If not forced, then there is a remote chance of losing some mail if the
system crashes at an inopportune time, and you are not using a journaled
filesystem (such as ext3).
The default is "off".
Force synchronous updates on mail queue?
                <Yes>                         <No>
```

Because nearly all current distributions use the *ext3* journaling filesystem by default, you can answer <No> here.

At this point, the installation finishes and writes the Postfix configuration file. The parameters and values printed here may not make sense to you right now, but you'll find them in the configuration file and will be able to change them if necessary.

Basic Postfix Configuration

The following is a minimal Postfix configuration file, */etc/postfix/main.cf*:

```
smtpd_banner = $myhostname ESMTP $mail_name (Debian/GNU)
biff = no
append_dot_mydomain = no
myhostname =
mydomain =
myorigin = $mydomain
inet_interfaces =
mydestination = $mydomain, localhost.$mydomain, localhost
mynetworks = 127.0.0.0/8
```

If you were building Postfix by hand, you would have to fill in many of these values yourself. The provision of this file makes one appreciate Debian's installation process.

Postfix uses a simple syntax in which each line consists of a configuration parameter followed by an equal sign and a value. Once a parameter is defined, later lines in the file can refer to the parameter by prefixing it with a dollar sign. Thus:

```
mydomain = centralsoft.org
myorigin = $mydomain
```

ends up assigning the value `centralsoft.org` to both the `mydomain` and `myorigin` parameters.

A basic configuration file performs local delivery only. It expects mail recipients to have shell accounts and home directories on the mail server itself. It doesn't require the system to append the `@` suffix (as would be specified by the `append_dot_mydomain` parameter). That's also why the Debian installation process asks you for domains, hostnames, and destination addresses.

Debian's package manager configures many of the parameters in */etc/postfix/main.cf* for you. Table 5-1 shows the key lines. A fuller listing of parameters can be found on the Debian system in the sample file */usr/share/postfix/main.cf.dist*.

Table 5-1. Key Postfix configuration parameters

Parameter	Explanation
`.smtpd_banner = $myhostname ESMTP $mail_name (Debian/GNU)`	Specifies the text in a banner that identifies this server when it's communicating over SMTP with another server. The use of a banner is mandatory according to SMTP specifications.
`biff = no`	*biff* is a small Postfix process that can notify local users that mail has arrived. If you do not have local users, you should turn it off. The default in the Debian install is off.
`append_dot_mydomain = no`	In an environment like ours, appending the domain name to an email address is the MUA's job. This value means that Postfix will not append a suffix such as *@centralsoft.org*.
`#delay_warning_time = 4h`	Uncomment this line to generate "delayed mail" warnings. We will not enable this option because we'll start with a low volume of users and don't expect delays.
`myhostname = server2.centralsoft.org`	Specifies the Internet hostname of this mail system. The default is to use the fully qualified domain name. `$myhostname` is used as a default value for many other configuration parameters.
`alias_maps = hash:/etc/aliases` `alias_database = hash:/etc/aliases`	Specifies the alias databases used by the local delivery agent. An alias is simply an alternative name that one uses instead of the original. For instance, you might specify *admin* as an alias for *root*. The roles of these two parameters are not important to understand at this point; just be aware that Postfix keeps a list of all the aliases in a single file and that these parameters tell the system where it's located and the format of the database file used.
`myorigin = mydomain`	Specifies the domain from which locally posted mail appears.
`mydestination = server2.centralsoft.org, localhost.centralsoft.org, , localhost`	Specifies a list of host or domain names, separated by commas and/or whitespace, for which this server will accept mail.
`relayhost =`	Specifies a default host that this server will use to forward mail when it doesn't know how to reach the recipient. We leave this blank, relying just on the `mynetworks` parameter that follows.

Table 5-1. Key Postfix configuration parameters (continued)

Parameter	Explanation
`mynetworks = 127.0.0.0/8`	Specifies hosts that this server trusts not to be spammers. Here, we've specified only our local host. You can instead specify the `mynetworks_style = class` parameter when Postfix should trust SMTP clients in the same network class (A/B/C) as the local machine. Don't trust the whole class at a dial-up site, because that would cause Postfix to become an open relay for your provider's entire network.
`mailbox_command = procmail -a "$EXTENSION"`	Specifies the optional external command to use to deliver to a local user's mailbox. The command is run as the recipient with proper `HOME`, `SHELL`, and `LOGNAME` environment settings.
`mailbox_size_limit = 0`	Sets a quota on the mail stored for each user. `0` disables the quota limit altogether.
`recipient_delimiter = +`	Specifies the separator used between usernames and address extensions in a lookup table.
`inet_interfaces = all`	Specifies the network interface (network card) addresses on which this mail system receives mail. This is useful only if you have more than one network card.

Some simple and useful customizations you may need to make include the following:

- Typically, `mydestination` lists the domains that appear in the email addresses of local users; that is, the domains for which Postfix accepts and delivers mail. By default, Postfix accepts mail destined for `$myhostname` and `localhost.$mydomain`, the host on which Postfix is running. You can specify that the system should accept mail for your whole domain by adding `$mydomain` to the list:

  ```
  mydestination = $myhostname, localhost.$mydomain, $mydomain
  ```

- You can tell Postfix which hosts you want to allow to relay mail by setting the `mynetworks` parameter. (If you set `mynetworks`, Postfix ignores the `mynetworks_style` parameter.) You can provide one or more IP addresses and/or use the network/netmask notation (e.g., `151.164.28.0/28`). This parameter is useful when you wish to provide relaying to hosts outside your network—for example, to executives working at home, salesmen on the road, etc.

We will make some other changes to */etc/postfix/main.cf* later in this chapter, to add allow authentication and password encryption.

Testing Mail

With Debian's configuration in place, you can receive and send email from your shell account. The following is an example of two test messages sent by one of this book's authors. First, I used a Gmail account to send a mail message to a user account on the *server2.centralsoft.org* system. I read the message from the shell using the standard Unix *mail* command:

```
~$ mail
Message 1:
```

```
Date: Tue, 11 Jul 2006 17:38:32 -0500
From: "Tom Adelstein" <tadelstein@gmail.com>
To: tadelste@server2.centralsoft.org
Subject: Testing simple STMP services
We're sending this email to test our mail server's capability to send
and receive simple SMTP mail.
```

Then I replied to the original email and received it in my Gmail account:

```
Delivered-To: tadelstein@gmail.com
Received: from server2.centralsoft.org
        Tue, 11 Jul 2006 16:10:44 -0700 (PDT)
To:tadelstein@gmail.com
Subject: Re: testing simple SMTP mail
In-Reply-To
tadelste@server2.centralsoft.org (Tom Adelstein)

We're sending this email to test our mail server's capability to send
and receive simple SMTP mail
```

Using the *mail* command is a primitive way to way to manage large volumes of mail, even in a shell account. An alternative is *mutt*, which has a robust interface and significantly more features. As an administrator, you may want to use one of these command-line mail user agents when receiving mail from your Linux system service accounts.

Adding Authentication and Encryption

We've now configured a default SMTP server. What else can we do with Postfix? In this section we will add authentication (using SASL) and encryption (using TLS) to our configuration file, */etc/postfix/main.cf*. With authentication, we make sure only users with proper credentials can use our SMTP server. With encryption, we make sure we do not send users' IDs and passwords across the network in clear text.

SASL Authentication

Figure 5-1 depicted a group of mobile users who needed to relay mail through a mail server from outside the server's local network. This is a common scenario. To distinguish these legitimate users from random spammers, you need a security mechanism on your backend. The Simple Authentication and Security Layer, developed as part of Carnegie Mellon University's Cyrus project, provides Postfix with a means to identify the sources of mail sent to the server and control mail relaying.

System administrators can use SASL to add authentication to many client/server interactions, but each service using SASL on a Linux operating system requires a different configuration file. You can't just install SASL and configure it system-wide.

How did SASL become a part of Postfix's solution? To find the answer, we have to go back to 1999, when the IETF wrote a standard called SMTP's Service Extension for Authentication. You'll see its handiwork if you spot the acronym *ESMTP*—for instance, it's on the first line of the */etc/postfix/main.cf* file (see Table 5-1). ESMTP prevents bulk mailers and/or attackers from using unknowing MTAs as their relays. It also provides security by authenticating users and logging their activities.

The IETF based its ESMTP service extension on SASL. As part of the SMTP protocol, ESMTP simply adds a command called *AUTH* to the commands servers use to connect and exchange data.

SASL's authentication framework allows a variety of ways to store and exchange user credentials. It can use Linux system passwords (*/etc/passwd*, */etc/shadow*, or Pluggable Authentication Modules); separate files; or external services such as LDAP, Kerberos, or *sasldb* (a directory developed by the Cyrus project and included with SASL).

In this chapter we'll show two ways to use Postfix with SASL. First, we'll configure a simple method that works well on small sites where you can give every mail user a user account on the Linux server; this method uses PAM, the default authentication used for the logins. Second, we'll configure a more complex system that lets you authenticate users who don't have accounts on the server.

Logging in can be considered a two-stage process. First, it establishes that the requesting user is whom he claims to be. Secondly, it provides him with the requested service, which can be a command shell (*bash*, *tcsh*, *zsh*, *etc.*) or X Window session running under his identity.

Configuring Postfix with SASL to authenticate users with accounts

Fortunately, Debian packages SASL with Postfix. You can utilize Debian's SASL libraries to allow mobile users to authenticate from outside the network. In the following example we'll use SASL to verify that people who are trying to connect have valid accounts on the Linux server; that is, our system will allow only people with accounts on the server to connect and send mail. We'll use the default Linux login mechanism, PAM, to accomplish this.

When you installed your packages earlier, you provided the necessary SASL extensions and libraries (*postfix-tls*, *libsasl2*, *sasl2-bin*, and *libsasl2-modules*). Now you need to configure */etc/postfix/main.cf*. First, we'll show you how to add parameters to the file using *postconf* commands; then we'll show you an alternative way that involves simply editing */etc/postfix/main.cf* directly.

Turn on authentication in the Postfix SMTP server by adding the `smtpd` (server) parameters to your *main.cf* file with this *postconf* command:

```
# postconf -e 'smtpd_sasl_auth_enable = yes'
```

Next, add a parameter to accommodate some nonstandard clients that don't follow SMTP authentication correctly:

```
# postconf -e 'broken_sasl_auth_clients = yes'
```

The `smtpd_sasl_security_options` parameter lets you control password mechanisms when clients connect to your SMTP server. The following configuration blocks anonymous authentication:

```
# postconf -e 'smtpd_sasl_security_options = noanonymous'
```

Postfix does not allow unauthorized relaying of mail by default. So, to allow your email users to deploy your server from the Internet, you need to add another parameter (note: this should appear on a single line):

```
# postconf -e 'smtpd_recipient_restrictions =
permit_mynetworks,permit_sasl_authenticated,reject_unauth_destination'
```

Finally, the `smtpd_sasl_local_domain` parameter stipulates the name of the local authentication domain. By default, Postfix considers the name of the machine to be the local authentication domain name. To use the default behavior, specify a null string:

```
# postconf -e 'smtpd_sasl_local_domain ='
```

That completes the SASL configuration for Postfix. Alternatively, instead of executing the preceding *postconf* commands, you can edit the */etc/postfix/main.cf* file, add the following entries, and reload Postfix:

```
smtpd_sasl_local_domain = $myhostname
smtpd_sasl_auth_enable = yes
broken_sasl_auth_clients = yes
smtpd_sasl_security_options = noanonymous
smtpd_recipient_restrictions =
    permit_sasl_authenticated,permit_mynetworks,reject_unauth_destination
smtpd_sasl_local_domain =
```

You've just about finished configuring SASL so you can begin using it. Before we discuss the last steps, run these commands to create a SASL configuration file in the directory where Postfix searches for it (the *-p* avoids an error if the directory already exists):

```
# mkdir -p /etc/postfix/sasl
# cd /etc/postfix/sasl
Create the smtpd.conf file with these two lines:
pwcheck_method: saslauthd
mech_list: plain login
```

You can now restart Postfix:

```
# postfix reload
```

The saslauthd daemon

In the *smtpd.conf* file, we specified *saslauthd* as our method for verifying user credentials. Why?

Our password backend uses PAM, and unprivileged processes don't have access to password files. Because the Postfix service account runs with limited privileges, it cannot directly authenticate users.

The SASL libraries packaged with Debian handle this situation by adding an authentication daemon called *saslauthd* that handles requests for Postfix. The daemon runs with superuser privileges in a separate process from Postfix, so a compromised mail server cannot benefit from *saslauthd*'s privileges.

saslauthd doesn't communicate outside of your network, so you can consider the security impact of running the daemon to be minimal even though *saslauthd* uses plain-text passwords. *saslauthd* needs the actual passwords because it uses the same login service you use to open your Linux console session.

Now, let's configure *saslauthd* to run with the mail server. The following directions are tailored for Debian, but you can do the same things with minor changes to directories and commands on other Linux systems.

Debian's port of Postfix runs chrooted in */var/spool/postfix*. Consequently, you need to put your *saslauthd* daemon in the same namespace. Follow these steps:

1. Create the necessary directory for the daemon:

   ```
   # mkdir -p /var/spool/postfix/var/run/saslauthd
   ```

2. Edit */etc/default/saslauthd* to activate *saslauthd*. Remove the comment marker (#) from the line `START=yes`, then add the line:

   ```
   PARAMS="-m /var/spool/postfix/var/run/saslauthd -r"
   ```

3. Your file should now look like this:

   ```
   # This needs to be uncommented before saslauthd will be run automatically
   START=yes
   PARAMS="-m /var/spool/postfix/var/run/saslauthd -r"
   # You must specify the authentication mechanisms you wish to use.
   # This defaults to "pam" for PAM support, but may also include
   # "shadow" or "sasldb", like this:
   # MECHANISMS="pam shadow"
   MECHANISMS="pam"
   ```

4. Next, edit */etc/init.d/saslauthd* to change the location of *saslauthd*'s process ID file. Change the value of `PIDFILE` to the following:

   ```
   PIDFILE="/var/spool/postfix/var/run/${NAME}/saslauthd.pid"
   ```

5. Start *saslauthd*:

   ```
   # /etc/init.d/saslauthd start
   ```

If you use a Linux distribution other than Debian, you'll work with different files, directories, and commands. For example, on many systems the standard way to start *saslauthd* for the first time is via this command:

```
# saslauthd -a pam
```

Debian specifies the use of PAM through the configuration file instead.

Configuring Postfix with SASL to authenticate users without accounts

Using the password file for Postfix authentication on a Linux system requires each person who relays mail via the server to have a user account. Obviously, this solution lacks scalability and requires more administrative time. To support users who don't have accounts on the SMTP server, SASL lets you use other storage options; popular options include *sasldb*, LDAP, Kerberos, and MySQL. The *saslauthd* daemon does not run when Postfix uses one of these methods; the separate program with superuser privileges is not needed because SASL does not need access to the operating system's password file.

When using *saslauthd*, you are limited to plain-text password transmission and login authentication. Therefore, Postfix also offers an alternative *auxprop* method, which supports plain-text, login, CramMD5, DigestMD5, OPT, and NTLM authentication methods.

Of all the authentication mechanisms discussed in this chapter, LDAP is the most robust and scalable, but it has the limitation of using primarily plain-text passwords. To deal with this problem, system administrators typically use Transport Layer Security to encrypt passwords moving from the client to the server (as discussed in the next section). The combination of LDAP and TLS currently provides the best security.

In a small network, *sasldb* can provide a simple solution to enable a few remote users. For really large sites with more users, you might find MySQL more scalable and easier to use and manage.

The *sasldb* and MySQL directory methods require you to install extra software called *auxiliary property plug-ins*. If you configure *sasldb* or MySQL, you have to edit the *smtpd.conf* file and change the line:

```
pwcheck_method: saslauthd
```

to the following, which provides a framework for the auxiliary property plug-ins:

```
pwcheck_method: auxprop
```

TLS Encryption

The drawback of using the *auxprop* method for user validation is that, without additional protections, it uses plain-text validation. When you log into your own workstation, that doesn't present a problem. But when you send your user ID and password over a network in plain text to send an email, whether inside a local network or over the Internet, anyone can easily obtain your credentials.

In Chapter 2 we discussed using TLS, an updated version of SSL encryption, to send passwords from your workstation to your mail server safely. Here, we'll extend this solution to encrypt identifying information by creating a certificate using OpenSSL.

The previous section on SASL and the current section both deal with security, but with different goals. The SASL section handles *authentication*, which determines who has the right to send mail through your server. This section handles *password protection*, which ensures that potential intruders can't read the users' secret credentials. You need both services for secure email.

Start by creating a directory for SSL certificates. Make it a subdirectory under the primary Postfix location in Debian:

```
# mkdir /etc/postfix/ssl
# cd /etc/postfix/ssl/
```

Next, generate two certificates and two encryption keys. You need a private key that no one knows and a public key that allows others to send secure credentials to you. Start with the server's key:

```
# openssl genrsa -des3 -rand /etc/hosts -out smtpd.key 1024
293 semi-random bytes loaded
Generating RSA private key, 1024 bit long modulus
..........................................++++++
......................................++++++
e is 65537 (0x10001)
Enter pass phrase for smtpd.key:
Verifying - Enter pass phrase for smtpd.key:
```

Change permissions on the resulting file that contains the OpenSSL server's key:

```
# chmod 600 smtpd.key
```

Next, generate another key and a certificate:

```
# openssl req -new -key smtpd.key -out smtpd.csr
You are about to be asked to enter information that will be incorporated
into your certificate request.
What you are about to enter is what is called a Distinguished Name or a DN.
There are quite a few fields but you can leave some blank
For some fields there will be a default value,
If you enter '.', the field will be left blank.
Country Name (2 letter code) [AU]:
State or Province Name (full name) [Some-State]:
Locality Name (eg, city) []:
Organization Name (eg, company) [Internet Widgits Pty Ltd]: centralsoft.org
Organizational Unit Name (eg, section) []: web
Common Name (eg, YOUR name) []:
Email Address []:
```

```
Please enter the following 'extra' attributes
to be sent with your certificate request
A challenge password []:
An optional company name []: cso
```

Some debate exists as to whether or not self-generated certificates require the information requested at the prompts. We recommend that you enter the appropriate information for your production site.

The next commands generate a signature key and change the existing keys to the new ones:

```
# openssl x509 -req -days 3650 -in smtpd.csr -signkey smtpd.key -out \
smtpd.crt
Signature ok
subject=/C=US/ST=Texas/L=Dallas/O=centralsoft.org/OU=web/CN=Tom_Adelstein/
emailAddress=tom.adelstein@gmail.com
Getting Private key
Enter pass phrase for smtpd.key:
# openssl rsa -in smtpd.key -out smtpd.key.unencrypted
Enter pass phrase for smtpd.key:
writing RSA key
# mv -f smtpd.key.unencrypted smtpd.key
# chmod 600 smtpd.key
# openssl req -new -x509 -extensions v3_ca -keyout cakey.pem -out \
cacert.pem -days 3650
Generating a 1024 bit RSA private key
.....................++++++
..........................++++++
writing new private key to 'cakey.pem'
Enter PEM pass phrase:
Verifying - Enter PEM pass phrase:
-----
You are about to be asked to enter information that will be incorporated
into your certificate request.
What you are about to enter is what is called a Distinguished Name or a DN.
There are quite a few fields but you can leave some blank
For some fields there will be a default value,
If you enter '.', the field will be left blank
Country Name (2 letter code) [AU]:
State or Province Name (full name) [Some-State]:
Locality Name (eg, city) []:
Organization Name (eg, company) [Internet Widgits Pty Ltd]:
Organizational Unit Name (eg, section) []:
Common Name (eg, YOUR name) []:
Email Address []:
```

Now you need to tell Postfix about your keys and certificates using the following *postconf* commands:

```
# postconf -e 'smtpd_tls_auth_only = no'
# postconf -e 'smtp_use_tls = yes'
# postconf -e 'smtpd_use_tls = yes'
```

```
# postconf -e 'smtp_tls_note_starttls_offer = yes'
# postconf -e 'smtpd_tls_key_file = /etc/postfix/ssl/smtpd.key'
# postconf -e 'smtpd_tls_cert_file = /etc/postfix/ssl/smtpd.crt'
# postconf -e 'smtpd_tls_CAfile = /etc/postfix/ssl/cacert.pem'
# postconf -e 'smtpd_tls_loglevel = 1'
# postconf -e 'smtpd_tls_received_header = yes'
# postconf -e 'smtpd_tls_session_cache_timeout = 3600s'
# postconf -e 'tls_random_source = dev:/dev/urandom'
```

The */etc/postfix/main.cf* file should now look like this:

```
# See /usr/share/postfix/main.cf.dist for a commented, more complete version
smtpd_banner = $myhostname ESMTP $mail_name (Debian/GNU)
biff = no
# appending .domain is the MUA's job.
append_dot_mydomain = no
# Uncomment the next line to generate "delayed mail" warnings
#delay_warning_time = 4h
myhostname = server1.example.com
alias_maps = hash:/etc/aliases
alias_database = hash:/etc/aliases
myorigin = /etc/mailname
mydestination = server1.example.com, localhost.example.com, localhost
relayhost =
mynetworks = 127.0.0.0/8
mailbox_command = procmail -a "$EXTENSION"
mailbox_size_limit = 0
recipient_delimiter = +
inet_interfaces = all
smtpd_sasl_local_domain =
smtpd_sasl_auth_enable = yes
smtpd_sasl_security_options = noanonymous
broken_sasl_auth_clients = yes
smtpd_recipient_restrictions = permit_sasl_authenticated,permit_mynetworks,reject_
unauth_destination
smtpd_tls_auth_only = no
smtp_use_tls = yes
smtpd_use_tls = yes
smtp_tls_note_starttls_offer = yes
smtpd_tls_key_file = /etc/postfix/ssl/smtpd.key
smtpd_tls_cert_file = /etc/postfix/ssl/smtpd.crt
smtpd_tls_CAfile = /etc/postfix/ssl/cacert.pem
smtpd_tls_loglevel = 1
smtpd_tls_received_header = yes
smtpd_tls_session_cache_timeout = 3600s
tls_random_source = dev:/dev/urandom
```

You can now restart the Postfix daemon:

```
# /etc/init.d/postfix restart
Stopping mail transport agent: Postfix.
Starting mail transport agent: Postfix.
```

Configuring POP3 and IMAP Mail Delivery Agents

In this section we'll add email delivery agents to complement Postfix. Use the following command on Debian to add an IMAP and a POP3 server:

```
# apt-get install ipopd-ssl uw-imapd-ssl
```

We've chosen *ipopd-ssl* to provide POP2 and POP3 mail delivery agents and *uw-imapd-ssl* for IMAP. Don't let the *ssl* suffixes fool you—both packages provide unencrypted services as well as encrypted ones. Standard IMAP uses port 143, and POP3 uses port 110. The encrypted protocols and ports are POP3S (port 995) and IMAPS (port 993).

Originally from the University of Washington, the *ipopd-ssl* package is now maintained by Debian. You just need to install it; it basically configures itself to use the home mail directory that exists on a mail server like the one we set up in Chapter 4. ISPs continue to use POP3, but it is rarely used in enterprises.

uw-imapd-ssl provides an IMAP server. Although it requires more disk space, IMAP is superior to POP because it leaves mail on the server and allows users to view messages from any location that has Internet access and a mail client. We don't know of any current mail clients unable to understand IMAP, so most mail users will want to use it.

You can also provide webmail on your mail server using SSL (*https*), making it convenient for users to access their email from a web browser.

In our configuration, users need standard Linux accounts on your email server, even though they read their mail with an email client on another system. Postfix usually allows local delivery inside a domain, but it requires backend relaying (as previously discussed in the section "Configuring Postfix with SASL to authenticate users without accounts") if users are outside the domain.

uw-imapd has advantages and disadvantages. On the plus side, it uses Unix-style *mbox* email storage, which maintains all of a user's mail in a single file in his home directory. You will also find this service easy to administer.

On the minus side, *uw-imapd* does not allow virtual users or those without shell accounts and home directories to access mail. In addition, many administrators don't like the simple *mbox* storage format, preferring the more hierarchical *maildir* format. As a single-file format, *mbox* allows only one application to access it at the same time, which requires file locking and might slow the system under heavy load.

File locking is a mechanism that enforces access to a computer file by only one user or process at any specific time. The purpose of locking is to prevent conflicting updates.

Many people consider file locking a problem in the case of mail. Many distributed filesystems lack reliable locking mechanisms. Some people also believe file locking is insufficient to prevent occasional *mbox* corruption. With Linux, corruption is possible if a mail process is terminated in the middle of updating an *mbox*.

The *maildir* format, in contrast, allows concurrent access by multiple applications and does not require file locking.

Other IMAP servers, such as Cyrus, Courier, and Dovecot, use the *maildir* format and allow virtual users and user accounts without shell access and home directories to access mail. Configured in conjunction with Postfix, the user accounts have only mailboxes. This allows the administrator to maintain the MTA and MDA without having to manage standard user accounts on the server itself.

IMAP servers other than *uw-imapd* are difficult and require significant knowledge to configure, so you will have to judge for yourself whether the size of your organization warrants their use. If so, you'll need to look at other sources of information, such as *The Book of Postfix* by Ralf Hildebrandt and Patrick Katter (No Starch Press).

Email Client Configuration

In our introduction to the */etc/postfix/main.cf* Postfix configuration file earlier in this chapter, we left it up to the user's email client to add the domain name when a user typed in an account name:

```
append_dot_mydomain = no
```

This matches the behavior of most clients, which can tack on a domain such as *@centralsoft.org* when the user types an account name into the "To" field of an email message.

If you configure Postfix to use encryption, as demonstrated earlier in this chapter, the email user also has to configure her MUA to use TLS encryption for sending mail. Most modern clients support this and provide a graphical interface to enable TLS for use with the outgoing server.

When you are not on Postfix's defined network and are stationary (as opposed to a mobile user), use your ISP's outgoing server for SMTP. In that case, you should select TLS if your server provider uses it. In the vast majority of cases, your ID and password will travel over your ISP's lines in clear text.

For your mail server to receive mail, you'll need to set up the incoming server with DNS, as discussed in Chapter 3. As a brief reminder, you'll use `MX` records to do this. A typical `MX` record looks like this:

```
MX 10 server1.centralsoft.org.
```

This record says that email addressed to the domain *centralsoft.org* should be delivered to *server1.centralsoft.org* (which is the mail server for the domain).

What's Next

At this point, you've installed and configured Postfix and an IMAP and POP3 service. You have the essential components of a mail system you can use in a corporate environment.

If this is your first exposure to mail, you may now understand why enterprises spend large amounts of money to buy packaged systems licensed on a per-seat basis. You may also understand why they hire a dozen or more system administrators to manage their email communication infrastructures. This area requires special expertise. After you've mastered the information in this book, you may want to study more components of advanced email systems. You should understand how to install and configure a scalable and secure mail server and how much effort is required to gain expertise in this area. You will also need an understanding of directory services such as OpenLDAP or Fedora Directory Server to validate large numbers of users and provide a listing of mail users in your enterprise.

The next chapter discusses the service most people see as an organization's most critical offering: a web server. After we introduce the setup of the Web's most popular server, Apache, we'll proceed to add on a range of important features, such as support for dynamic web sites and reporting statistics, and give you some troubleshooting tips.

CHAPTER 6

Administering Apache

In this chapter, we'll build a Linux web server from scratch. You'll learn how to:

- Install and configure Apache, PHP, and MySQL
- Manage multiple web sites with virtual hosts
- Encrypt sensitive pages with SSL
- Enable server-side includes and CGI scripts
- Test for performance and security problems
- Install *vlogger* and Webalizer to view site statistics
- Install Drupal, a content management system that you'll find useful in many environments and that uses many of these elements

This chapter describes an environment with a single web server; in Chapter 7, we'll show you how to set up a pair of web servers for load balancing.

Web servers are large and complex, and when configuring them it isn't always clear how or why things are done. Along the way, we'll point out why we have chosen some alternatives and passed by others. To keep explanations short and simple, we'll use standard Debian procedures and defaults. We'll secure the installations as we go, to underscore the lesson that you have to think about security and build it in from the start. Toward the end of the chapter, you'll find the "Troubleshooting" section.

Static and Dynamic Files

A basic web site consists of files: HTML, graphics, JavaScript, stylesheets, and other types. The contents of these files are *static*—they don't change on the server, and the only job of the web server is to return them to the browser on request. A web server needs only a little configuration to serve static files.

Many sites have some *dynamic* aspects, too, including content generation, access control, and database storage and retrieval. The simplest way to make static HTML files dynamic is with *server-side includes* (SSI), which are specially formatted HTML comments that Apache interprets to echo the values of variables or include the contents of other HTML files. SSI file inclusion is a simple way for a site to define a common header and footer for its pages, for instance.

SSI has its limits, though, and most dynamic sites use the far more powerful *Common Gateway Interface* (CGI) programs. These executable programs can be written in any language that Linux supports, although the most popular choices are dynamic ("scripting") languages such as Perl, PHP, Python, and Ruby, followed by Java. CGI is a protocol that specifies how web clients and servers should exchange requests and responses.

When CGI first appeared on the Web, CGI programs were completely separate from web servers. Each request caused the web server to start up a new CGI process. The startup cost increased system load as sites got busier, so alternatives were developed.

People often confuse the CGI protocol with this early implementation method and think that CGI is inherently slow. However, the CGI standard does not define implementation. There are faster methods that follow the same CGI protocol.

One faster method is FastCGI, which starts up the CGI program as a separate long-running process and manages two-way communications between it and the web server. This avoids the constant reload cost, and the process separation ensures that if the CGI program crashes, it won't bring down the web server with it. FastCGI does have one drawback, though: FastCGI programs, like standalone CGI programs, can't access web server internals, which might be required by some complex applications.

Some CGI programs have evolved into Apache modules that are loaded as part of the web server itself: the Perl interpreter became *mod_perl*, PHP became *mod_php*, and *mod_squad* became a terrible '70s pun. The performance of FastCGI programs and Apache modules is roughly similar, and modules have both advantages and disadvantages. They have access to all of the server's internal data structures and functions, so they can be used in various stages of web transactions, not just to generate HTML content. However, modules also increase the size and memory usage of the web server, and module bugs can crash the web server.

A Simple LAMP Setup

The standard *LAMP* (Linux, Apache, MySQL, PHP/Perl/Python) setup uses Apache modules to perform CGI functions. This approach performs and scales well, although there are limits to everything. We'll point out some of those limits in this chapter, but you can skip those sections if you prefer to learn through bitter experience. We already have the L, so let's explore the A; M and P won't be far behind.

Apache isn't the fastest web server, or the easiest to configure, or the most secure, but it's good enough to dominate all others. According to Netcraft, Apache powers more than 60 percent of all public web sites (*http://news.netcraft.com/archives/web_server_survey.html*). Apache runs on Linux, Mac OS X, and all other Unix-like systems, as well as the many incarnations of Microsoft Windows.

Like other Unix programs, Apache can be built with all of its modules combined into one big program (*static linking*), or with modules that are loaded into memory as needed (*dynamic shared objects*, or DSOs). The DSO method is easier and more flexible, since it allows you to add modules to Apache after you've built it. The Debian installation for PHP and other Apache modules uses the DSO method.

Installation

In this section, we'll install Apache, PHP, and MySQL. We'll test each with its default setup to ensure they're all running correctly. In the following section, we'll dive into Apache configuration files and explore how to customize our setup.

Apache

You need to be the *root* user to install packages. First get the Apache server:

```
# apt-get install apache2
```

This should install Apache and start it. Did it work? To find out, enter your site's URL in a web browser. For the examples in this chapter, we'll use the name of our test server (*http://server1.centralsoft.org*). When you see this URL in the examples, substitute the URL of your own server. If you're running your browser on the same machine as your web server and might have problems with DNS resolution of your server's name, you can use *http://localhost* or *http://127.0.0.1*. If you're testing from outside, you can use the server's IP address, such as *http://70.253.158.41*.

Type your server's URL into a web browser, and you should see a page that proudly starts with:

```
If you can see this, it means that the installation of the Apache
web server software on this system was successful. You may now add
content to this directory and replace this page.
```

Your browser should also show that Apache has remapped the address you typed as follows: *http://server1.centralsoft.org/apache2-default*.

We'll explain this a little later when we get into Apache configuration files. But for now, let's create our first web file. Go to the directory that Apache considers the home directory for your web site and create a little text file:

```
# cd /var/www
# echo testing > test.html
```

Then type its URL (e.g., *http://server1.centralsoft.org/test.html*) into your browser.

You should see the word `testing` on the screen. Your Apache server is running with no access restrictions, serving any files and directories that exist under */var/www*.

PHP

PHP is the most popular Apache CGI module. In this chapter, we'll use PHP 4, which remains more popular than its eventual successor, PHP 5. Using either version is a good way to create dynamic web pages, and the large library of PHP modules adds many useful functions. Begin by getting the PHP program and libraries:

```
# apt-get install php4
```

Now get the PHP Apache module, *mod_php*. This command will install *mod_php* and tell Apache to let it execute files with a *.php* suffix:

```
# apt-get install libapache2-mod-php4
```

Create this test PHP script and save it to */var/www/info.php*:

```
<?php
phpinfo( );
?>
```

Then enter the script's URL (*http://server1.centralsoft.org/info.php*) in your browser.

You should see a page with tables full of PHP configuration information. This information tells a lot about your machine that you may not want to share with the world, so you should delete this script after testing it. If you don't see anything, take a look at the"Troubleshooting" section at the end of this chapter.

By the way, if you're a newbie, you just wrote your first CGI script! (In the later section on CGI, we'll provide more details about how web servers run external programs and scripts.)

MySQL

If you don't need a database, you have a *LAP* platform and you can skip this section. For the full *LAMP* set, get the MySQL database server and the PHP MySQL module:

```
# apt-get install mysql-server
# apt-get install php4-mysql
```

This is all you need to create PHP CGI scripts that can access the MySQL database server, but we'll also install the standard MySQL command-line client (*mysql*) to help us test the database without involving PHP or Apache:

```
# apt-get install mysql-client
```

If you run the *mysql* client but don't specify a MySQL account name with the *-u* option, it tries to use your Linux account name. In our examples, we're logged in as *root*, so the name would be *root*. The MySQL administrator account happens also to be called *root*, and it has complete control of the database. However, the MySQL and Linux *root* accounts have nothing to do with one another. MySQL stores its account names and passwords in the database itself.

Use this command to see whether the database server is up and running:

```
# mysql -u root
Welcome to the MySQL monitor.  Commands end with ; or \g.
Your MySQL connection id is 5 to server version: 4.0.24_Debian-10sarge2-log

Type 'help;' or '\h' for help. Type '\c' to clear the buffer.

mysql> show databases;
+----------+
| Database |
+----------+
| mysql    |
| test     |
+----------+
2 rows in set (0.00 sec)

mysql> quit;
Bye
#
```

If this works, your MySQL server is running. The bad news is that the MySQL *root* user starts out with no password. Let's assign one (use some gibberish password of your choice where we've written *newmysqlpassword*):

```
# mysqladmin -u root password newmysqlpassword
```

Now try to get in again without the password:

```
# mysql -u root
ERROR 1045: Access denied for user: 'root@localhost' (Using password: NO)
```

For once, we're glad something failed, because it was supposed to. Try again:

```
# mysql -u root -p
Enter password: newmysqlpassword
Welcome to the MySQL monitor.  Commands end with ; or \g.
Your MySQL connection id is 8 to server version: 4.0.24_Debian-10sarge2-log

Type 'help;' or '\h' for help. Type '\c' to clear the buffer.

mysql> quit;
```

Make a note of this MySQL root password, because you'll need to provide it later in the chapter when we install the Drupal application, as well as whenever you want to access MySQL as the main administrator.

For security reasons, the default installation of MySQL that we've performed restricts the MySQL server to local clients such as PHP web scripts or the command-line *mysql* client. Otherwise, people could connect to your database through the Internet, which would be a cruel thing for an innocent database. You can check that the MySQL server's address is 127.0.0.1 (the local or *loopback* address) using this command:

```
# netstat -tlnp
Proto Recv-Q Send-Q Local Address    Foreign Address  StatePID/Program name
tcp        0      0 127.0.0.1:3306   0.0.0.0:*        LISTEN25948/mysqld
```

Apache Configuration Files

Apache uses plain ASCII configuration files. Their locations vary across Linux distributions; Table 6-1 shows where Debian puts them.

Table 6-1. Apache configuration files

File/Directory under /etc/apache2	Uses

apache2.conf	Main configuration file. Includes other files through the following directives:
	`# Include module configuration:`
	`Include /etc/apache2/mods-enabled/*.load`
	`Include /etc/apache2/mods-enabled/*.conf`
	
	`# Include all user configurations:`
	`Include /etc/apache2/httpd.conf`
	
	`# Include ports listing`
	`Include /etc/apache2/ports.conf`
	
	`# Include generic snippets of statements`
	`Include /etc/apache2/conf.d/[^.#]*`

*conf.d/**	Anything you like can go here. By default, it's empty.
mods-enabled/.conf*	Definitions for each enabled module. Debian includes the programs *a2enmod* to enable a module and *a2dismod* to disable one. The effect is to move *xyz.conf* and *xyz.load* files between */etc/apache/mods-available* and */etc/apache2/mods-enabled* for a module named *xyz*. The *apache2.conf* file uses the files under *mods-enabled*.
*sites-enabled/**	Definitions for each web site. The default is *000-default*, but there's nothing magic about that name. You can have as many files here as you like.
.htaccess	Definitions for a directory, contained in that directory. Overrides other configuration files because it's read last. Permitted only if `AllowOverride` is not set to none. Can be changed without reloading Apache. This is how many webmasters allow their clients to customize their sites without touching the main Apache configuration files.

If `AllowOverride` is enabled for any directory, on every client request Apache must check every directory from the document root down for any *.htaccess* files, and read them. This slows down Apache. More importantly, it spreads some of Apache's configuration across the filesystem, making it hard to know what options are in effect for a directory at any time. If you don't need *.htaccess* files, don't use them. They're disabled by default.

Configuration File Directives

Each Apache configuration file is divided into sections that contain Apache *directives* (commands or settings) and their values. Some directives are part of the Apache core, while only specific modules use others. If a directive refers to a module that you haven't configured Apache to use, Apache will fail to start, and a message containing the incorrect lines will be written to the error log.

After you have Apache running successfully, you can see which Apache directives are currently usable by typing this command:

```
# /usr/sbin/apache2 -L
```

The "Troubleshooting" section at the end of this chapter has step-by-step guidelines to help you diagnose web server problems.

Assuming the test file worked, you can now turn to configuring Apache. Following are the contents of the default Apache configuration file, */etc/apache2/sites-enabled/000-default*. Sections begin and end with HTML-style tags, such as:

```
<VirtualHost *>
...
</VirtualHost>
```

Here's a copy of the file that we've annotated with comment lines:

```
# Answer to any name or IP address:
NameVirtualHost *

# For any virtual host at any address, any port:
<VirtualHost *>
    # If Apache has problems, whom should it contact?
    ServerAdmin webmaster@localhost

    # Our web site files will be under this directory:
    DocumentRoot /var/www/

    # Overall directives, in case we move DocumentRoot
    # or forget to specify something later:
    <Directory />
        # Lets Apache follow symbolic links:
        Options FollowSymLinks
        # Disables .htaccess files in subdirectories:
        AllowOverride None
    </Directory>

    # DocumentRoot itself:
    <Directory /var/www/>
        Options Indexes FollowSymLinks MultiViews
        # Forbids .htaccess files:
        AllowOverride None
        Order allow,deny
        allow from all
        # Maps / to /apache2-default, the initial welcome
```

```
        # page that says "If you can see this...":
        RedirectMatch ^/$ /apache2-default/
    </Directory>

    # Permits CGI scripts:
    ScriptAlias /cgi-bin/ /usr/lib/cgi-bin/
    <Directory "/usr/lib/cgi-bin">
        AllowOverride None
        Options ExecCGI -MultiViews +SymLinksIfOwnerMatch
        Order allow,deny
        Allow from all
    </Directory>

    # Error log for a single site:
    ErrorLog /var/log/apache2/error.log

    # Possible values include: debug, info, notice,
    # warn, error, crit, alert, and emerg:
    LogLevel warn

    # Access log for a single site:
    CustomLog /var/log/apache2/access.log combined

    # Sends Apache and PHP version information to browsers;
    # Set to Off if you're paranoid, or have reason to be:
    ServerSignature On

    # Shows Apache docs (only to local users)
    # if you installed apache2-docs;
    # to suppress showing the documents,
    # you can comment these lines or delete them:
    Alias /doc/ "/usr/share/doc/"
    <Directory "/usr/share/doc/">
        Options Indexes MultiViews FollowSymLinks
        AllowOverride None
        Order deny,allow
        Deny from all
        Allow from 127.0.0.0/255.0.0.0 ::1/128
    </Directory>
</VirtualHost>
```

Most of the changes we'll make to the Apache configuration files in this section will be in this file. The overall server configuration file, */etc/apache2/apache2.conf*, contains many server-wide settings that usually don't need to be changed; a few notable exceptions follow.

User and Group directives

These important settings tell Apache to run with a particular user ID and group ID. The Debian default in */etc/apache2/apache2.conf* is:

```
User www-data
Group www-data
```

Any files and directories served by Apache need to be readable by this user and group. Incorrect file and directory permissions are very common causes of Apache errors, such as the inability to view a page (or the ability to view something that you should not).

Listen directive

Apache normally responds to requests on TCP port 80, but you can direct it to listen on other ports instead of, or in addition to, port 80. It's common to use another port for testing; many people use 81 because it's easy to remember and not used for anything else. To specify one or more ports, use one or more `Listen` directives:

```
Listen 81
```

If you will be using SSL encryption for some pages, you'll need to include this directive to use the standard secure web port:

```
Listen 443
```

DocumentRoot directive

Each web site has a document root, which is the directory that contains the site's content files and scripts. It's specified with the `DocumentRoot` directive. In the default Debian Apache setup, this is specified in */etc/apache2/sites-enabled/000-default*:

```
DocumentRoot /var/www/
```

Authentication and Authorization

Some parts of your web site may be open to the world, but you may want to restrict other parts to certain visitors. *Authentication* determines *who* a visitor is. *Authorization* determines *what* that visitor can do, such as:

- Read a file
- Use server-side includes
- Run a CGI program
- Generate an index page for a directory lacking one

In Apache, the usual place to store authentication information is in a plain-text *user file* (often called an *.htpasswd* file, after the program that modifies it). The user file contains user IDs and encrypted passwords. The optional *group file* contains plain-text group IDs and user IDs; it's useful for larger sites because it lets you specify permissions for a group as a whole rather than for each of the individual users.

User files

As an example, create a password-protected directory and place a small text file in it:

```
# cd /var/www
# mkdir secret
```

```
# cd secret
# echo "now you see it" > file.html
```

Since you haven't protected it yet, the file should be visible in your browser (*http://server1.centralsoft.org/secret/file.html*):

```
now you see it
```

Now make a user file:

```
# cd /tmp
# htpasswd -c /tmp/users jack
New password: black_pearl
Re-type new password: black_pearl
Adding password for user jack
```

Your password will not be echoed as you type it. You need to include the *-c* argument this first time you run the *htpasswd* program on the file, so that it will create the file.

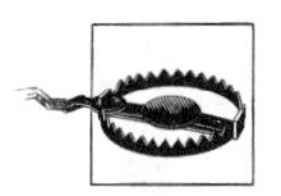

Don't use the *-c* argument when you add more users later, because doing so will cause the file to be overwritten.

If you want to change *jack*'s password later, enter:

```
# htpasswd /tmp/users jack
New password: kraken
Re-type new password: kraken
Updating password for user jack
```

The user file consists of lines that each contain a username and an encrypted password, separated by a colon, as follows:

```
jack:OSRBcYQOd/qsI
```

Now edit the Apache site configuration file */etc/apache2/sites-enabled/000-default* and add (before the final `</VirtualHost>` line):

```
<Location /secret>
    AuthName "test"
    AuthType Basic
    AuthUserFile /tmp/users
    Order deny,allow
    require valid-user
</Location>
```

`AuthName` is mandatory and must be followed by a quoted string. We used `"test"` here; you can use `""` if you want, but for some reason you can't omit this directive. `AuthType Basic` means we're using an *htpasswd*-style user file. `AuthUserFile` specifies the location of the user file. The `Order` directive says that Apache should deny access by default, and allow access only when specified in the user file. Lastly, the `require` directive says that any user in the user file is allowed. To allow only the user *jack* to see the secret, you would substitute:

```
require jack
```

And if you had more than one permitted user, you would add them like this:

```
require jack will elizabeth
```

Apache must be told to re-read its configuration file for these changes to take effect:

```
# /etc/init.d/apache2 reload
```

Now try to access this secret file (*http://www.example.com/secret/file.html*) from one of the accounts listed in the user file. You will get a dialog box that says something like this:

```
Enter username and password for "test" at server1.centralsoft.org
Username:
Password:
```

Enter the username and password (you will see asterisks as you enter the password), and click OK. You should see:

```
now you see it
```

Group files

Another way to handle multiple users is to use a group file. Create a */tmp/groups* file containing a group name, a colon, and one or more space-separated usernames:

```
pirates: jack will elizabeth
```

It's also legal to list the group and users individually:

```
pirates: jack
pirates: will
pirates: elizabeth
```

Then add an `AuthGroupFile` directive to *000-default*:

```
<Location /secret>
    AuthName "test"
    AuthType Basic
    AuthUserFile /tmp/users
    Order deny,allow
    AuthGroupFile /tmp/groups
    require group pirates
</Location>
```

Reload Apache as usual so your changes take effect:

```
# /etc/init.d/apache2 reload
```

Containers and Aliases

Apache applies authorization restrictions to *containers*, or files and directories on the server. One such container is the `Location` section discussed earlier. We'll review the various container directives here.

Absolute pathnames: Directory

This directive specifies a directory on the server. Here's an example from the original contents of our Apache configuration file:

```
<Directory />
    Options FollowSymLinks
    AllowOverride None
</Directory>
```

Relative pathnames: Location

This directive specifies files and directories relative to the document root. For instance, the following example:

```
<Location /cgi>
    Options ExecCGI
</Location>
```

allows CGI programs within */var/www/cgi*. We'll see this again in the section on CGI.

Pattern matching: Files and FilesMatch

You may need to specify a file or directory based on some text pattern. Here's an example that prevents people from downloading images from your site without authorization, by checking where the requests originate. It uses the `FilesMatch` directive, which lets you specify regular expressions (patterns) within the quotation marks:

```
# Some notes on the regular expression:
#   \. means a literal dot character.
#   (gif|jpg|jpeg|png) means any of these four strings.
#   $ means the end of the filename.
# The regular expression will match files with the suffix
#   .gif, .jpg, .jpeg, or .png.
<FilesMatch "\.(gif|jpg|jpeg|png)$">
    # Set the environment variable local to 1
    # if the referring page (the URL this image
    # was called from) is on this site.
    # Set local to 0 if the URL was on another site
    # that wants to steal our lovely images.
    SetEnvIfNoCase Referer "^http://server1.centralsoft.org/" local=1
    Order Allow, Deny
    # This checks the local variable and
    # allows access only if the referrer was local.
    Allow from env=local
</FilesMatch>
```

Aliases

The `Alias` directive assigns a name to a directory:

```
Alias /test /tmp/test
```

The alias (new name) comes first in the directive, followed by the actual location of the directory. The directory may be outside of the document root. In this case, the file */tmp/test/button.gif* would be accessible as the URL *http://www.example.com/test/button.gif*, even though it's not in */var/www/test*.

Limits

On a busy server, Apache can create many simultaneous child processes and use a lot of memory. This can increase the load average and make the system sluggish or even unresponsive. Table 6-2 shows how you can limit some of Apache's runtime values in the site configuration file.

Table 6-2. Apache resource directives

Directive	Default	Usage
`MaxClients`	256	Maximum simultaneous requests. If any more requests arrive, they'll be rejected.
`MaxRequestsPerChild`	0 (infinite)	Maximum requests served before a child Apache process is restarted. Used to avoid memory leaks.
`KeepAlive`	on	Reuse the TCP connection between the web client and Apache. Increases throughput by fetching all contents of a page over the same connection.
`KeepAliveTimeout`	15	Maximum seconds to wait for another request on the same connection.

Server-Side Includes

SSI can be used to include file contents, the output of programs, or the contents of environment variables as part of an HTML file. The syntax to specify SSI in Apache configuration files can be misleading. For example, to allow *only* server-side includes in */var/www/ssi* but no other options, create the directory:

```
# mkdir /var/www/ssi
```

and tell Apache to allow only SSI within it:

```
<Location /ssi>
    Options Includes
</Location>
```

To add SSI to existing options, use:

```
<Location /ssi>
    Options +Includes
</Location>
```

SSI lets you include file contents, but it can also run any program and include its output. This can be unsafe, so to restrict SSI inclusion to file contents only, use:

```
<Location /ssi>
    Options IncludesNoExec
</Location>
```

If you would like to have SSI files in various places rather than confined to this directory, you can tell Apache to associate a certain file suffix with SSI:

```
AddHandler server-parsed .shtml
```

For SSI to work, the Apache *include* module that runs it must be loaded. Since it was not loaded in the default Apache or PHP setups, we'll do it now:

```
# a2enmod include
Module include installed; run /etc/init.d/apache2 force-reload to enable.
# /etc/init.d/apache2 force-reload
```

SSI commands look like HTML comments. They have the form:

```
<!--#command argument="value"-->
```

Possible values of *command* are `include` (include file), `echo` (display environment variables), `exec` (include command output), and `config` (format some `echo` variables). Let's test file inclusion first. Create two files:

```
# cd /var/www/ssi
# echo "top stuff" > top.html
# echo "bottom stuff" > bottom.html
```

Now create the file *middle.shtml* with these contents:

```
<!--#include virtual="top.html"-->
middle stuff!
<!--#include virtual="bottom.html"-->
```

Note that the file doing the including (*middle.shtml*) needs the *.shtml* suffix, but the files that it's including (*top.html* and *bottom.html*) do not. Now point your hardworking browser to *http://server1.centralsoft.org/middle.shtml*, and you should see:

```
top stuff
middle stuff!
bottom stuff
```

If the `Includes` option is set for a container, SSI can also execute commands, but the user (typically, in a web browser) cannot pass any directives to them. SSI command execution is used for fairly simple things like directory listings:

```
<!--#exec cmd="ls -l /tmp"-->
```

A final use of SSI is to display CGI environment variables and some other handy variables. A quick way to print all of the variables is:

```
<!--#printenv-->
```

For a particular variable, this line:

```
<!--#echo var="DATE_GMT"-->
```

will display something like:

```
Tuesday, 01-Aug-2006 02:42:24 GMT
```

If you have only static files, or a mixture of static files and CGI scripts, it's safest to disable SSI command execution:

```
<Location />
    Options IncludesNoExec
</Location>
```

CGI

CGI is a much more flexible (and dangerous) way of running programs on web servers, since users can pass information to the programs. Apache has two ways of specifying what programs can be run as CGI programs.

Location

Either of the following directives will associate CGI programs in the */var/cgi* directory with URLs beginning with *http://server1.centralsoft.org/cgi/*:

```
ScriptAlias /cgi /var/cgi
```

or:

```
<Location /cgi>
    Options ExecCGI
</Location>
```

File suffix

The *suffix* method associates a *MIME type* (a file-type naming standard) with a suffix. The PHP module uses this method to get Apache to pass *.php* files to the *mod_php* interpreter:

```
AddType application/x-httpd-php .php
```

Here are the full contents of the Apache configuration file for *mod_php* (*/etc/apache2/mods-enabled/php4.conf*), which also treats files with the *.phtml* or *.php3* suffix as PHP:

```
<IfModule mod_php4.c>
    AddType application/x-httpd-php .php .phtml .php3
    AddType application/x-httpd-php-source .phps
</IfModule>
```

The first `AddType` line causes any files ending with *.php*, *.php3*, or *.phtml* to be executed as PHP CGI programs. The second `AddType` line causes Apache to pretty-print the contents of files with *.phps* suffixes, rather than running them and returning their output. Web authors use this to run a script (*.php*) and let users see a printable version (*.phps*). If you accidentally use the *.phps* suffix when you meant *.php*, your script will not execute; instead, its contents will be displayed.

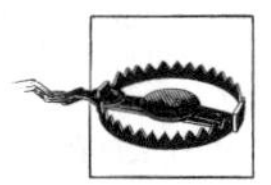

Never put a script interpreter like Perl, PHP, or a Linux shell in a CGI directory. Anyone could run these with the full permissions of the Apache user and group.

When testing your PHP installation earlier, you created this small PHP CGI program:

```
<?php
phpinfo();
?>
```

Now let's try something more interesting: we'll connect to the MySQL server, execute a SQL (database) query, and print the results as HTML. We'll again need the MySQL *root* user password. Save this file as */var/www/db.php*:

```
<?php
$link = mysql_connect("localhost", "root", "newmysqlpassword");
if (!$link) {
        echo "Can't connect to database.  Drat.\n";
        exit();
}
$result = mysql_query("show databases");
if (!$result) {
        echo "Arggh, a database error: ", mysql_error();
        exit();
}
# print_r prints all of a variable's contents
while ($row = mysql_fetch_assoc($result))
        print_r($row);
?>
```

Enter the URL *http://server1.centralsoft.org/db.php* in your browser, and it will display:

```
Array ( [Database] => mysql ) Array ( [Database] => test )
```

If you had used the same SQL command with the command-line *mysql* client, you'd get the same results (two databases, named *mysql* and *test*), but with a different format:

```
$ mysql -u root -p
Enter password:
Welcome to the MySQL monitor.  Commands end with ; or \g.
Your MySQL connection id is 2996 to server version: 4.0.24_Debian-10sarge2-log

Type 'help;' or '\h' for help. Type '\c' to clear the buffer.

mysql> show databases;
+----------+
| Database |
+----------+
| mysql    |
| test     |
+----------+
2 rows in set (0.00 sec)
```

PHP Module-Specific Directives

PHP directives may be placed in PHP's own configuration file (*/etc/php4/apache2/php.ini*), or in Apache configuration files. Normally you don't need to deal with them unless you install a PHP extension module or want to modify where PHP searches for libraries or tweak security settings (such as safe mode). The normal Apache modules have configuration files with a *.conf* suffix, located under */etc/apache2/mods-enabled*.

Virtual Hosts

Although you could devote an Apache server to a single site, you'll probably want to handle more than one site. Apache calls these *virtual hosts*, and it has more than one way to specify them. When a web client contacts a web server via HTTP, it sends the destination IP address and (in HTTP 1.1, the current web protocol standard) the name of a server at that address.

In the default Apache setup, there are no independent virtual hosts. Apache will happily serve web pages no matter how many names the server has, and all domain names share the same configuration.

In the following examples, let's assume we want to house each site in its own directory under */var/www/vhosts*.

IP-based virtual hosts

If you have more than one IP address on your server and want to dedicate certain addresses to certain sites, you may choose to use IP-based (or address-based) virtual hosts:

```
<VirtualHost 192.168.6.1>
    ServerName "www1"
    DocumentRoot "/var/www/vhosts/www1.example.com"
</VirtualHost>
<VirtualHost 192.168.6.2>
    ServerName "www2"
    DocumentRoot "/var/www/vhosts/www2.example.com"
</VirtualHost>
```

This was common in the early days of the Web, because HTTP 1.0 had no way to specify which server you wanted to reach at that address. With HTTP 1.1, name-based hosting is more popular.

Name-based virtual hosts

With this method, the `NameVirtualHost` directive defines which addresses can be virtual hosts; * means any name or address this server has, including *localhost*, *127.0.0.1*, *www.centralsoft.org*, *www2.centralsoft.org*, or others. Individual `ServerName` directives associate the server name from the browser's request with the proper directory storing files to be served:

```
# Accept any site name on any port:
NameVirtualHost *
<VirtualHost *>
    ServerName www1.example.com
    DocumentRoot "/var/www/vhosts/www1.example.com"
</VirtualHost>
<VirtualHost *>
    ServerName www2.example.com
    # A virtual host can have multiple names:
    ServerAlias backup.example.com
    DocumentRoot "/var/www/vhosts/www2.example.com"
</VirtualHost>
```

mod_vhost_alias

If you want to administer multiple hosts without needing to specify the names of each in configuration files, you can instead enable Apache's *mod_vhost_alias* module:

```
# a2enmod vhost_alias
```

and configure the names to be served in the designated file. The *vhost_alias* in the previous command expands to */etc/apache2/mods-enabled/vhost_alias.conf*. Sample contents might be:

```
UseCanonicalName    Off
VirtualDocumentRoot /var/www/vhosts/%0
```

The `VirtualDocumentRoot` directive is very flexible. The `%0` we specified here is expanded to the full site name (*server1.centralsoft.org*). We could have used `%2` to get the second part from the left (*centralsoft*), `%-2` for the second part from the right (also *centralsoft*), `%2+` for the second through the last parts (*centralsoft.org*), and so on. These alternatives are useful if you have many virtual hosts. If you always have the same base domain name, like *centralsoft.org*, and sites called *www1.centralsoft.org*, *www2.centralsoft.org*, and so on, you could use `%1` to get the directories */var/www/vhosts/www1*, */var/www/vhosts/www2*, etc.

For now, just use `%0` for the full name and create a directory for each virtual host:

```
# cd /var/www/vhosts
# mkdir www1.centralsoft.org
# echo "test www1.centralsoft.org" > www1.centralsoft.org/index.html
# mkdir www2.centralsoft.org
# echo "test www2.centralsoft.org" > www2.centralsoft.org/index.html
```

Then prod Apache to get its attention:

```
# /etc/init.d/apache2 reload
```

If you have DNS records that point *www1.centralsoft.org* and *www2.centralsoft.org* to your server, you can aim your browser at *http://www1.centralsoft.org/index.html* and *http://www2.centralsoft.org/index.html* and see the contents of the test *index.html* files that you just made.

Logfiles

Apache writes ASCII logfiles of two types: *access* (requests that come to the server) and *error* (errors that occur during requests). You control how much is written to these files, depending on what you want to know about visitors to your site, how much disk space you have (logs get big), and what log analysis tools you want to apply.

A typical access message (broken onto several lines to fit the page) is:

```
192.168.0.1 - - [22/Sep/2006:15:04:05 -0400] "GET / HTTP/1.1"
200 580 "-" "Mozilla/5.0 (Windows; U; Windows NT 5.0; en-US;
rv:1.8.0.7) Gecko/20060909 Firefox/1.5.0.7"
```

A typical error message is:

```
[Fri Sep 29 10:13:11 2006] [error]
[client www.centralsoft.org]
File does not exist: /var/www/index.html
```

The default logs are */var/log/apache2/access.log* and */var/log/apache2/error.log*.

Log Splitting and Rotation

The default Apache setup includes a daily *cron* job that rotates the access and error logs. It does the rotation as follows:

1. Renames *access.log* to *access.log.1* and *error.log* to *error.log.1*
2. Increments the number suffixes of the older rotated logs (e.g., *access.log.1* is incremented to *access.log.2*)
3. Deletes *access.log.7* and *error.log.7*
4. Creates a new *access.log* and *error.log*

By default, all of your virtual hosts share the same access and error logs. If you have more than one host, however, you'll probably want to split the logs to provide separate analyses for each.

Apache has two standard access logfile formats: *common* and *combined*. You'll find their definitions in the master Apache configuration file, */etc/apache2/apache.conf*:

```
# The following directives define some format nicknames for use with
# a CustomLog directive (see below).
LogFormat "%h %l %u %t \"%r\" %>s %b \"%{Referer}i\" \"%{User-Agent}i\"" combined
LogFormat "%h %l %u %t \"%r\" %>s %b" common
LogFormat "%{Referer}i -> %U" referer
LogFormat "%{User-agent}i" agent
```

All those % things stand for Apache configuration variables; for example, %h means hostname. The combined format is just the common format plus the *referer* and the *user agent* (browser). Unfortunately, neither format includes the name of the virtual host (a %v variable), which you need to split the log by host. Therefore, if you want to do this you'll need to define a new logfile type.

Rather than getting your fingerprints all over the master Apache configuration file, continue to make your changes to the site file we've been using thus far (*/etc/apache2/sites-enabled/000-default*). Put these lines above any of your VirtualHost directives:

```
# Define a new virtual host common log format:
LogFormat "%v %h %l %u %t \"%r\" %s %b" vcommon
```

Splitting Logs with vlogger

You may be wondering whether to split lines of logging information into separate files as Apache is being accessed, or to split the access file once a day with a utility such as Apache's *split-logfile*. We prefer the first option, because it diverts the lines into the proper access logs immediately, and we don't need to write *cron* jobs. A good splitter is the *vlogger* program. Apache allows you to pipe the log through some external program, which is just what we want. Add this right below the LogFormat line you just entered:

```
# Split log on the fly into virtual host directories
# under /var/log/apache2:
CustomLog "| /usr/sbin/vlogger -s access.log /var/log/apache2" vcommon
```

Since *vlogger* is not part of the standard Debian package, install it:

```
# apt-get install vlogger
```

Then tickle Apache:

```
# /etc/init.d/apache2 restart
```

vlogger will create a directory under */var/log/apache2* for each virtual host that you've defined. It will create daily time-stamped access logs, with a symbolic link from *access.log* to the most recent one:

```
# cd /var/log/apache2/www1.example.com
# ls -l
total 4
-rw-r--r--  1 root root 984 Aug  3 23:19 08032006-access.log
lrwxrwxrwx  1 root root  19 Aug  3 23:19 access.log -> 08032006-access.log
```

Analyzing Logs with Webalizer

Many open source and commercial Apache log analyzers are available. We think Webalizer is a good choice because it's easy to install, runs well, and produces useful output.

Let's try it:

```
# apt-get install webalizer
...
Which directory should webalizer put the output in?
/var/www/webalizer
Enter the title of the reports webalizer will generate.
Usage Statistics for server1.centralsoft.org
What is the filename of the rotated webserver log?
/var/log/apache2/access.log.1
```

Access it with the URL *http://server1.centralsoft.org/webalizer*.

The next day (after the Webalizer daily *cron* job */etc/cron.daily/webalizer* first runs), you should see pages of tables describing accesses to your web server. You don't need to edit the configuration file (*/etc/webalizer.conf*) unless you want to change the settings you gave during the installation.

Spammers have ways of manipulating web logs such as Webalizer's, so it's good practice to restrict access to the Webalizer output pages.

SSL/TLS Encryption

Willie Sutton once said that he robbed banks because "that's where the money is." Internet attacks are increasingly being aimed at the application level for the same reason. It's become essential to encrypt sensitive data such as credit card numbers and passwords.

When you request a page from a web server with the *http://* prefix, all data passing between the server and your web browser is unencrypted. Anyone with access to the intervening networks can snoop the contents. Think of plain web access (like standard email) as a postcard rather than a letter.

The Secure Sockets Layer standard was developed to encrypt web traffic, and it's been critical in enabling the explosion of commercial sites and e-commerce on the Web. Apache has the ability to encrypt web traffic with SSL, which, with slight modifications, is known as Transport Layer Security. You get this encryption when you access a site with the *https://* prefix. Think of encrypted web traffic as a sealed envelope.

Let's set up SSL for Apache. Edit */etc/apache2/ports.conf* and add this line:

```
Listen 443
```

Then turn on the Apache SSL module and tell Apache to use it:

```
# a2enmod ssl
Module ssl installed; run /etc/init.d/apache2 force-reload to enable.
# /etc/init.d/apache2 force-reload
```

Now try accessing your home page with an *https://* URL (for example, *https://server1.centralsoft.org*).

For SSL to work, your server also needs a *certificate*. This is an encrypted file that proves to the user's browser that you are who you claim to be. How does the browser know whom to trust? Web browsers have built-in lists of trusted *certificate authorities* (CAs). The command/option/tab chain to view them is:

Firefox 2.0
: Tools → Advanced → Encryption → View Certificates → Authorities

Internet Explorer 6.0
: Tools → Internet Options → Content → Certificates → Trusted Root Certification Authorities

CAs are companies that sell your organization a certificate and want cash for doing the legwork to verify your identity. Commercial web sites almost always use commercial CAs, because the browser silently accepts certificates issued by its trusted CAs.

Alternatively, you can be your own CA and create a *self-signed certificate*. This works with SSL just as well as a commercial certificate, but the web browser will prompt the user about whether or not to accept your certificate. Self-signed certs are common in small open source projects and during testing of larger projects.

suEXEC Support

Apache can serve multiple sites at the same time, but the individual sites will have different pages, CGI scripts, users, and so on. Because Apache runs as a particular user and group (our defaults are each *www-data*), that user can read and write the contents of all of the sites. But we want to ensure that only the members of a particular site can run that site's programs and access that site's data. As usual, there's more than one way to do this, using various combinations of Apache, PHP, and other tools.

A popular method is to use *suEXEC*, a program that runs with *root* permissions and makes CGI programs run with the user and group IDs of a specific user, not the user and group running the Apache server. For example, using our unimaginatively named second virtual host *www2.example.com*, user account *www-user2*, and group *www-group2*, we can change the permissions for that virtual host by specifying:

```
<VirtualHost www2.example.com>
    SuExecUserGroup www-user2 www-group2
</VirtualHost>
```

Benchmarking

Our primary goal was to install and configure our web server correctly and securely. Beyond this, we want to ensure that it can handle the expected load for our web sites. The Web has many moving parts, and it's easy for one to get stuck or fly off with a faint whistle. To see how our system performs, we'll use benchmarking tools to simulate hundreds of fast-typing users (which is much cheaper than actually hiring hundreds of fast-typing users).

Apache can run with different versions, called *models*. The default installation under Debian is the *prefork* model, in which multiple Apache processes are started to handle requests. This seems to be the model that works best under Linux.

At least one static HTML file is required for benchmarking. Create a file called */var/www/bench.html*. It should be roughly the size you expect a typical web page on your site to be. You can impress your friends by generating Latin text at *http://www.lipsum.com* to cut and paste into *bench.html*. The benchmarking program, *ab*, is in the *apache2-utils* package, and it should have been installed with Apache. Let's make 1,000 separate requests for the same file, with a concurrency (simultaneous requests) of 5:

```
# ab -n 1000 -c 5 http://server1.centralsoft.org/bench.html
This is ApacheBench, Version 2.0.41-dev <$Revision$> apache-2.0
Copyright (c) 1996 Adam Twiss, Zeus Technology Ltd, http://www.zeustech.net/
Copyright (c) 1998-2002 The Apache Software Foundation, http://www.apache.org/

Benchmarking server1.centralsoft.org (be patient)
Completed 100 requests
Completed 200 requests
Completed 300 requests
Completed 400 requests
Completed 500 requests
Completed 600 requests
Completed 700 requests
Completed 800 requests
Completed 900 requests
Finished 1000 requests


Server Software:        Apache/2.0.54
Server Hostname:        server1.centralsoft.org
Server Port:            80

Document Path:          /bench.html
Document Length:        1090 bytes

Concurrency Level:      5
Time taken for tests:   2.799386 seconds
```

```
Complete requests:      1000
Failed requests:        0
Write errors:           0
Non-2xx responses:      1000
Total transferred:      1425000 bytes
HTML transferred:       1090000 bytes
Requests per second:    357.22 [#/sec] (mean)
Time per request:       13.997 [ms] (mean)
Time per request:       2.799 [ms] (mean, across all concurrent requests)
Transfer rate:          496.89 [Kbytes/sec] received

Connection Times (ms)
              min  mean[+/-sd] median   max
Connect:        0    0   0.1      0       3
Processing:     6   11   2.2     11      22
Waiting:        5   10   2.3     11      18
Total:          6   11   2.2     11      22

Percentage of the requests served within a certain time (ms)
  50%     11
  66%     12
  75%     13
  80%     13
  90%     14
  95%     14
  98%     15
  99%     16
 100%     22 (longest request)
```

People usually want to see requests per second or its converse, time per request. These numbers will tell you the best you can do with your server hardware and Apache configuration.

Installing and Administering Drupal

Now that we have Apache, PHP, and MySQL running, let's install a package that uses them. Sadly, we don't get paid for product placement here, so we'll choose something that's open source, big enough to represent typical real-world software, and useful in its own right. According to its web site (*http://www.drupal.org*):

> Drupal is software that allows an individual or a community of users to easily publish, manage and organize a great variety of content on a website.

This includes weblogs, forums, document management, galleries, newsletters, and other forms of web-based collaboration.

The following two sections describe two installation methods for Drupal:

apt-get
: Easier, so try this first. However, we've had some problems with Debian Drupal packages.

Source
: More work, but you can see what's happening; try this if the *apt-get* method fails.

Installing Drupal with apt-get

The easiest way to install Drupal is with *apt-get*. You can go to the Drupal web site and look for a package to download, or you can ask *apt-cache* whether it's in a Debian repository:

```
# apt-cache search drupal
drupal - fully-featured content management/discussion engine
drupal-theme-marvinclassic - "Marvin Classic" theme for Drupal
drupal-theme-unconed - "UnConeD" theme for Drupal
```

The first one is what we want, so let's install it:

```
# apt-get install drupal
```

The installation process tells you that it needs some packages you don't have, gets them, and chatters some more as it installs them. Then it asks you to configure Drupal through a sequence of text menus. Use the Tab key to move between choices, the Space bar to toggle a choice, and Enter to go to the next page. We'll include only the last line or two of each screen here, and the recommended responses:

```
Automatically create Drupal database?
Yes

Run database update script?
Yes

Database engine to be used with Drupal
MySQL

Database server for Drupal's database
localhost

Database server administrator user name on host localhost
root

Password for database server administrator root on localhost
newmysqlpassword

Drupal database name
drupal

Remove Drupal database when the package is renoved?
No

Remove former database backups when the package is removed?
Yes
```

```
Web server(s) that should be configured automatically
[ ] apache
[ ] apache-ssl
[ ] apache-perl
[*] apache2
```

The installation will copy the program files, create a MySQL database, and create an Apache configuration file (*/etc/apache2/conf.d/drupal.conf*):

```
Alias /drupal /usr/share/drupal
<Directory /usr/share/drupal/>
    Options +FollowSymLinks
    AllowOverride All
    order allow,deny
    allow from all
</Directory>
```

If you run into an odd complaint like this one:

```
An override for "/var/lib/drupal/files" already exists, but -force
specified so lets ignore it.
```

you can smack your head repeatedly as we have, or install from source. If everything looks good, skip the next section.

Installing Drupal from Source

Download the latest source distribution and move its directory to your web document root directory:

```
# wget http://ftp.osuosl.org/pub/drupal/files/projects/drupal-4.7.3.tar.gz
# tar xvzf drupal-4.7.3.tar.gz
# mv drupal-4.7.3 /var/www/drupal
# cd /var/www/drupal
```

We'll excerpt the installation steps from *INSTALL.txt* and *INSTALL.mysql.txt*. Create the Drupal database (we'll call it *drupal*), administrative user (also *drupal*, since we have no imagination), and administrative password (please use something other than *drupalpw*):

```
# mysql -u root -p
Enter password:
Welcome to the MySQL monitor.  Commands end with ; or \g.
Your MySQL connection id is 37 to server version: 4.0.24_Debian-10sarge2-log

Type 'help;' or '\h' for help. Type '\c' to clear the buffer.

mysql> create database drupal;
Query OK, 1 row affected (0.00 sec)

mysql> GRANT SELECT, INSERT, UPDATE, DELETE, CREATE, DROP,
    -> INDEX, ALTER, CREATE TEMPORARY TABLES, LOCK TABLES
    -> on drupal.* to
    -> "drupal"@"localhost" identified by "drupalpw";
```

```
Query OK, 0 rows affected (0.01 sec)

mysql>  FLUSH PRIVILEGES;
Query OK, 0 rows affected (0.00 sec)

mysql> quit;
Bye
```

Next, load the Drupal database definitions into MySQL:

```
# mysql -u root -p drupal < database/database.4.0.mysql
Enter password:
#
```

Then edit the file *sites/default/config.php* and change the line:

```
$db_url = 'mysql://username:password@localhost/databasename';
```

to:

```
$db_url = 'mysql://drupal:drupalpw@localhost/drupal';
```

Configuring Drupal

In your web browser, go to *http://server1.centralsoft.org/drupal*. The first page (in the version we tested) says:

```
Welcome to your new Drupal website!
Please follow these steps to set up and start using your website:
Create your administrator account
To begin, create the first account. This account will have full administration rights
and will allow you to configure your website.
```

Click on the "create the first account" link. On this second page, type your desired account name (or your full name) in the "Username" text field and your email address in the "E-mail address" field. Then press the "Create new account" button. You'll be sent back to the first page, which now says at the top:

```
Your password and further instructions have been sent to your e-mail address.
```

Check your email for the generated one-time password, and log into Drupal in the "User login" area. You'll be sent to a page to specify a permanent password. After setting this, you can go to your home page, where you'll see these choices:

1. **Create your administrator account**

   To begin, create the first account. This account will have full administration rights and will allow you to configure your website.

2. **Configure your website**

   Once logged in, visit the administration section, where you can customize and configure all aspects of your website.

3. **Enable additional functionality**

   Next, visit the module list and enable features that suit your specific needs. You can find additional modules in the Drupal modules download section.

4. **Customize your website design**

   To change the "look and feel" of your website, visit the themes section. You may choose from one of the included themes or download additional themes from the Drupal themes download section.

5. **Start posting content**

   Finally, you can create content for your website. This message will disappear once you have published your first post.

   For more information, please refer to the Help section, or the online Drupal handbooks. You may also post at the Drupal forum or view the wide range of other support options available.

Since you've already created the first (administrator) account, you're now on your own to try all the other functions. Drupal on.

Troubleshooting

If you like diagnosing problems, you'll love the Web. There are so many things to break, in so many places and in so many ways, that you'll be kept busy for ages.

Let's look at some classic web problems. (The browser error messages are those used by the Firefox browser, but Internet Explorer's messages are similar.)

Web Page Doesn't Appear in Browser

Let's assume your document root is */var/www*, your file is *test.html*, and your server is *server1.centralsoft.org*. When you use an external web browser to access *http://server1.centralsoft.org/test.html*, you get an error page in your browser window.

A browser error message like "Server Not Found" implies a DNS problem. First, ensure that *server1.centralsoft.org* has DNS entries in a public nameserver:

```
# dig server1.centralsoft.org
...
;; ANSWER SECTION:
server1.centralsoft.org.        106489  IN      A       192.0.34.166
...
```

Then see whether the server can be reached from the Internet. If your firewall allows pings, poke the server from the outside to see if it's alive:

```
# ping server1.centralsoft.org
PING server1.centralsoft.org (192.0.34.166) 56(84) bytes of data.
64 bytes from server1.centralsoft.org (192.0.34.166): icmp_seq=1 ttl=49
time=81.6 ms
```

Check that port 80 is open and not blocked. From an external machine, try *nmap*:

```
# nmap -P0 -p 80 server1.centralsoft.org

Starting nmap 3.81 ( http://www.insecure.org/nmap/ ) at 2006-07-25 23:50 CDT
Interesting ports on server1.centralsoft.org (192.0.34.166):
PORT   STATE SERVICE
80/tcp open  http

Nmap finished: 1 IP address (1 host up) scanned in 0.186 seconds
```

If you don't have *nmap*, pretend to be a web browser. Use *telnet* to connect to the standard web port (80) and make the simplest HTTP request possible:

```
# telnet server1.centralsoft.org 80
Trying 192.0.34.166...
Connected to server1.centralsoft.org.
Escape character is '^]'.
HEAD / HTTP/1.0

HTTP/1.1 200 OK
Date: Wed, 26 Jul 2006 04:52:13 GMT
Server: Apache/2.0.54 (Fedora)
Last-Modified: Tue, 15 Nov 2005 13:24:10 GMT
ETag: "63ffd-1b6-80bfd280"
Accept-Ranges: bytes
Content-Length: 438
Connection: close
Content-Type: text/html; charset=UTF-8

Connection closed by foreign host.
```

If that doesn't work, make sure this line is in */etc/apache2/ports.conf*:

```
Listen 80
```

and see whether anything else is hogging port 80:

```
# lsof -i :80
COMMAND   PID     USER   FD   TYPE DEVICE SIZE NODE NAME
apache2 10678 www-data    3u  IPv6 300791       TCP *:www (LISTEN)
apache2 10679 www-data    3u  IPv6 300791       TCP *:www (LISTEN)
apache2 10680 www-data    3u  IPv6 300791       TCP *:www (LISTEN)
apache2 20188     root    3u  IPv6 300791       TCP *:www (LISTEN)
apache2 20190 www-data    3u  IPv6 300791       TCP *:www (LISTEN)
apache2 20191 www-data    3u  IPv6 300791       TCP *:www (LISTEN)
apache2 20192 www-data    3u  IPv6 300791       TCP *:www (LISTEN)
apache2 20194 www-data    3u  IPv6 300791       TCP *:www (LISTEN)
apache2 20197 www-data    3u  IPv6 300791       TCP *:www (LISTEN)
apache2 20198 www-data    3u  IPv6 300791       TCP *:www (LISTEN)
apache2 20199 www-data    3u  IPv6 300791       TCP *:www (LISTEN)
```

If you don't see *apache2* in this output, find out whether Apache is running:

```
# ps -efl | grep apache2
```

If the output contains lines like this:

```
5 S root       7692      1  0  76    0 -  2991 415244 Jul16 ?        00:00:00
/usr/sbin/apache2 -k start -DSSL
```

Apache is running. If it isn't, kick it in the pants:

```
# /etc/init.d/apache2 start
```

Then run the *ps* command again. If Apache still does not appear, look at the error log:

```
# tail -f /var/log/apache2/error.log
```

If you don't have permission to view this file, you're definitely having a hard day. If the error log is empty, it may also have the wrong permissions. Confirm that the */var/log/apache2* directory and the */var/log/apache2/error.logfile* exist:

```
# ls -l /var/log/apache2
total 84
-rw-r-----  1 root adm 31923 Jul 25 23:09 access.log
-rw-r-----  1 root adm 32974 Jul 22 20:50 access.log.1
-rw-r-----  1 root adm   379 Jul 23 06:25 access.log.2.gz
-rw-r-----  1 root adm  1969 Jul 25 23:09 error.log
-rw-r-----  1 root adm  1492 Jul 23 06:25 error.log.1
-rw-r-----  1 root adm   306 Jul 23 06:25 error.log.2.gz
```

If the *tail* of the error log showed old information, you may be out of disk space. It's surprising how often we forget to check this before investigating more esoteric suspects, such as firewalls. Type:

```
# df
Filesystem           1K-blocks      Used Available Use% Mounted on
/dev/hda1            193406200    455292 183126360   1% /
tmpfs                   453368         0    453368   0% /dev/shm
```

If you used a different `User` or `Group` directive in your Apache configuration, check that the user and group exist:

```
# id www-data
uid=33(www-data) gid=33(www-data) groups=33(www-data)
```

If the browser returned an Apache error message, you have some more digging to do. If the display says:

```
Not Found
The requested URL /wrong.html was not found on this server.
```

the URL was probably mistyped. If you see:

```
Forbidden
You don't have permission to access /permissions.html on this server.
```

the file is there, but the Apache user can't read it:

```
# cd /var/www
# ls -l permissions.html
-rw-------  1 root root 0 Jul 26 00:01 permissions.html
```

Permissions problems can be fixed by changing the owner of the file to the process running Apache.

Virtual Hosts Don't Work

Use

```
# apache2ctl -S
```

for a quick check of your virtual host directives.

SSI Doesn't Work

If you see lines like this in your error log (*/var/log/apache2/error.log*):

```
[error] an unknown filter was not added: INCLUDES
```

you didn't enable *mod_include*. Run the command:

```
# a2enmod include
```

CGI Program Doesn't Run

If you can't get a CGI program to run, work through the following checklist:

- Has CGI been enabled, by one of the methods discussed earlier?
- Is the CGI program in a CGI directory like */var/cgi-bin*, or does it have a suffix like *.php*?
- Is the file readable? If not, use *chmod*.
- What does the Apache error log say?
- How about the system error log, */var/log/messages*?

SSL Doesn't Work

Check that you enabled the Apache SSL module (*a2enmod ssl*) and told Apache to listen to port 443 in */etc/apache2/ports.conf*:

```
Listen 443
```

If the directive wasn't there, add it and restart Apache. Then try to access this URL in your browser: *https://server1.centralsoft.org*. If it still doesn't work, port 443 may be blocked by a firewall. You can check this with *nmap*:

```
# nmap -PO -p 443 server1.centralsoft.org

Starting nmap 3.70 ( http://www.insecure.org/nmap/ ) at 2006-08-01 22:38 CDT
Interesting ports on ... (...):
PORT    STATE SERVICE
443/tcp open  https

Nmap run completed -- 1 IP address (1 host up) scanned in 0.254 seconds
```

Further Reading

You can explore the shadowed recesses of the Web in books like *Apache Cookbook* by Ken Coar and Rich Bowen (O'Reilly), *Pro Apache* by Peter Wainwright (Apress), and *Run Your Own Web Server Using Linux & Apache* by Stuart Langridge and Tony Steidler-Dennison (SitePoint).

CHAPTER 7

Load-Balanced Clusters

More than 10 years ago, people discovered they could connect multiple cheap machines to perform computing tasks that would normally require a mainframe or supercomputer. NASA's *Beowulf* cluster was an early example that is still in use today (*http://www.beowulf.org*). A Wikipedia entry (*http://en.wikipedia.org/wiki/Computer_cluster*) lays out the chief characteristics of a cluster succinctly:

> A *computer cluster* is a group of loosely coupled computers that work together closely so that in many respects they can be viewed as though they are a single computer. Clusters are commonly, but not always, connected through fast local area networks. Clusters are usually deployed to improve speed and/or reliability over that provided by a single computer, while typically being much more cost-effective than single computers of comparable speed or reliability.

Clusters are a good solution when you're looking to improve speed, reliability, and scalability for a reasonable price. Amazon, Yahoo!, and Google have built their businesses on thousands of commodity servers in redundant cluster configurations. It's cheaper and easier to scale *out* (horizontally, by just adding more servers) than it is to scale *up* (vertically, to more expensive machines). There are many Linux cluster solutions, both open source and commercial. In this chapter we'll discuss clusters based on the free Linux Virtual Server (*http://www.linuxvirtualserver.org*). We'll show how to combine cereal boxes, rubber bands, and three computers into a load-balanced Apache web server cluster. We'll also discuss high availability and, finally, alternatives to clusters. We won't cover high-performance computing clusters, grid computing, parallelization, or distributed computing; in these areas, hardware and software are often specialized for the subject (say, weather modeling or graphics rendering).

Load Balancing and High Availability

Load balancing (LB) provides *scalability*: the distribution of requests across multiple servers. LB consists of packet forwarding plus some knowledge of the service being balanced (in this chapter, HTTP). It relies on an external monitor to report the loads on the physical servers so it can decide where to send packets.

High availability (HA) provides *reliability*: keeping services running. It relies on redundant servers, a *heartbeat* exchange to say "I'm still alive," and a *failover* procedure to quickly substitute a healthy server for an ailing one.

In this chapter, we're mainly concerned with LB, which administrators will generally encounter first and need more often. As sites become more critical to an organization, HA may also become necessary. Toward the end of this chapter, we'll provide some useful links for information on setting up combined LB/HA systems.

The example LB configuration we'll use in this chapter is a simple one consisting of three public addresses and one virtual address, all listed in Table 7-1.

Table 7-1. Addresses and roles for servers in our cluster

Name	IP address	Description
lb	70.253.158.44	Load balancer—public web service address
web1	70.253.158.41	First web server—one of the real IPs (RIPs)
web2	70.253.158.45	Second web server—another RIP
(VIP)	70.253.158.42	Virtual IP (VIP) shared by *lb*, *web1*, and *web2*, in addition to their real IP addresses

The VIP is the address exposed to external clients by the load balancer, which will relay requests to the web servers.

Load-Balancing Software

The simplest form of load balancing is *round-robin DNS*, where multiple `A` records are defined for the same name; this results in the servers taking turns responding to any incoming requests. This doesn't work well if a server fails, though, and it doesn't take into account any special needs the service may have. With HTTP, for example, we might need to maintain session data such as authentication or cookies and ensure that the same client always connects to the same server. To meet these needs, we'll get a little more sophisticated and use two tools:

- IP Virtual Server (IPVS), a transport-level (TCP) load-balancer module that is now a standard Linux component
- *ldirectord*, a utility that monitors the health of the load-balanced physical servers

The installation instructions are based on the Debian 3.1 (Sarge) Linux distribution.

IPVS on the Load Balancer

Since IPVS is already in the Linux kernel, we don't need to install any software, but we do need to configure it.

On *lb*, add these lines to */etc/modules*.

```
ip_vs_dh
ip_vs_ftp
ip_vs
ip_vs_lblc
ip_vs_lblcr
ip_vs_lc
ip_vs_nq
ip_vs_rr
ip_vs_sed
ip_vs_sh
ip_vs_wlc
ip_vs_wrr
```

Then load the modules into the kernel:

```
# modprobe ip_vs_dh
# modprobe ip_vs_ftp
# modprobe ip_vs
# modprobe ip_vs_lblc
# modprobe ip_vs_lblcr
# modprobe ip_vs_lc
# modprobe ip_vs_nq
# modprobe ip_vs_rr
# modprobe ip_vs_sed
# modprobe ip_vs_sh
# modprobe ip_vs_wlc
# modprobe ip_vs_wrr
```

To enable packet forwarding in the Linux kernel on *lb*, edit the file */etc/sysctl.conf* and add this line:

```
net.ipv4.ip_forward = 1
```

Then load this setting into the kernel:

```
# sysctl -p
net.ipv4.ip_forward = 1
```

ldirectord

Although we could obtain *ldirectord* on its own, we'll get it as part of the *Ultra Monkey* package, which includes the heartbeat software for HA. Because Ultra Monkey isn't a part of the standard Debian distribution, you'll need to add these two lines to your Debian repository file (*/etc/apt/sources.list*) on the *lb* machine:

```
deb http://www.ultramonkey.org/download/3/ sarge main
deb-src http://www.ultramonkey.org/download/3 sarge main
```

Then update the repository and get the package:

```
# apt-get update
# apt-get install ultramonkey
```

The installation process will ask you some questions:

```
Do you want to automatically load IPVS rules on boot?
No
Select a daemon method.
none
```

Our configuration will have one virtual server (the address that clients see, running *ldirectord*), which we'll call the *director*, and two *realservers* (running Apache). The realservers can be connected to the director in one of three ways:

LVS-NAT
: The realservers are in a NAT subnet behind the director and route their responses back through the director.

LVS-DR
: The realservers route their responses directly back to the client. All machines are on the same subnet and can find each other's level-2 (Ethernet) addresses. They do not need to be pingable from outside their subnet.

LVS-TUN
: The realservers can be on a different network from the director. They communicate by tunneling with IP-over-IP (IPIP) encapsulation.

We're going to use DR, because it's easy, it's fast, and it scales well. With this method, we designate a VIP that is shared by the load balancer and the realservers. This causes an immediate problem: if all machines share the same VIP, how do we resolve the VIP to a single physical MAC address? This is called *the ARP problem*, because systems on the same LAN use the Address Resolution Protocol (ARP) to find each other, and ARP expects each system to have a unique IP address.

Many solutions require kernel patches or modules, and change along with changes to the Linux kernel. In 2.6 and above, a popular solution is to let the load balancer handle the ARP for the VIP and, on the realservers, to configure the VIP on aliases of the loopback device. The reason is that loopback devices do not respond to ARP requests.

That's the approach we'll take. We'll configure the web servers first.

Configuring the Realservers (Apache Nodes)

On each realserver (*web1* and *web2*), do the following:

1. If the server doesn't already have Apache installed, install it:

   ```
   # apt-get install apache2
   ```

   If you haven't installed the content files for your web site, you can do it now or after load balancing is set up.

2. Install *iproute* (a Linux networking package with more features than older utilities such as *ifconfig* and *route*):

   ```
   # apt-get install iproute
   ```

3. Add these lines to */etc/sysctl.conf*:

```
net.ipv4.conf.all.arp_ignore = 1
net.ipv4.conf.eth0.arp_ignore = 1
net.ipv4.conf.all.arp_announce = 2
net.ipv4.conf.eth0.arp_announce = 2
```

4. Get the changes into the kernel:

```
# sysctl -p
net.ipv4.conf.all.arp_ignore = 1
net.ipv4.conf.eth0.arp_ignore = 1
net.ipv4.conf.all.arp_announce = 2
net.ipv4.conf.eth0.arp_announce = 2
```

5. Assuming that your realserver is a Debian system, edit the */etc/network/interfaces* file, associating the VIP (70.253.15.42) with the loopback alias `lo:0`:

```
auto lo:0
iface lo:0 inet static
    address 70.253.15.42
    netmask 255.255.255.255
    pre-up sysctl -p > /dev/null
```

6. Enable the loopback alias:

```
# ifup lo:0
```

7. Create the file */var/www/ldirector.html* with the contents:

```
I'm alive!
```

8. On *web1*:

```
# echo "I'm web1" > /var/www/which.html
```

9. On *web2*:

```
# echo "I'm web2" > /var/www/which.html
```

10. Start Apache, or restart it if it's already running:

```
# /etc/init.d/apache2 restart
```

The Apache access logs should not yet show any activity, because *lb* is not talking to them yet.

Configuring the Load Balancer

On *lb*, create the load balancer configuration file, */etc/ha.d/ldirectord.cf*:

```
checktimeout=10
checkinterval=2
autoreload=no
logfile="local0"
quiescent=no
virtual=70.253.158.42:80
        real=70.253.158.41:80 gate
        real=70.253.158.45:80 gate
        service=http
        request="director.html"
        receive="I'm alive!"
```

```
        scheduler=rr
        protocol=tcp
        checktype=negotiate
```

If quiescent is yes, a faulty realserver gets a weight of 0 but remains in the LVS routing table; we've set it to no, so dead servers will be removed from the pool. The *weight* of a server reflects its capacity relative to the other servers. For a simple LB scheme like ours, all live servers have a weight of 1 and dead ones have a weight of 0.

If checktype is negotiate, the director will make an HTTP request to each of the realservers for the URL request, and see if its contents contain the string value for receive. If the value is check, only a quick TCP check will be done, and request and receive will be ignored.

The system startup files in */etc* for *ldirectord* should have already been created during the installation. Ultra Monkey also installed Heartbeat, which we aren't using yet, so let's disable it for now:

```
# update-rc.d heartbeat remove
update-rc.d: /etc/init.d/heartbeat exists during rc.d purge (use -f to force)
```

The load balancer monitors the health of the web servers by regularly requesting the file we specified in *ldirectord.cf* (request="director.html").

Since this server will be responding to web requests at the VIP address (70.253.158.42), we'd better tell the server about it. Edit */etc/network/interfaces* and add these lines to create the alias device eth0:0:

```
auto eth0:0
iface eth0:0 inet static
        address 70.253.158.42
        netmask 255.255.255.248
    # These should have the same values as for eth0:
        network ...
        broadcast ...
        gateway ...
```

Now, fire up this new IP address:

```
# ifup eth0:0
```

Finally, start your engines on *lb*:

```
# /etc/init.d/ldirectord start
Starting ldirectord... success
```

Testing the System

Let's check that the load balancer is running on *lb*:

```
# ldirectord ldirectord.cf status
```

You should see something like this:

```
ldirectord for /etc/ha.d/ldirectord.cf is running with pid:
1455
```

If you see something like this instead:

```
ldirectord is stopped for /etc/ha.d/ldirectord.cf
```

there's some problem. You can stop the director and restart it with the debug flag *-d*, and see whether any errors appear in the output:

```
# /usr/sbin/ldirectord /etc/ha.d/ldirectord.cf stop
# /usr/sbin/ldirectord -d /etc/ha.d/ldirectord.cf start
DEBUG2: Running exec(/usr/sbin/ldirectord -d /etc/ha.d/ldirectord.cf start)
Running exec(/usr/sbin/ldirectord -d /etc/ha.d/ldirectord.cf start)
DEBUG2: Starting Linux Director v1.77.2.32 with pid: 12984
Starting Linux Director v1.77.2.32 with pid: 12984
DEBUG2: Running system(/sbin/ipvsadm -A -t 70.253.158.42:80 -s rr )
Running system(/sbin/ipvsadm -A -t 70.253.158.42:80 -s rr )
DEBUG2: Added virtual server: 70.253.158.42:80
Added virtual server: 70.253.158.42:80
DEBUG2: Disabled server=70.253.158.45
DEBUG2: Disabled server=70.253.158.41
DEBUG2: Checking negotiate: real
server=negotiate:http:tcp:70.253.158.41:80:::\/director\.html:I\'m\ alive\!
(virtual=tcp:70.253.158.42:80)
DEBUG2: check_http: url="http://70.253.158.41:80/director.html"
virtualhost="70.253.158.41"
LWP::UserAgent::new: ()
LWP::UserAgent::request: ()
LWP::UserAgent::send_request: GET http://70.253.158.41:80/director.html
LWP::UserAgent::_need_proxy: Not proxied
LWP::Protocol::http::request: ()
LWP::Protocol::collect: read 11 bytes
LWP::UserAgent::request: Simple response: OK
45:80/director.html is up
```

The output is shorter if checktype is check.

Just to be nosy, we'll see what the lower-level IP virtual server says:

```
# ipvsadm -L -n
IP Virtual Server version 1.2.0 (size=4096)
Prot LocalAddress:Port Scheduler Flags
  -> RemoteAddress:Port           Forward Weight ActiveConn InActConn
TCP  70.253.158.42:80 rr
  -> 70.253.158.45:80             Route   1      1          2
  -> 70.253.158.41:80             Route   1      0          3
```

This shows that our first realserver is active, but the second is not.

We'll also check the system logs on *lb*:

```
# tail /var/log/syslog
Sep 11 22:59:45 mail ldirectord[8543]: Added virtual server:
70.253.158.44:80
Sep 11 22:59:45 mail ldirectord[8543]: Added fallback server: 127.0.0.1:80
( x 70.253.158.44:80) (Weight set to 1)
Sep 11 22:59:45 mail ldirectord[8543]: Added real server: 70.253.158.41:80
( x 70.253.158.44:80) (Weight set to 1)
```

```
Sep 11 22:59:45 mail ldirectord[8543]: Deleted fallback server: 127.0.0.1:80
( x 70.253.158.44:80)
Sep 11 22:59:46 mail ldirectord[8543]: Added real server: 70.253.158.45:80
( x 70.253.158.44:80) (Weight set to 1)
```

Back on *web1* and *web2*, check the Apache access logs. The director should demand *director.html* every `checkinterval` seconds:

```
70.253.158.44 - - [11/Sep/2006:22:49:37 -0500] "GET /director.html HTTP/1.1"
200 11 "-" "libwww-perl/5.803"
70.253.158.44 - - [11/Sep/2006:22:49:39 -0500] "GET /director.html HTTP/1.1"
200 11 "-" "libwww-perl/5.803"
```

In your browser, go to the virtual site URL *http://70.253.158.42/which.html*, and you should see either:

```
I'm web1
```

or:

```
I'm web2
```

If the load balancer is broken or one of the web servers is down, you might always get a response from the same web server.

Now, stop Apache on *web1*:

```
# /etc/init.d/apache stop
```

Reload/refresh your browser page to access *http://70.253.158.42/which.html* again. You should always get the response:

```
I'm web2
```

Adding HA to LB

The load balancer is a single point of failure. If it starts pining for the fjords, the web servers behind it will become inaccessible. To make the system more reliable, you can install a second load balancer in an HA configuration with the first. Detailed instructions, which use the Ultra Monkey package that you've already installed, can be found in "How To Set Up A Loadbalanced High-Availability Apache Cluster," (*http://www.howtoforge.com/high_availability_loadbalanced_apache_cluster*).

You may not need HA for the Apache servers themselves, because *ldirectord* is already prodding them every `checkinterval` seconds for status and adjusting weights, which is similar in effect to the heartbeat of HA.

Adding Other LB Services

We've used Apache web servers as this chapter's example because they're the most likely to be part of a server farm. Other services that could benefit from LB/HA include MySQL, email servers, or LDAP servers. See "How To Set Up A Load-Balanced MySQL Cluster" (*http://www.howtoforge.com/loadbalanced_mysql_cluster_debian*) for a MySQL example.

Scaling Without LB and HA

If you offered a wonderful service, would your server survive a Slashdotting (i.e., a huge activity spike)? If not, your credibility could suffer and many visitors might never return. But because implementing LB and HA requires significant effort and hardware investments, it's worth considering other solutions. There are ways to get more from your present server. For instance, you can disable *.htaccess* files in your Apache configuration (`AllowOverride None`), and use *mod_expires* to avoid *stat* calls for infrequently changed files such as images. Apache books and web sites contain many such optimization tips.

Once you reach the limits of your web server software, consider alternatives. In many cases, web servers such as *lighttpd* (*http://www.lighttpd.net*), *Zeus* (*http://www.zeustech.net*), and *litespeed* (*http://litespeedtech.com*) are faster than Apache and use less memory.

You can also get huge boosts from caching. *Code caches*, which include PHP accelerators such as e-accelerator (*http://eaccelerator.net*) and APC (*http://apc.communityconnect.com*), save PHP bytecode and avoid parsing overhead on each page access. *Data caches* such as MySQL's query cache save the results of identical queries. *Replication* is a form of LB. *memcached* (*http://danga.com/memcached*) is a fast way to cache data such as database lookup results. Squid (*http://www.squid-cache.org*), when used as a caching reverse proxy, is a page cache that can bypass the web server entirely.

When servers are in separate tiers (e.g., MySQL → PHP → Apache), improvements are multiplicative; for example, the presentation "Getting Rich with PHP 5" (*http://talks.php.net/show/oscon06*) combines many small fixes to scale a PHP application from 17 calls/second to 1,100 calls/second on a single machine.

If you're already using these techniques and are still straining to meet demand, definitely try LB, and provide HA if stability is critical.

Further Reading

More details on the software used in this chapter are available via the products' web pages:

- The Linux Virtual Server Project (*http://www.linuxvirtualserver.org*)
- Ultra Monkey (*http://www.ultramonkey.org*)
- Heartbeat/The High-Availability Linux Project (*http://linux-ha.orgS*)

You may also want to check out the Red Hat Cluster Suite (*http://www.redhat.com/software/rha/cluster*), a commercial LB/HA product for Linux built on LVS. The same software is freely available (but without support) in CentOS.

CHAPTER 8

Local Network Services

In this chapter we'll look at some skills a system administrator needs to manage a host behind the firewall or gateway of a company, an organization, or even a home network.

Some of us prefer reading about developments in Internet technology rather than local area networks, which we think of as routine and unchallenging. But when we need to configure or fix something central to our working environment, local networking moves up the value chain. For example, little else seems to matter when the CEO's email doesn't work.

Local networking can take up the majority of a system administrator's time if she isn't smart about it. So, if you've just started in system administration, you'll want a primer on LANs and how to install, configure, and maintain a number of different servers you'll find there. For the basics, take a look at the most recent edition of the *Linux Network Administrator's Guide* Terry Dawson, et al (O'Reilly). As long as you possess basic Linux user skills, though, even without such background the topics in this chapter shouldn't be over your head—and we find them exciting.

In this chapter, we'll explore distributed filesystems with a unique slant, how to set up DHCP and gateway services (including routing between a LAN and the Internet), the craziness of corporate printing, and user management. Local email services fit under the umbrella of LAN topics, too, but we covered those issues in Chapter 5.

We'll use the Fedora Core Linux distribution for this chapter. Red Hat sponsors the Fedora project and typically uses it for testing its next stable enterprise release. Fedora is not the ultra-stable version of Red Hat Enterprise Linux, but it's reasonably stable and robust. Red Hat provides native packages of many tools for Fedora, putting Fedora on the leading edge of free Linux distributions available for commercial use.

Whether you like the Red Hat model or not, you can apply the material in this chapter to other distributions of Linux. We suggest you dig into this material: it's fun, you'll need it in practically any environment you work in, and you won't find the bulk of this material elsewhere.

Distributed Filesystems

You may find it difficult to imagine a time when PCs simply stood alone without the benefit of a network or a connection to the Internet. But PCs were not originally designed with networking in mind. You may or may not remember when people transferred files by walking floppy disks from one PC to another, or flipped a switch so two to four users could share a printer. Those were painful times.

After the introduction of the PC, it took a number of years and innovations to create such basic networking conveniences as distributed filesystems. Getting those filesystems working on PCs transformed the landscape of business, because it allowed us to put a computer on everyone's desk. No longer did we have to manually fill out forms for keypunch operators to funnel into batch mainframe systems.

Networking became more available and affordable when an IBM researcher, Barry Feigenbaum, turned a local DOS filesystem into a distributed one. His efforts helped create the Server Message Block (SMB) application protocol, and the era of system administrators and network engineers began.

Distributed filesystems let users open, read, and write files stored on computers other than their own. In some environments, a single large computer stores files accessed by all users on the LAN; the central computer can even store the users' home directories, so that all their work is essentially stored on it. In other environments, users store files on their PCs but allow others to access those files. The two environments can be mixed, too. Whatever the configuration, this practice is called *file sharing*, and the directories (folders, in PC lingo) that users can access on the remote machines are called *shares*.

PCs became prevalent in businesses toward the end of the 1980s, and local area networks came into existence as PC use evolved and people discovered the need to share resources.

Try to imagine what the introduction of a LAN must have been like to a closely situated group of PC users who had never had network services. Suddenly, coworkers could conveniently share documents, print to devices some distance away from their desks, and answer emails from supervisors located across the office, campus, or country. That opened a lot of people's eyes.

Today, many sites store their users' critical files on central servers, which control users' access rights to the files. We'll discuss user management later in this chapter.

Introduction to Samba

SMB file and printer sharing evolved under Microsoft's guidance into the Common Internet File System (CIFS) protocol. CIFS has been published as a standard, but it's poorly documented and contains lots of secret behaviors that Microsoft continues to evolve. However, an intrepid team of developers keeps reverse engineering the protocol, and it has created one of the most popular free-software projects to implement Microsoft file sharing on non-Microsoft systems: *Samba*. Samba is increasingly popular; it has significant support for Windows and Linux desktops and is even used on Mac OS X.

As a Linux system administrator, you will need at least a high-level understanding of Samba. If you wish to drill down deeper into Samba (and you should), many excellent books exist on the subject, including the online documentation guides at *http://samba.org*. To use a common phrase, "An in-depth discussion of this topic goes far beyond the scope of this book." Actually, we don't see any reason to duplicate the excellent material already available. However, we do want to discuss Samba in enough detail for you to make it functional in your environment. Luckily, most distributions provide simple, graphical frontends to Samba, and we'll discuss some of those here.

Certain central functions in CIFS networks (mostly involving the way systems find each other) take place on *domain controllers*: servers that provide files, printers, and various controlling operations. Samba can integrate Linux machines into Microsoft networks as file and print servers, domain controllers, or workgroup members.

The latest iteration of Samba interoperates with Microsoft's Active Directory. Samba combined with LDAP can also function as a robust authentication server, replacing both Microsoft NT domain controllers and Active Directory servers.

Samba can also play a file-sharing role in simpler environments where members of small offices and/or departments of larger organizations use peer-to-peer networking. Desktop users can share their printers and files with others without those others having to authenticate. If sensitive functions such as financial accounting and record keeping are handled on one machine, stronger machine-level security policies can be implemented to shield that machine from other users without compromising its ability to access the resources of the peer-to-peer network.

Now, let's take a look at a Linux/Windows network and see how you can set up Samba for your desktop users.

Configuring the Network

Figure 8-1 represents a network as it might be seen from a Linux system (the Xandros distribution, which is a convenient desktop Linux suitable for corporate environments). The tree view on the left side of the screen shows four computers named *Athlon*, *Atlanta*, *Dallas*, and *Dell*. *Dallas* offers a printer, along with several directories, to the other systems; *Dell* also hosts a printer. One of the other computers runs Windows XP, and the other two run Windows 98. Linux ties them all together. The Linux system looks the same as a Windows system when viewed from the Network Neighborhood or My Network Places on one of those systems.

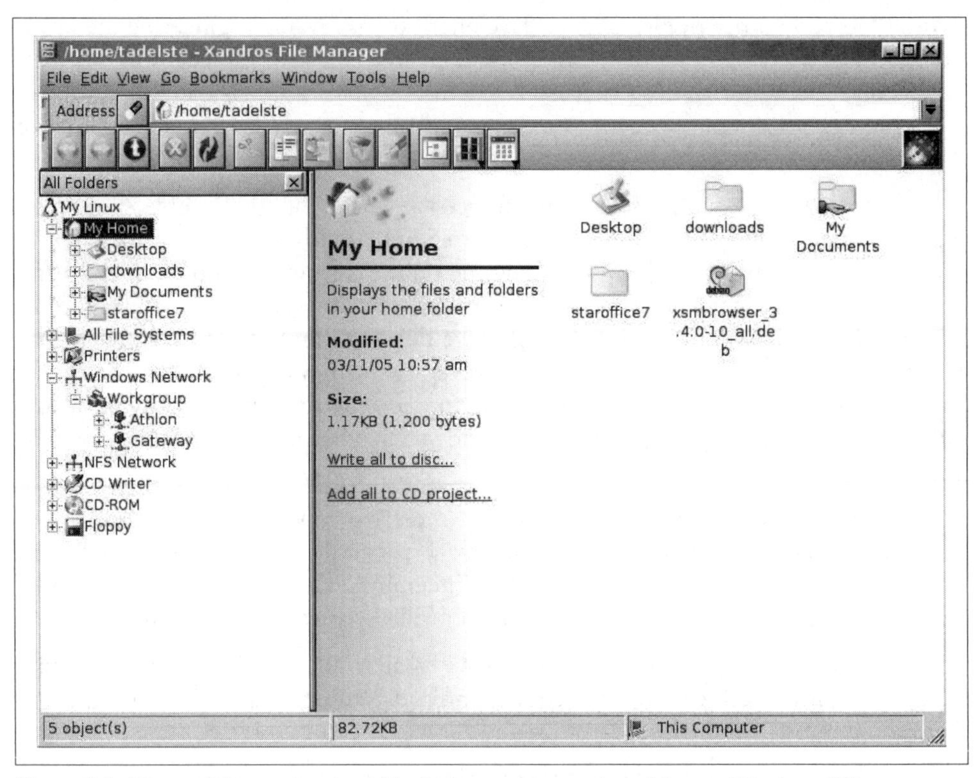

Figure 8-1. Files and directories shared by Linux system, as viewed from a Windows PC

The right side of the screen in Figure 8-1 highlights the shared documents folders on the node called *Dallas*, which is a Windows XP system. You also can see a word processor file named *xp_network_setup.sxw*, which was saved in a native OpenOffice.org Writer format (Version 1).

How difficult was it to set up this network? Aside from the standard wiring, Ethernet connections, and installation of the firewall and modem, the system basically installed itself. We followed standard setup procedures on both Windows 98 machines. The systems used DHCP to obtain their IP addresses, DNS servers, and routes to a gateway. The router provided DHCP services and a private Internet address scheme using a Class C network (192.168.0.0 through 192.168.0.255). (We'll discuss DHCP in the next section.)

Once the Windows systems established their network configurations and could reach the Internet, we right-clicked Network Neighborhood, selected Properties, and changed the dynamic addresses to static ones. This allowed the workstations to act as print servers and provide shared access to the Internet.

Setting up the Windows XP systems was slightly more complicated, because at first the XP and (now unsupported) Windows 98 machines didn't see each other. To make them aware of each other, we had to enable Simple File Sharing via XP's control panel and run the Network Setup Wizard. The wizard asked us if we wanted to enable sharing on other computers, referring to Windows 98 machines. Answering yes enabled us to create a floppy disk that we could use to install the XP protocols on the Windows 98 computers. This process upgraded the older systems to the newer protocols, enabling the XP and Windows 98 boxes to communicate. (The program furnished by Microsoft is called *netsetup.exe*.)

We then installed the Xandros Linux desktop and enabled Windows Networking on it, as shown in Figure 8-2.

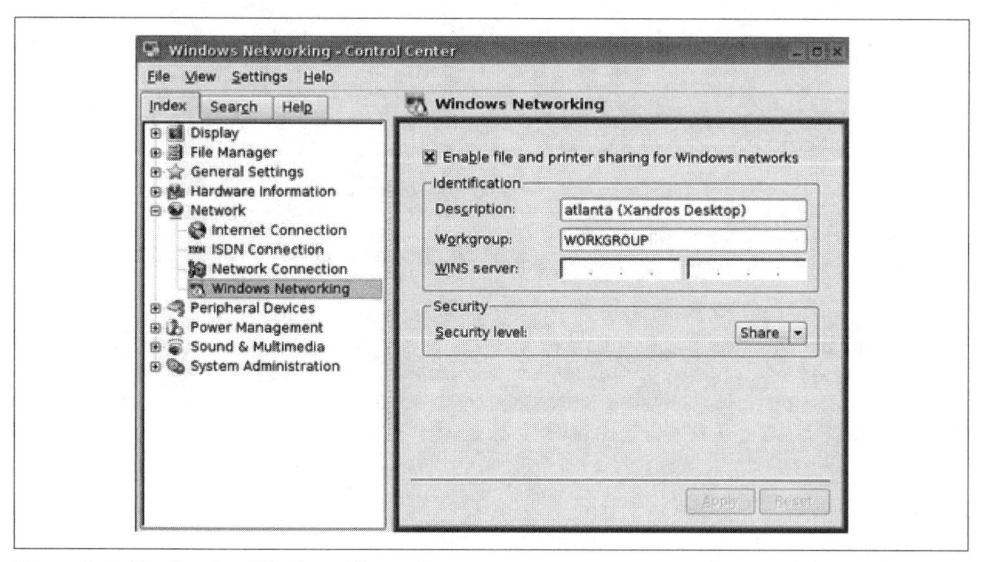

Figure 8-2. Configuring Windows Networking

Notice that we were able to configure Windows Networking via a dialog box. The Linux desktop allowed us to enable file and printer sharing, name the computer, define the workgroup, and enable share-level security, which allows the Windows nodes to use CIFS functionality.

Other Linux distributions, such as Fedora and Ubuntu, also offer easy tools for setting up Windows file sharing. Figure 8-3 shows two configuration screens for the Ubuntu desktop.

Ubuntu also gives you the option of setting up the Network File System (NFS), a popular Unix-to-Unix file-sharing system that is incompatible with CIFS. The dialog box in Figure 8-4 lets you choose either or both systems; you can use Samba to interoperate with Windows and Mac OS X, while using NFS to interoperate with other Unix/Linux systems. Sharing services in Ubuntu are not installed by default, but if you select Shared Folders (under the Administration menu in Ubuntu 6.10), Ubuntu downloads the necessary files; you're then ready to become a member of the domain or workgroup.

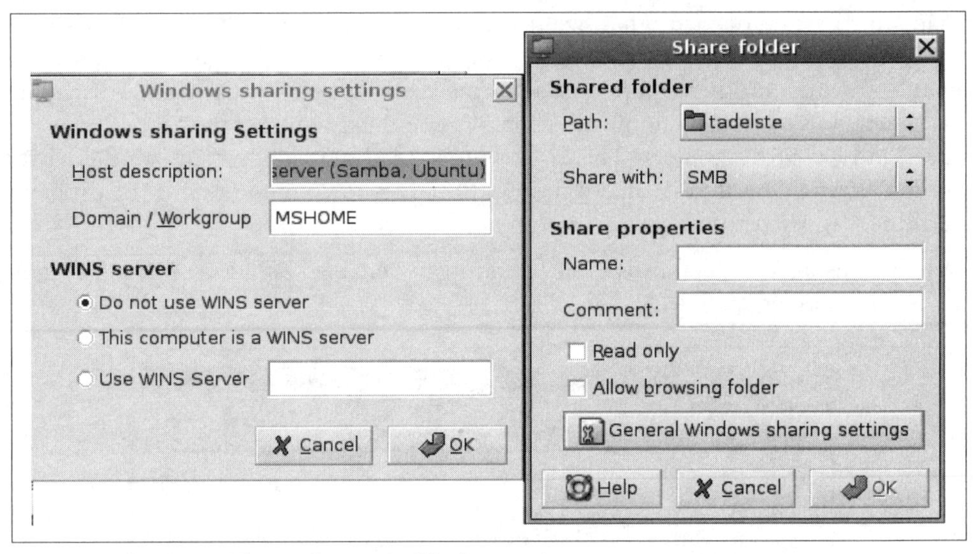

Figure 8-3. Setting up Ubuntu shares in a Windows environment

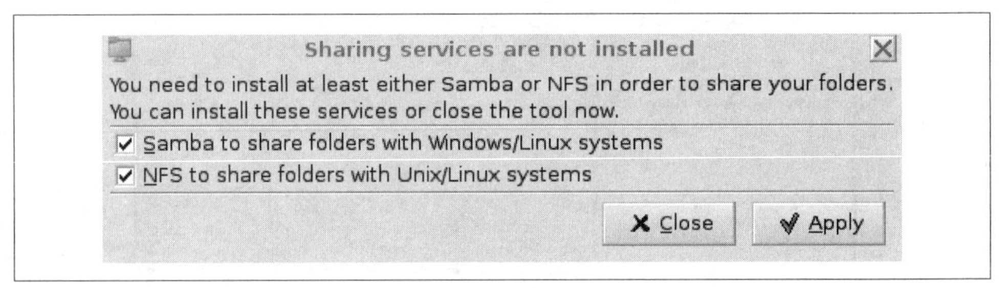

Figure 8-4. Ubuntu's setup screen for file-sharing services

We'll dig deeper into Samba issues in the section"Print Services" later in this chapter,

DHCP

Dynamic Host Configuration Protocol (DHCP) services can help you with a number of problems associated with local network environments, including IP address assignment problems and administration issues. It's difficult to imagine a network without DHCP.

Let's look at some issues you may face, and consider how DHCP can help:

- PCs and workstations require unique IP addresses, DNS information, and the locations of gateways.
- Manually tracking IP addresses causes excessive work.
- Accidental duplication of IP addresses creates conflicts on the network.

- Troubleshooting address problems (such as duplicate addresses) and changes in location creates unnecessary work.
- Changes in personnel usually mean that someone will have to check each computer to configure a new database of IP assignments.
- Frequent movement of mobile users creates a need to reconfigure networking on laptops.

DHCP solves these problems by handing out IP addresses as needed to each system on a LAN when those systems boot up. The DHCP server ensures that all IP addresses are unique. The service requires little human involvement in the assignment and maintenance of IP addresses. Administrators can write the configuration files and leave the rest up to the DHCP server (*dhcpd*). This server manages the IP address pool, freeing a human network administrator from that task.

Installing DHCP

To get started with DHCP, you first need to install the DHCP server. Because this chapter focuses on Fedora, you can install the RPM package with Yum or the package manager */usr/bin/gnome-app-install*; the current version of the package is *dhcp-3.0.3-28.i386*. (Debian users can install the *dhcp3-server* package and edit the configuration file */etc/dhcp3/dhcpd.conf*). The software originates from the Internet Systems Consortium.

Once you've installed it, configure DHCP in */etc/dhcpd.conf*. As a first step, copy the file */usr/share/doc/dhcp/dhcpd.conf.sample* to */etc/dhcpd.conf*. Next, edit the file to fit your network. The following example is typical. The syntax uses pound signs (#) for comments:

```
ddns-update-style interim;
ignore client-updates;

subnet 192.168.1.0 netmask 255.255.255.0 {

# --- default gateway
    option routers 192.168.1.1;
    option subnet-mask 255.255.255.0;

# ---     option nis-domain "domain.org";
# ---     option domain-name "domain.org";
    option domain-name-servers 192.168.1.1;

# ---     option time-offset -18000;     # Eastern Standard Time
#    option ntp-servers 192.168.1.1;
#    option netbios-name-servers 192.168.1.1;
# --- Selects point-to-point node (default is hybrid). Don't change this
# -- unless you understand Netbios very well
#    option netbios-node-type 2;
```

```
# ---    range dynamic-bootp 192.168.0.128 192.168.0.254;
    default-lease-time 21600;
    max-lease-time 43200;

    # we want the nameserver to appear at a fixed address
    host ns {
        next-server server1.centralsoft.org;
        hardware ethernet 00:16:3E:63:C7:76;
        fixed-address 70.253.158.42;
    }
}
```

We configured a few items in our configuration file after we copied it to the */etc* directory:

```
subnet 192.168.1.0 netmask 255.255.255.0 {
    option routers 192.168.1.1;
    option domain-name-servers 192.168.1.1;
    option subnet-mask 255.255.255.0;
    default-lease-time 21600;
    max-lease-time 43200;
```

The first line sets the range or pool of IP addresses available for the users in the subnet of the LAN. In this case we used the reserved private Class C network 192.168.1.0, which provides 254 nodes (192.168.1.1 through 192.168.1.254). This netmask must match the netmask used to define your LAN.

We specified the gateway address in the second line, `option routers`, and a caching nameserver in the third line, `option domain-name-servers`. The IP address is the same on both lines, which reflects common practice.

A single server with two network cards often acts as a gateway in a local area network. One card, represented by a device name such as *eth0*, has an address on the Internet, while the other card (say, *eth1*) has an address on the private network.

When packet forwarding and *iptables* firewalling are enabled, any Linux server can act as a gateway/firewall. In this case, we also enabled BIND in caching mode to function as the network's DNS server.

The last two lines specify the amount of time a client can keep the address, measured in seconds.

In our DHCP configuration file, we also added a clause to specify a static address for a corporate DNS server:

```
# we want the nameserver to appear at a fixed address
host ns {
    next-server server1.centralsoft.org;
    hardware ethernet 00:16:3E:63:C7:76;
    fixed-address 70.253.158.42;}
```

In the upcoming section "Assigning IPv6 Addresses with radvd" we'll discuss how to use *dhcpd* to hand out static IP addresses based on the MAC address of a client's network card. But before we do, let's look at a simple version of */etc/dhcpd.conf*:

```
ddns-update-style interim;

default-lease-time              600;
max-lease-time                  7200;

subnet 192.168.1.0 netmask 255.255.255.0 {
    option routers 192.168.1.1;
    option subnet-mask 255.255.255.0;
    option domain-name-servers server.centralsoft.org,
        server2.centralsoft.org;
    range 192.168.1.2 192.168.1.254;
}
```

For simple DHCP servers, maintenance may actually be easier if you omit comments and keep the configuration file short.

Starting Your DHCP Service

Some DHCP services require a *dhcpd.leases* file. Use the *touch* command to create an empty file in the same directory as the *dhcpd.conf* file:

```
# touch /var/lib/dhcp/dhcpd.leases
```

You'll want to start your DHCP server now, to check whether the configuration is correct. You'll also want to configure the server to start on boot. To accomplish the first task, enter:

```
[root@host2 ~]# service dhcpd start
Starting dhcpd:                                         [  OK  ]
[root@host2 ~]#
```

You can also test whether the DHCP process is running with the following command (if the service is running, a line will be displayed with the process's statistics):

```
# ps aux | grep dhcpd
root    9028  0.0  0.0   2552   636    Ss    09:40   0:00 /usr/sbin/dhcpd
```

Use the *chkconfig* command to get DHCP to start at boot time:

```
# chkconfig dhcpd on
# chkconfig --list
....from the list:
dhcpd           0:off   1:off   2:on    3:on    4:on    5:on    6:off
```

As with other services under Linux, you'll need to restart the DHCP daemon whenever you make changes to your configuration files. You can set other options in the *dhcpd.conf* file globally or for a client machine or subnet. This means you can establish useful defaults for your network, then override them for a certain group of machines or even individual machines. Here's an example of a global configuration section at the top of a *dhcpd.conf* file:

```
option domain name "host2.centralsoft.org";
```

Providing Static IP Addresses

Workstations usually function fine with dynamic addresses (that is, addresses that can change periodically or upon reboot), but servers usually benefit from static addresses so that their addresses don't change while they're in the middle of a session with a client. Thus, DHCP lets you specify static IP addresses for particular systems in *dhcpd.conf*. Let's do this in steps.

First, set up the subnet, broadcast address, and routers:

```
subnet 192.168.1.0 netmask 255.255.255.0
option broadcast-address 192.168.1.255;
option routers 192.168.1.1;
```

Next, add a `host` section for each machine on your network. To do this, you need to know the hardware address (often called the *MAC address*) for each network card, which you can determine by using the *ifconfig* command on the host. Here's an example `host` section:

```
# ethernet MAC address as follows (Host's name is "laser-printer"):

host laser-printer {
    hardware ethernet 08:00:2b:4c:59:23;
    fixed-address 192.168.1.10;
}

host1.centralsoft.com {
    hardware ethernet 01:0:c0:2d:8c:33;
    fixed-address 192.168.1.5;
}
```

Create a configuration clause like this for each server needing a static lP address, and add it to the configuration file.

Assigning IPv6 Addresses with radvd

Back in 1995, Steve Deering and Robert Hinden realized the need for a new Internet Protocol addressing system. Their first specification for IPv6 appeared in 1995, in IETF Request for Comments (RFC) 1883; the second in appeared in 1998, in RFC 2460. Deering and Hinden articulated what many people already knew: that lPv4's 32-bit address space would limit the explosive growth of the Internet.

Few system administrators realize that IPv6 and its new methods for assigning IP addresses have started gaining in popularity. Although many people scoff at IPv6, saying either that it is unnecessary or that the weight of existing practice will prevent it from ever entering the mainstream, enough applications and environments require it that the tide is turning in its direction.

An extensive discussion of IPv6 is, again, out of this book's scope; for more information on the IPv6 protocol and daemon, as well as on obtaining public IPv6 addresses, you'll have to look elsewhere.

IPv6 addresses often include the hardware addresses of network cards. This property allows IPv6 users to obtain static IP addresses without requiring any configuration on the server side to support those addresses. Automatic assignment of IPv6 addresses can be done with the help of the router-advertising daemon *radvd*.

Fedora users can install the *radvd-0.9.1* package from their Yum repositories. Debian users can install the *radvd* package and read the file */usr/share/doc/radvd/README.Debian*.

radvd listens to router solicitations and sends router advertisements as described in RFC 2461, "Neighbor Discovery for IP Version 6 (IPv6)." Hosts can automatically configure their addresses and choose their default routers based on these advertisements.

radvd supports a simple protocol. You'll also find its configuration simple. An example of a fully configured */etc/radvd.conf* file looks like this:

```
interface eth0
{
    AdvSendAdvert on;
    prefix 0:70:1f0Q:96::/64
    {
    };
};
```

If you wish to use *radvd*, you'll need to change the `prefix` to the one for your network and set up the service. You will also need to configure DNS on your client workstations separately.

You can find the *radvd* project home page at *http://www.litech.org/radvd*.

Gateway Services

Linux has facilities for LAN users to browse the Internet without exposing their individual IP addresses to the public. The typical setup hides activities inside an organization from the public by using Linux as a router. On the private side of the router, local activities go undetected by anyone on the public side.

People sometimes also refer to a gateway as a *bastion host*. You might think of it as a network entity that provides a single entrance and exit point to the Internet. Bastion hosts help prevent the cracking of a network by providing a barrier between private and public areas. We refer to the services they provide as *gateway services*.

Linux system administrators implement gateway services by using a combination of packet forwarding and firewall rules known as *iptables*. You might also see other names for gateway services, such as *masquerading* or Network Address Translation (NAT).

In small organizations and home networks, a gateway can exist on a single server and include basic security, a firewall, and DHCP, caching DNS, and mail services. In larger organizations, such services are generally spread across several servers, with a demilitarized zone (DMZ) isolating the gateway.

Role of a DMZ

In computer security, the term *demilitarized zone* refers to a perimeter network, which is a subnet or network that sits between an internal network and the Internet. For example, your private network might use an internal network of 192.168.1.0, the DMZ 10.0.0.0, and the public Internet block 70.253.158.0.

DMZs are used to contain servers that need to be accessible from the outside world, such as email, web, and DNS servers. Connections from the Internet to the DMZ are usually controlled using *Port Address Translation* (PAT).

The source and destination for every IP packet contain an IP address and a port. Port translation makes changes to both the sender's and recipient's addresses on data packets. Port numbers, not IP addresses, are used to designate different computers on the inside network.

A DMZ typically sits in the middle of two gateways or firewalls and connects to both, with one network interface card connected to the internal network and the other to the Internet. A DMZ can prevent accidental misconfiguration that would allow access from the Internet to the internal network. We call this a *screened-subnet firewall*.

For our purposes, we'll limit the gateway configuration to packet forwarding; we won't spend time on a DMZ, which requires more equipment and effort. To build a gateway, you need:

- A dedicated computer to act as the gateway
- A connection to the Internet and two network cards
- A small switch for client machines to connect to the gateway
- *iptables* installed

We'll assume that *eth0* is your Internet connection and *eth1* is your internal gateway in this configuration. Edit the configuration file for *eth0*, which is in */etc/sysconfig/networking/devices/ifcfg-eth0*, to include the following lines:

```
ONBOOT=yes
USERCTL=no
IPV6INIT=no
```

```
PEERDNS=yes
GATEWAY=70.253.158.46
TYPE=Ethernet
DEVICE=eth0
HWADDR=00:04:61:43:75:ee
BOOTPROTO=none
NETMASK=255.255.255.248
IPADDR=70.253.158.43
```

Similarly, the configuration for *eth1* should look like this:

```
ONBOOT=yes
USERCTL=no
IPV6INIT=no
PEERDNS=yes
TYPE=Ethernet
DEVICE=eth1
HWADDR=00:13:46:e6:e5:83
BOOTPROTO=none
NETMASK=255.255.255.0
IPADDR=192.168.1.1
```

Information on these configuration parameters can be found in the file *sysconfig.txt*, which you'll find in a directory with a name similar to */usr/share/doc/initscripts-7.93.7*.

With your network cards configured, you need to make sure you've installed *iptables*. You should see the following result:

```
[root@host2 devices]# rpm -q iptables
iptables-1.3.5-1.2
[root@host2 devices]#
```

If you don't have *iptables* installed, install it now and load the modules.

Fedora 5 will install *iptables* using the Add/Remove Software application, located directly above the Applications menu on the GNOME panel. It also loads the kernel modules as part of the installation process.

Then run:

```
# iptables -t nat -A POSTROUTING -o eth0 -j MASQUERADE
# service iptables save
# echo 1 > /proc/sys/net/ipv4/ip_forward
```

Now edit */etc/sysctl.conf*, changing `net.ipv4.ip_forward = 0` to `1` to keep this enabled at reboot. You make the system re-read */etc/sysctl.conf* by typing:

```
# sysctl -p
```

Finally, if you have a small organization, you can add DHCP to the server using a simple version of *dhcpd.conf*:

```
ddns-update-style interim;

default-lease-time              600;
max-lease-time                  7200;
```

```
subnet 192.168.1.0 netmask 255.255.255.0 {
    option routers 192.168.1.1;
    option subnet-mask 255.255.255.0;
    option domain-name-servers server1.centralsoft.org,
        server2.centralsoft.org;
    range 192.168.1.2 192.168.100.254;
}
```

Another Approach to Gateway Services

This section covers the use of packaged gateway and firewall combination products with multiple feature sets. Several free packages exist, such as Firestarter, IPCop, Netfilter, and Shorewall. You will see Smoothwall and ClarkConnect mentioned in Linux literature, but these are commercial products that install an entire Linux distribution, not standalone applications.

For use in this chapter, we chose Firestarter. However, you may want to take a look at Shorewall, a configuration utility for Netfilter (a command-line tool).

You can download Firestarter from the Fedora repositories. Our installation had the following package:

```
[root@host2 ~]# rpm -q firestarter
firestarter-1.0.3-11.fc5
[root@host2 ~]#
```

The Firestarter Firewall Wizard (Figure 8-5) launches when an administrator starts the program the first time. You can relaunch the wizard from the Firewall menu in the main interface, as well as change the choices through the Preferences option.

Figure 8-5. The Firestarter Firewall Wizard

After the initial splash screen there will be a series of configuration screens, starting with the Network device setup screen (Figure 8-6), which can setup dual network cards.

Figure 8-6. The Network device setup screen

Firestarter refers to its primary function as *connection sharing*. However, since it uses NAT it functions as a gateway, so client PCs on an internal LAN look like a single machine with a single IP address to the Internet. This becomes evident, for example, in the preferences screen shown in Figure 8-7. Notice that the first device description refers to the "Internet connected network device" and the second description refers to the "local network connected device."

You can also see toward the bottom of Figure 8-7 that Firestarter allows the administrator to use an existing DHCP configuration or create a new one. Here's Firestarter's *dhcpd.conf* file:

```
# DHCP configuration generated by Firestarter
ddns-update-style interim;
ignore client-updates;

subnet 192.168.1.0 netmask 255.255.255.0 {
    option routers 192.168.1.1;
    option subnet-mask 255.255.255.0;
    option domain-name-servers 70.253.158.42, 70.253.158.45, 151.164.1.8;
    option ip-forwarding off;
    range dynamic-bootp 192.168.1.10 192.168.1.254;
    default-lease-time 21600;
    max-lease-time 43200;
}
```

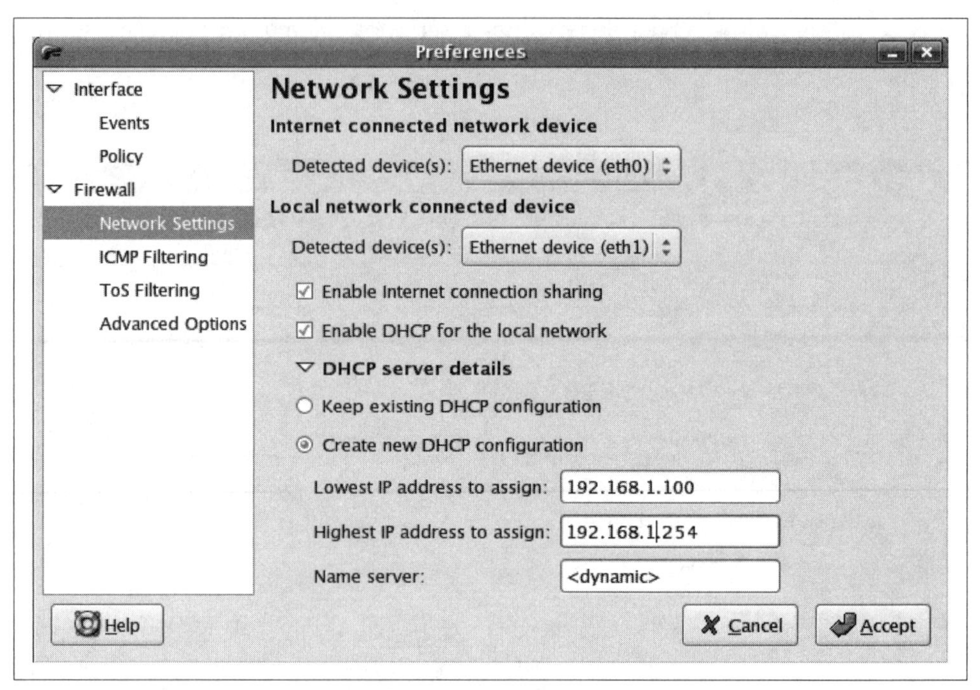

Figure 8-7. Firestarter Preferences screen

The *resolv.conf* file on the gateway shows up on DHCP client machine configuration settings as Firestarter reads that file and places the DNS server addresses in *dhcpd.conf*.

The main interface of Firestarter provides a view of the gateway's status and connections to DHCP hosts. It also provides a summary of events and activity, as shown in Figure 8-8.

In Figure 8-9, you can see a view of events from the second tab of the main interface. In this view, you can see the blocked connections.

The Events panel provides a log of attempts to exploit the firewall. You might find it useful when intruders attempt to break into your systems. If they seem to persist, add their IP addresses to the */etc/hosts.deny* file. If someone attempts to enter through *ssh*'s port 22 using a dictionary attack, you can simply close the port with Firestarter.

The Firestarter icon turns red when it sees a potential exploit in the making. Notice the message above it in Figure 8-10: "Hit from 221.237.38.68 detected." That's worth investigating.

The third tab on the main interface allows you to set policies for services you will or will not allow. For example, we allow SSH connections into the firewall from the outside, so we set a policy to allow SSH on port 22.

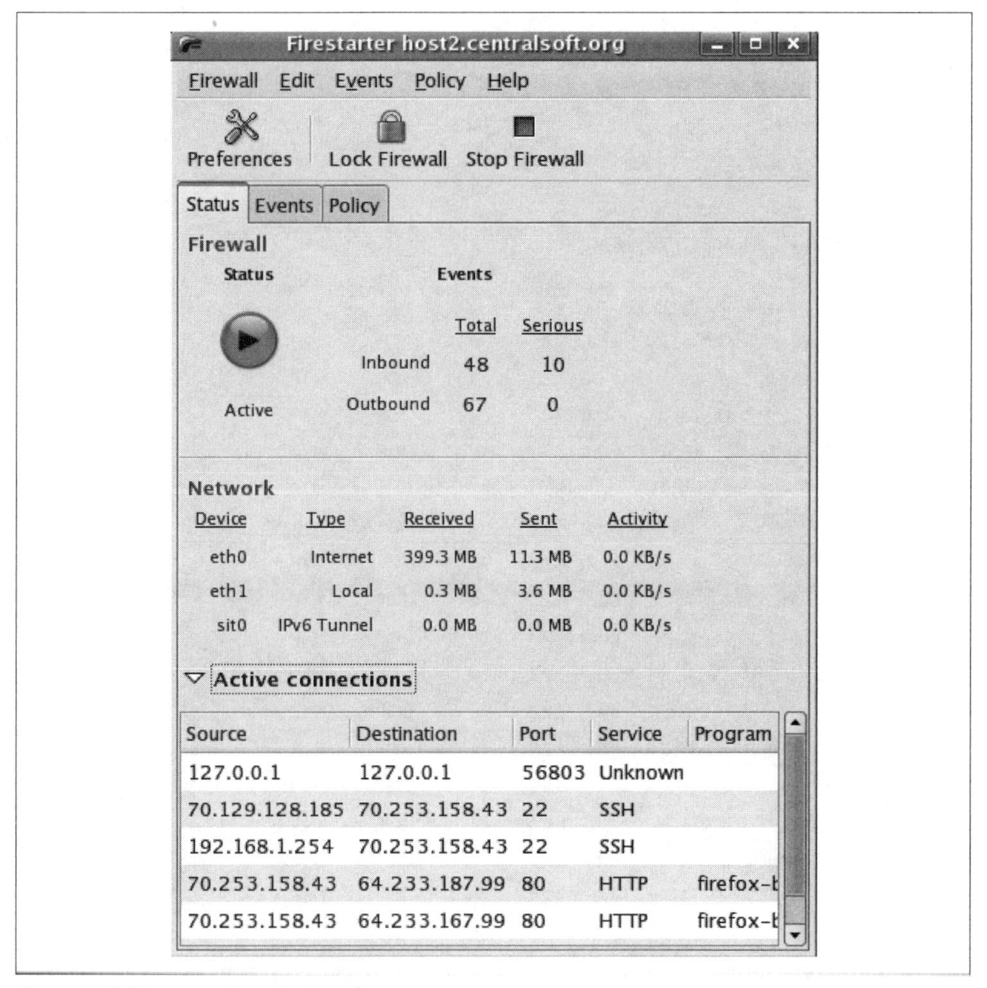

Figure 8-8. Firestarter's main interface

Firestarter uses a wizard to configure gateway policies. You can get a glimpse of how this works in Figure 8-11.

Figure 8-11 shows a window named "Add new inbound rule." This screen appears after you select Add Rule on the Policy tab. In this window, you can see a selection of options you can use to allow services into the network. A similiar screen eixts for outbound services you provide your users.

You will find Firestarter an easy application to configure. The project community has done an outstanding job of documenting the procedures in a well-written and succinct user guide, which you can find at *http://fs-security.com/docs.php*.

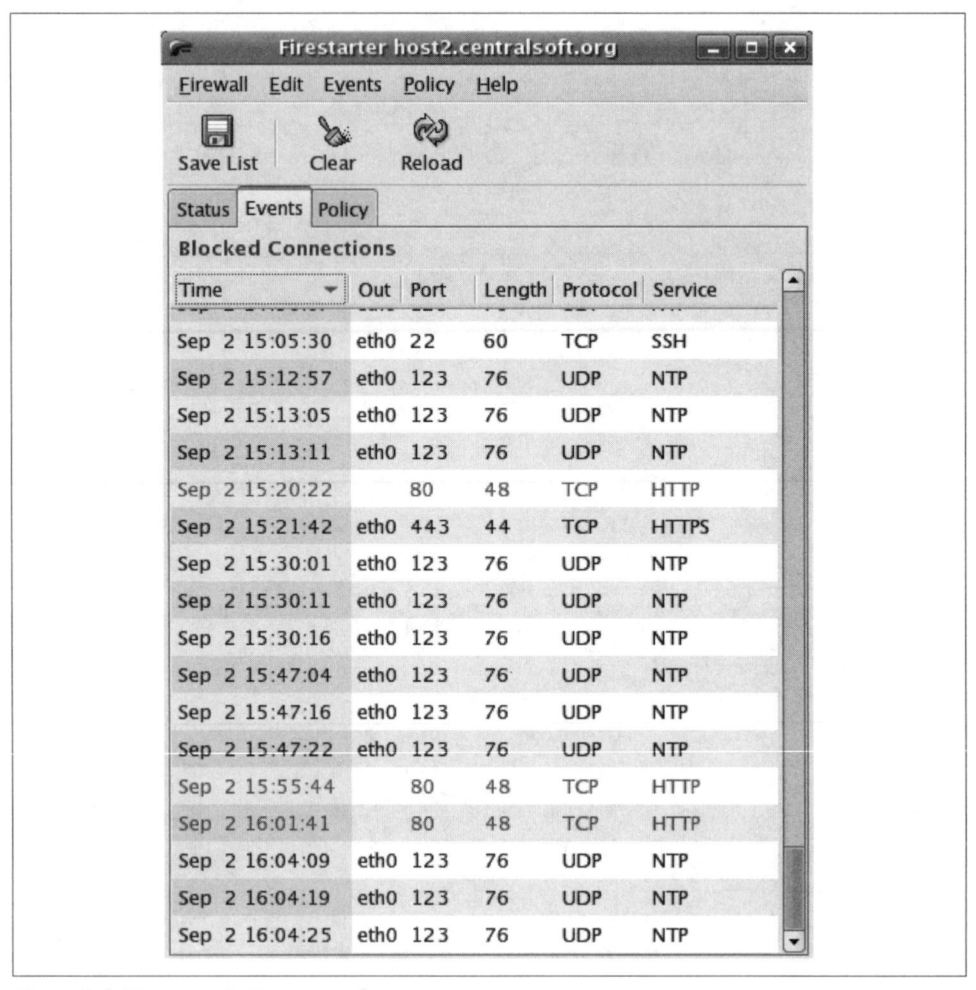

Figure 8-9. Firestarter's Events panel

Figure 8-10. Panel icons showing an attempted intrusion

At this point, you may be wondering why we've included an application dependent on the GNOME desktop. Recall that when we chose Fedora as the distribution for local networking, we did so because of its extensive tool set. Adding Firestarter fits into our philosophy without removing our ability to use the command-line interface.

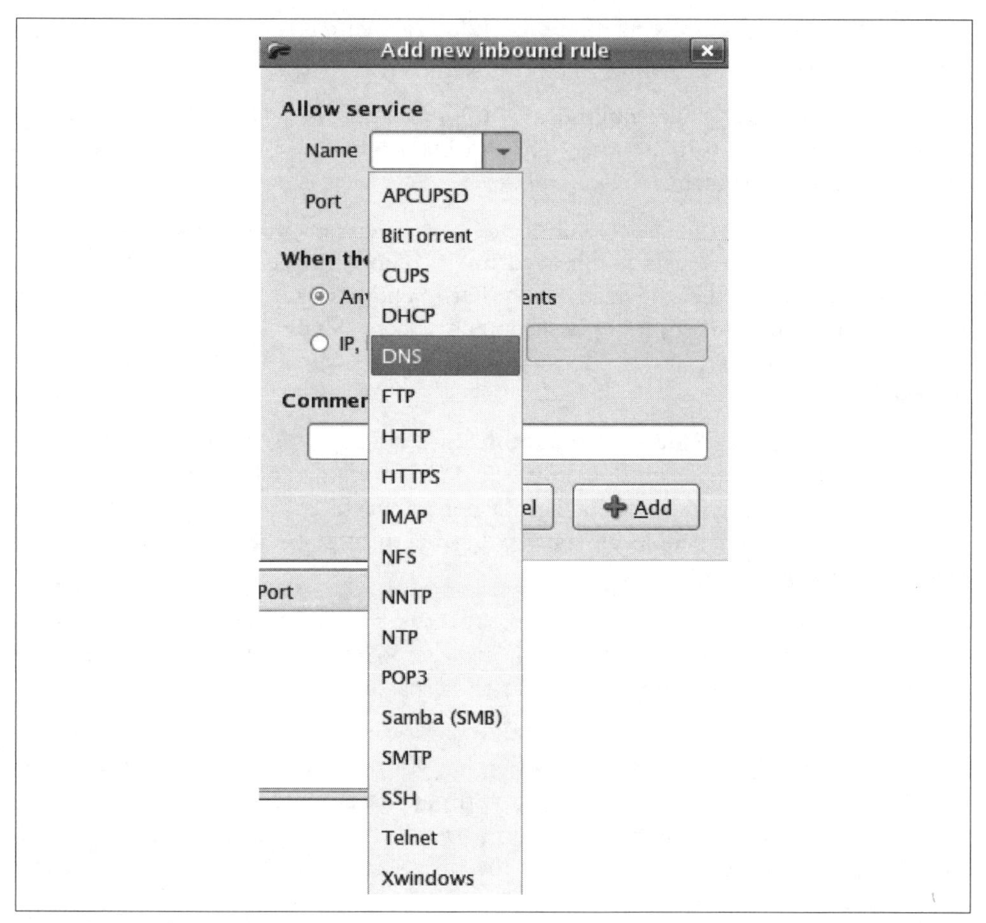

Figure 8-11. Policy configurations for Firestarter

Print Services

As a Linux system administrator, printers can cause you serious headaches. You're bound to find hardware, software, and operating system incompatibilities. Because such a wide variety of systems and methods of configuring printers exists, this area of administration has the potential to put you in a bad mood for months—or at least until you get a handle on the situation.

Let's start with hardware. Most system administrators will discover four types of hardware for networking printers. In existing networks, you may find any combination of these configured:

- Printers attached to users' PCs
- Dedicated PCs used as printer servers

- Network-enabled printers with built-in Ethernet cards
- Printer server devices connecting printers directly to a LAN

In most medium-sized office buildings, you'll probably see several of these solutions in use every time you turn a corner. The flexibility provided by modern desktop systems often causes problems.

Let's say that one of your users, Sally Jean, buys an inkjet printer, goes down to the petty cash window and gets reimbursed for it, then connects it directly to her PC. Billy Bob, who's seated at the desk next to her, then asks if he can use her printer. So, she right clicks the printer on her desktop and selects "Share." Billy Bob tries to connect to Sally's printer, but it doesn't work. Why? He doesn't have the driver installed.

So, these two users call the system administrator (that's you) to come fix the problem. You install the driver on Billy Bob's PC, and suddenly, just like magic, it works. Later, Sally Jean calls and complains that her PC needs more memory and a faster processor. Why? Ten people are now using her printer because she has an open share, and it's slowing her down.

When you check out the situation, you see that just around the corner a large-volume laser printer with a print direct card is sitting idle. Why aren't all those users printing to that printer? As it turns out, it doesn't show up on the network because no one's bothered to add it to the domain controller.

What this hypothetical anecdote shows is that you, as a system administrator, need to prepare a strategy for managing your printer infrastructure. This section of the chapter will provide you with a high-level overview and enough practical information to get you started. You can begin the process with a hardware inventory and some decision making regarding software and operating systems.

Because there are so many types of printers and combinations of devices, operating systems, and software out there, you'll have to do most of your printing-related learning on the job. The best approach to learning about printing involves developing a strategy for your own infrastructure. That narrows down the amount of information you'll need to digest.

Printing Software Considerations

Linux and Windows started off with completely different printing models. Fortunately, progress has been made in getting everyone to cooperate and play nicely. But until you configure the printers in your network, they're still not likely to work together.

Originally, Linux used the Unix standard for printing known as Line Printer Daemon (LPD); later, an upgraded daemon called LPRng was added. Linux distributions also used the LPD tools for printing and interoperability with Unix variants.

Linux distributors continue to ship LPDs and their tools, but they've also added support for a new system known as the Common Unix Printing System (CUPS). Unlike LPD, CUPS is also compatible with the Windows and Mac OSs. CUPS and LPD use different network printing protocols. Whereas LDP cannot query a print job for basic characteristics, CUPS can. CUPS also works directly in heterogeneous networks and can couple with Samba if necessary. Not all Linux distributions enable the interface, but Red Hat includes CUPS in Fedora by default.

As a system administrator, you will want to familiarize yourself with CUPS administrative tools. In Fedora, simply type *http://localhost:631* in a browser, and you will see the management interface presented in Figure 8-12.

Figure 8-12. The CUPS configuration interface

The interface is self-explanatory, so we'll leave its exploration up to you. If you lack familiarity with CUPS, take a look at the management interface or go to the project web site at *http://www.cups.org/book/index.php* and read the book.

Cross-Platform Printing

Now, let's consider some of the printing dilemmas you're likely to face in today's enterprise environments. You'll almost certainly find situations where you want to share Linux printers with Windows machines. (In fact, you'll probably want to use

Linux as a print server in a Windows network to save license fees.) You may also want to share Windows printers with Linux machines. How do you do that?

First, let's look at giving Windows users access to Linux-connected printers. Typically, you'll need to set up a Samba workgroup or domain, and you will need to install CUPS on your Linux PCs. You'll also need to configure CUPS for Samba, which you can do with the following command:

```
# ln -s `which smbspool` /usr/lib/cups/backend/smb
```

Edit */etc/samba/smb.conf* to create a printer share on a Samba server. In a real-life situation you're likely to restrict access to certain systems or users for each printer, but in the following example the Linux PC will share all of its printers with any systems on your network that you've configured Samba to serve:

```
[printers]
    comment = All Printers
    printing = cups
    printcap name = cups
```

Your Windows PCs can now access printers over the network. You will probably need the Windows print drivers, either from your Windows version's media or the media that came with your printer.

In the next scenario, you need to enable your Linux users to use printers connected to Windows servers. Again, you need CUPS and Samba to do this. On the Windows PCs, share the printers as you normally would: under Windows NT, 2000, and/or XP, enable the *guest* account and provide permissions for everyone to access the shared printers. Then install CUPS on the Samba server and configure it for Samba as described earlier.

Now install the Windows printers you want to make available on the Samba server with CUPS, using the CUPS web interface.

You will need to log in as *root*. On some Linux systems, you need to set up *root* as the CUPS system admin first. You can do that with the *adduser* command:

```
~$ su
Password:
# adduser cupsys shadow
Adding user `cupsys' to group `shadow'...
Done.
# /etc/init.d/cupsys restart
Restarting Common Unix Printing System: cupsd                    [ ok ]
#
```

Then you can log in as *root*.

Click on "Add Printer" and enter the printer name from the Windows system. We'll use "BrotherHL1440" (see Figure 8-13). Then enter the location and description. When you get to the device window, click on the drop-down menu and select "Windows Printer via SAMBA."

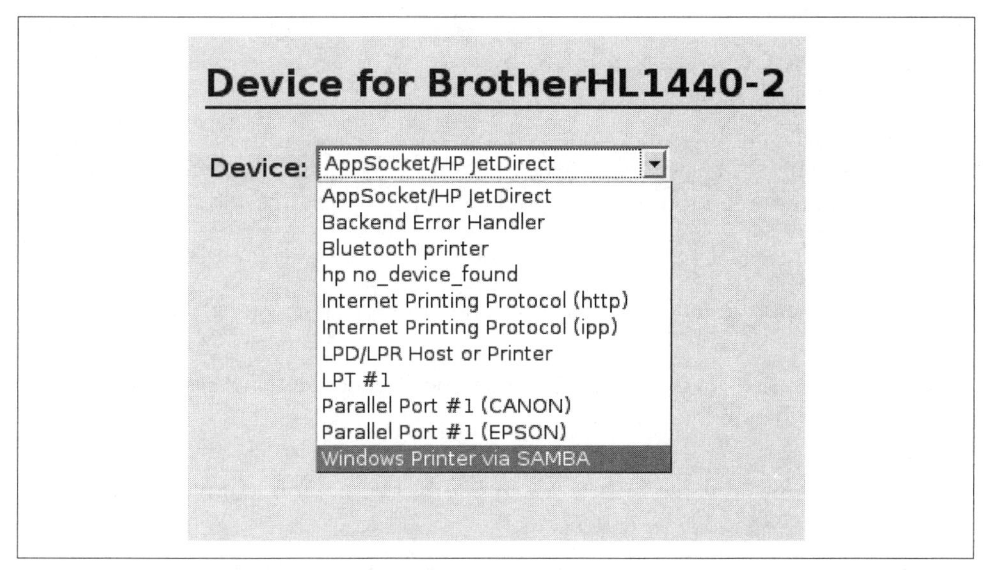

Figure 8-13. Adding Windows printers

In the next window, "Device URI for," enter the device URI. "BrotherHL1440-2" is connected to Philadelphia on Windows 2003, so you must enter the "guest" username and hostname:

```
smb://guest@philadelphia/brotherhl1440-2
```

At this point, you have to select the printer driver. You should also print a test page. On your Linux client, open the CUPS interface, and you should see the printer. Linux clients on the LAN can now use this printer.

Controlling Print Queues from the Command Line

You can *ssh* to a remote Linux print server and use CUPS commands to control print queues. CUPS CLI commands usually require *root* privileges.

Let's take a brief look at those commands:

lpc
: Allows various forms of control over printers. With *lpc status*, you can see a list of available queues and the status of each.

lpstat
: Displays a list of jobs queued for printing on the system's printers. You can use various options to modify this command's output.

lpq
: Displays the status of the current queue or the queue specified with the *-P queue* option.

lppasswd
: Changes the CUPS password used by the system. Set `AuthType` to `Digest` in the *cupsd.conf* configuration file.

enable and disable
: Starts or stops the specified queue. The most frequently used command is *disable* with the *-c* option, to stop a queue and cancel all the jobs currently in the queue.

accept and reject
: Causes the print queue to begin accepting or rejecting new jobs.

lprm
: Removes a job from the queue. You can specify the queue (*-P queue*) and the job identifier (obtained with *lpstat*).

lpmove
: Moves a print job from one queue to another with a job identifier and a queue name (e.g., *lpmove queue1-46 queue2*).

You can try these commands on your own. Here's an example of the first one on the printer we just set up using the CUPS interface:

```
# lpc status
BrotherHL1440:
        printer is on device 'parallel' speed -1
        queuing is enabled
        printing is enabled
        no entries
        daemon present
```

User Management

In Linux, you can manage users (add, change, delete) in many ways. In the beginning of this section, we're going to assume that each server you administer has its own database of users, found in the */etc/passwd* file. We're also going to assume that you know the basics of adding and deleting user accounts with the commands *adduser* and *useradd* for whatever distribution you use, since they differ from distro to distro.

Different Linux distributions have changed the default behavior of the *adduser/useradd* commands. You can access manual pages for either command, but they probably won't work as the manpages indicate. You'll have to experiment to see how your distribution behaves. In Fedora, the two commands seem to behave the same: they both add an account and a user directory. If you type either *adduser tadelste* or *useradd tadelste*, the commands will add the user and create a home directory, but they won't ask for a temporary password or go through the standard Linux questions you might expect to see.

On other distributions, you might see output like this:

```
... # adduser tadelste
Adding user `tadelste'...
Adding new group `tadelste' (1001).
Adding new user `tadelste' (1001) with group `tadelste'.
Creating home directory `/home/tadelste'.
Copying files from `/etc/skel'
Enter new UNIX password: passwd1
Retype new UNIX password: passwd1
passwd: password updated successfully
Changing the user information for tadelste
Enter the new value, or press ENTER for the default
        Full Name []: New User
        Room Number []:
        Work Phone []: 999-555-1212
        Home Phone []:
        Other []:
Is the information correct? [y/N] y
```

On Fedora, however, the output stops at the "Copying files..." line. The administrator is then expected to create the first password for the user. But what if the administrator doesn't immediately assign the new user a password? Could the added user access the server through *ssh*, for instance? Let's try it:

```
$ ssh tadelste@host2.centralsoft.org
tadelste@host2.centralsoft.org's password:
Permission denied, please try again.
tadelste@host2.centralsoft.org's password:
Permission denied, please try again.
tadelste@host2.centralsoft.org's password:
Permission denied (publickey,gssapi-with-mic,password).
$
```

As you can see, the answer is no. The user doesn't just have a blank password; he doesn't have a password at all. The *ssh_config* file has the password requirement enabled, so the user can't use SSH to log in either.

The *root* user must therefore add a password for the user, which an administrator can do as follows:

```
[root@host2 ~]# passwd tadelste
Changing password for user tadelste.
New UNIX password: passwd1
Retype new UNIX password: passwd1
passwd: all authentication tokens updated successfully.
[root@host2 ~]#
```

The output states that the *passwd* command is changing the password for the user, but it's not; it does not ask for the (nonexistent) original password.

As a user, once you've been assigned a password, you can change it yourself:

```
$ passwd
Changing password for user tadelste.
Changing password for tadelste
```

```
(current) UNIX password: passwd1
New UNIX password: passwd1
Password unchanged
New UNIX password: passwd2
Retype new UNIX password: passwd2
passwd: all authentication tokens updated successfully.
$
```

Fedora first verifies that you have a password (if you don't, you won't be able to log onto the server). It also verifies that the new password you enter is different from your existing password. If you enter the same password, Fedora does not accept it and prompts you again.

Since Fedora uses Red Hat's protocol, you have to assume that some security issues must exist around the adding of users and setting of passwords.

When you installed Fedora, the installation script prompted you to create a password for the *root* account and an optional primary user account besides *root*. Other than that, you may have only scant experience with adding users, and little if any with group administration.

System administrators need to know:

- How to create and set up accounts
- How to delete or disable accounts
- The potential for security exploits associated with user management, and how to remedy them

You should also be aware that user accounts serve a number of purposes on Linux systems, and that some "users" are not people. You'll see two major types of accounts:

Accounts for real people
: Each user is given an account that is associated with a few configuration options, such as a password, a home directory, and a shell that runs when the user logs in. Providing separate accounts for each user allows people to set permissions on their files, so they can control who has access to them.

Accounts for system services such as mail or a database server
: These accounts ensure that services run with very restricted privileges and have access only to a few necessary files, in case a programming error or a malicious intruder causes them to try to affect other parts of the system. Typically, when a service is installed, the installation process or the system administrator creates a user and group of the same name (*postfix*, *mysql*, etc.) and assigns them to all files and directories controlled by the service. Services are not given passwords, home directories, or shells, because only intruders would be likely to use these.

As stated previously, if you're reading this book, you should already know how to add users, set passwords, and so on. Now, we want to focus on the issues an administrator needs to know about users from a security point of view.

Removing a User

Employee turnover in many organizations runs high. So, unless you run a small shop with a stable user base, you need to learn how to clean up after an employee leaves. Too many so-called system administrators do not understand the stakes involved when they manage users. Disgruntled former employees can often cause significant trouble for a company by gaining access to the network.

Removing a user isn't a one-step process—you need to manage all of the user's files, mailboxes, mail aliases, print jobs, recurring (automatic) personal processes (such as the backing up of data or remote syncing of directories), and other references to the user. It is a good idea to first disable the user's account in */etc/passwd*; after that, you can search for the user's files and other references. Once all traces of the user have been cleaned up, you can remove the user completely (if you remove the entry from */etc/passwd* while these other references exist, you have a harder time specifying them).

When you remove a user, it's a good idea to follow a predetermined course of action so you don't forget any important steps; you may even want to make a checklist so that you have a routine laid out.

The first task is to disable the user's password, effectively locking him out. You can do this with a command like the following:

```
# passwd -l tadelste
```

Sometimes it's necessary to temporarily disable an account without removing it. For example, a user might go on maternity leave or take a post for 90 days in another country. You may also discover from your system logs that someone has gained unauthorized control of an account by guessing its password. The *passwd -l* command is useful for these situations as well.

Next, you have to decide what to do with the user's files. Remember that users may have files outside their home directories. The *find* command can find them:

```
# find / -user tadelste
[root@host2 ~]# find / -user tadelste
/home/tadelste
/home/tadelste/.zshrc
/home/tadelste/.bashrc
/home/tadelste/.bash_profile
/home/tadelste/.gtkrc
/home/tadelste/.bash_logout.......
```

You can then decide whether to delete these files or keep them. If you decide to delete them, back them up in case you need data from them later.

As extra security, you can change the user's login shell to a dummy value. Simply change the last field in the *passwd* file to `/bin/false`.

If your organization uses Secure Shell (SSH, usually provided on Linux by *OpenSSH-server*) and you allow remote RSA or DSA key authentication, a user can get access to your system even if his password is disabled. This is because SSH uses separate keys.

For instance, even after you have disabled Tom Adelstein's password, he can get on another computer somewhere and run a command such as:

```
$ ssh -f -N -L8000:intranet.yourcompany.com:80 my.domain.com
```

This forwards traffic to port 80 (the port on which a web server usually listens) on your internal server.

Obviously, if your system offers SSH, you should remove authorized keys from the appropriate directories (e.g., *~tadelste/.ssh* or *.~tadelste/.ssh2*) in order to stop the user from regaining access to his account this way:

```
$ cd .ssh
:~/.ssh$ ls
authorized_keys known_hosts
:~/.ssh$ rm authorized_keys
:~/.ssh$ ls
known_hosts
:~/.ssh$
```

Likewise, look for *.shosts* and *.rhosts* files in the user's home directory (for example, *~tadelste/.shosts* and *~tadelste/.rhosts*).

Also, check to see if the user still has any processes running on the system. Such processes might act as a backdoor to allow the user into your network. The following command will tell you if a user currently has any running processes:

```
# ps aux |grep -i ^tadelste
```

Some other questions a system administrator might ask about a personal user who has left the company include:

- Could the user execute CGI scripts from his home directory or on one of the company's web servers?
- Do any email forwarding files such as *~tadelste/.forward* exist? Users can use forwarders to send mail to their accounts and cause programs to be executed on the system where they supposedly do not have access.

Sealing the Home Directory

You will often find that management wants to retain the information in the home directory of an employee who leaves. All the email and other documents in a personal user's account belong to the company. In the event that a disgruntled former employee becomes litigious, the company's legal counsel may want access to these files. Many analysts consider the keeping such directories good practice.

You can save the contents of a user's home directory by renaming it. Simply execute a move command:

```
# mv /home/tadelste /home/tadelste.locked
```

This prevents the former employee from logging in or making use of configuration files such as the *.forward* file discussed in the previous section. The contents remain intact in case they're needed later.

Graphical User Managers

As Linux's market penetration began to increase earlier in the decade, companies such as Sun Microsystems, Novell, Computer Associates, HP, and IBM started porting their administrative toolkits to Red Hat, SUSE, and other Linux platforms. Additionally, the administrative tools bundled with Linux distributions began to mature, with increases in both function and usability.

Since you now have some knowledge of the commands and processes required to create and clean up a personal user account, you should find these utilities easy to use. Generally, though, you will find them less flexible than using the command line.

Let's take a look at an example of one such tool, originally built on a SUSE utility called YaST2. Sun's Java Desktop Configurator is pictured in Figure 8-14. Descriptions of the functions you can perform with this tool are provided in the panel on the left.

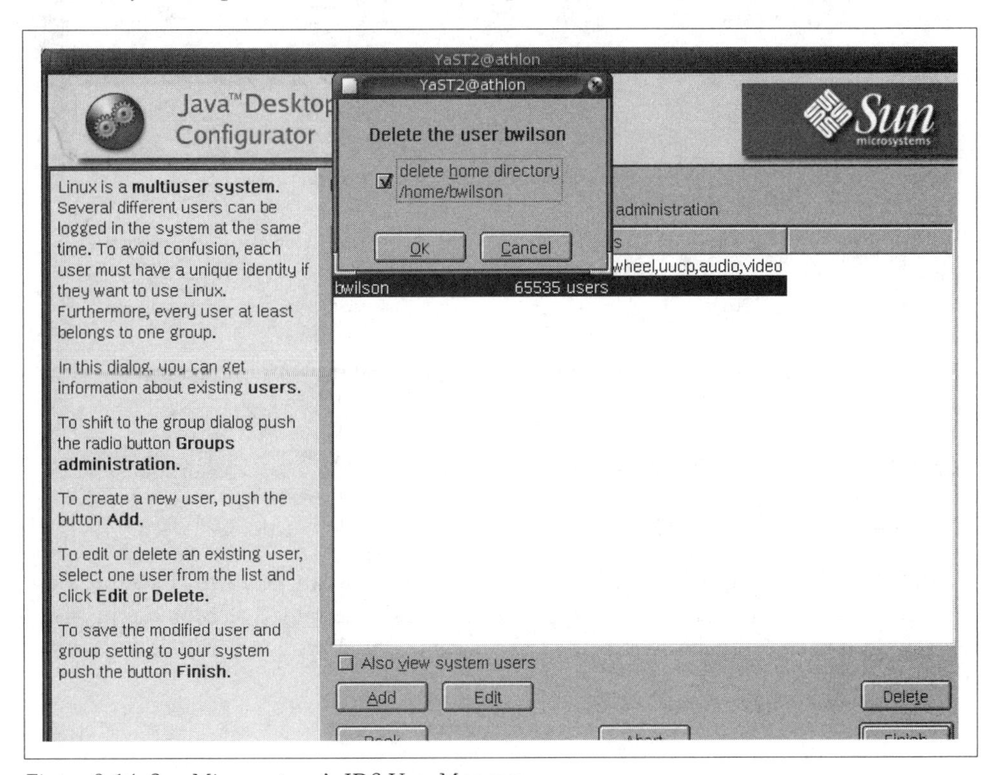

Figure 8-14. Sun Microsystems's JDS User Manager

Notice that the dialog box at the top is asking whether you want to delete the directory */home/tadelste*. As we discussed previously, your company may wish to retain the home directories of former employees. In this case, the graphical tool gives you only two options: either to delete the directory or not. It does not give you the option of renaming the directory, which, as we discussed earlier, may be the most secure and convenient course to take.

In Figure 8-15, you can see another example taken from our Fedora system.

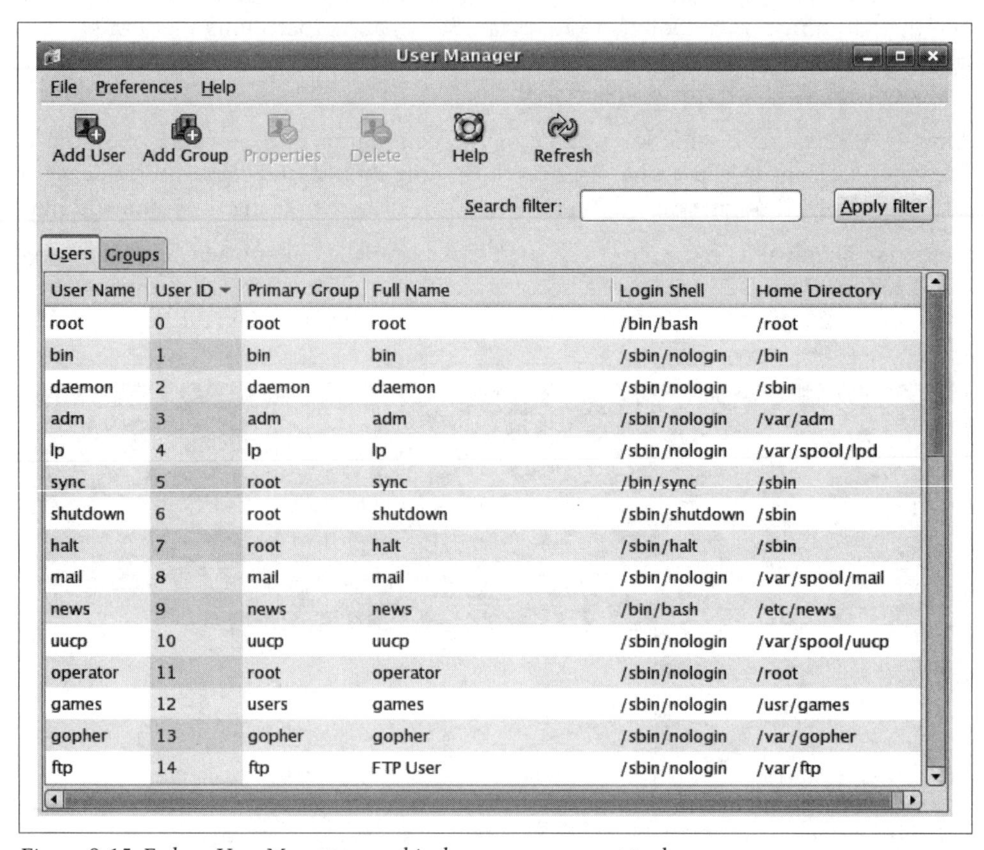

Figure 8-15. Fedora User Manager graphical user management tool

With the Fedora graphical user management tool, you can perform the same basic functions as the ones outlined in Figure 8-14. Again, it may not provide all of the options you need to properly manage the accounts of departing users.

Although it's not technically a user manager, Fedora offers another tool that you can use to configure a number of services related to users. Take a look at Figure 8-16, the graphical tool provided by Fedora when you type the text command *setup*.

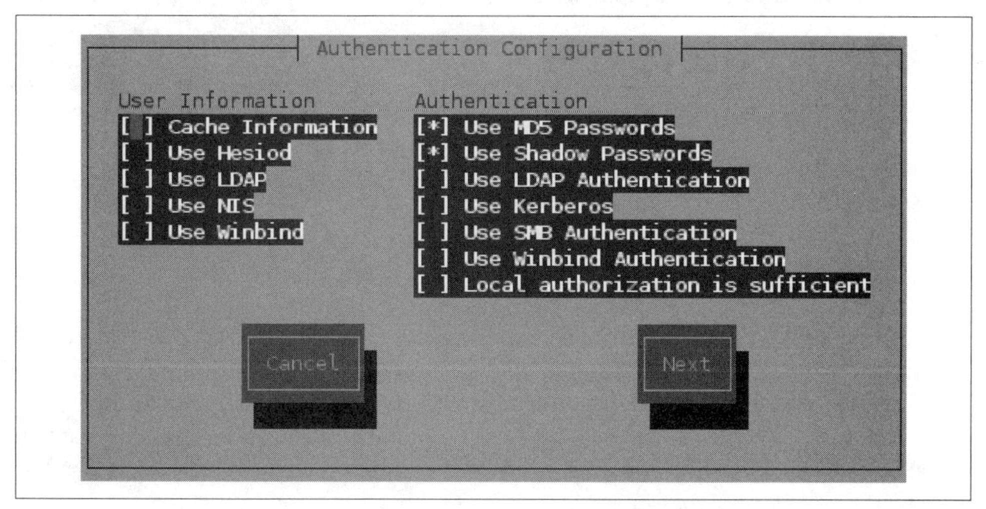

Figure 8-16. Red Hat Authentication Configurator

This is another example of the many ways Linux provides to manage user accounts. It does not require you to run the X Window System.

CHAPTER 9

Virtualization in the Modern Enterprise

In this chapter, we address an area experiencing explosive growth in demand for Linux system administrators. Linux virtualization lies at the heart of today's trends in data center consolidation, high-performance computing, rapid provisioning, business continuity, and workload management. Enterprises are seeing real cost savings because of Linux virtualization, and analysts are noting that the technology is changing the business landscape.

Virtualization is a concept that has gained popularity thanks to the successful company VMware (*http://www.vmware.com*) and the open source project Xen (*http://www.cl.cam.ac.uk/research/srg/netos/xen*). It refers to one piece of hardware running multiple kernels (which are sometimes all the same and sometimes from completely different operating systems) on top of a lower layer of software that manages their access to the hardware. Each kernel, called a *guest*, acts as if it has the whole processor to itself.

The different guests are isolated from each other much more than processes are isolated within a single operating system. This isolation provides security and robustness, because a failure or compromise in one guest doesn't affect the others. The virtualization layer performs many functions of an operating system, managing access to processor time, devices, and memory for each guest.

At the time of this writing, the Linux developers are working on a new system called the Kernal-based Virtual Machine (KVM), which will be part of the kernal.

Why Virtualization Is Popular

To understand who is using virtualization and the environments in which it's valuable, you should understand a bit about current business needs. This section provides that background before we explain how Linux virtualization works.

The entire field of information technology has grown exponentially since the advent of common distributed filesystems. Organizations have seen their infrastructures expand year by year. Many attribute this growth to constant improvements in computer components and software. But that's not the whole picture.

Computer technology has evolved from a focus on managing transactions to harnessing business processes. Some firms specialize in human resource management, others in finance and accounting, and still others in manufacturing and supply chain management. This specialization has created fiefdoms in data centers and among IT staffs.

Traditional networks are now able to capture and manage more and different kinds of transactions than ever before, and this has created the need for increased computing power and subsequently more storage. Growth has also occurred in the number of places and ways we store data, which in itself has created server sprawl (see Figure 9-1).

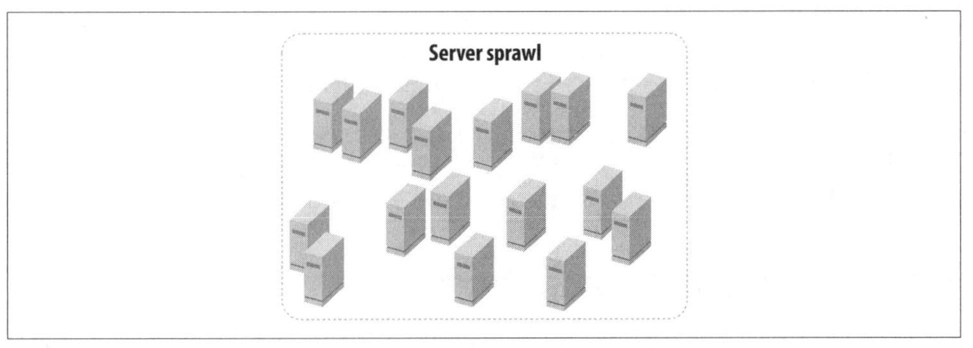

Figure 9-1. Sprawling server farms, one operating system per box

Now add another piece to the mix: specialized applications for fields such as accounting and finance nearly always run on separate, highly available servers with redundant hardware for the sake of ensuring business continuity. This combination of factors has transformed the IT landscape into a welter of isolated, single function, oversized and underutilized physical servers.

On top of all this comes the increasing burden of regulatory compliance, which causes costs to grow again: you have to increase your capacity to store and retrieve documents, and in many cases you're expected to store them for up to 25 years.

Consider what that means. Your successors won't necessarily have the technology available to produce the documents an auditor or attorney might want a decade from now, much less in a quarter of a century.

Let's take another look at the results of computer growth. We have:

- Single-function servers and applications (often known as "silos") with underused capacity
- Additional cost increases because of the complexity of software and the need to manage ever-increasing amounts of data

- The need for staff to specialize into functional areas where you will find a lack of documentation and high levels of personnel turnover
- The need to train and support users and administrators and keep software up-to-date

Now you might understand why enterprise virtualization has gained popularity and become one of the few areas where technology can change the business landscape. With virtual images, you can easily compress your data together with all the programs, configuration settings, operating system libraries, and other metadata that make a whole system. Restoring an image restores the system exactly as it was running at the time, thus making it easier to reproduce documents. Virtualization has the following benefits:

- It replaces wasteful arrays of systems with fewer, better-utilized systems.
- It simplifies administration, because separate kernels with one application running on each are more secure and manageable than one kernel running many applications. It also maintains the environment in which documents were created, to meet regulatory requirements.
- Reduced hardware and complexity allows reduced staff.
- Virtualization may help reverse the trend of server sprawl.

High-Performance Computing

Linux has become the preferred host operating system for virtual machines because of its ability to run and manage massive PC clusters and grids. It took a while for the major hardware vendors to catch on, but once they did they saw big dollar signs. For several years Linux has enjoyed benefactors willing to contribute personnel and advanced technology to its development effort. Such contributors include IBM, Intel, AMD, HP, Novell, Red Hat, Unisys, Fujitsu, and dozens of others.

For example, IBM needed a utility operating system for its OpenPower initiative. Suddenly, Linux ran on Big Blue's Virtualization Engine in the form of an open source hypervisor and accompanying technologies. IBM's engine allows Linux to create and manage partitions and dynamically allocate I/O resources to them.

Then Linux kernel developers announced their new simultaneous multi-threading (SMT) and hyper-threading technology. Linux can now enable two threads to execute simultaneously on the same processor—an essential technology to act as a host for guest operating systems. Thus, VMware runs well on top of Linux and provides a virtualization layer for other instances of Linux or other operating systems. User-Mode Linux (UML) is another example of Linux forming a foundation for virtualization.

The 2.6 Linux kernel fits well with IBM's SMT technology. Prior to this version of the kernel, Linux had insufficient thread-scheduling and arbitration-response characteristics. The 2.6 kernel fixed that problem and greatly expanded the number of processors on which the kernel could run.

This is important for two reasons. First, as a host for virtual machines, Linux has to perform well and excel at managing its hardware. Second, as a guest divorced from its physical hardware, it has to maintain its performance and capacity to handle various processes as the host. Today, Linux makes both a great host and a great guest OS. It manages hardware and virtual partitioning and runs well in the guest partitions, thanks to HP and IBM.

If you've ever wondered why companies like XenSource and Virtual Iron suddenly appeared out of thin air, now you know: it's because of open source hypervisor contributions. Like the hardware vendors that realized Linux could enhance PC and data center component sales, software vendors jumped on the bandwagon. Even Microsoft eventually realized it needed to get in on the Linux game, contributing to both XenSource and Virtual Iron.

Business Continuity and Workload Management

Even on a small scale, your organization will benefit from separating email, DNS, and web servers and directories, gateways, and databases. Placing each of these services on a unique server ensures that if one server goes down, your entire infrastructure doesn't collapse. But separating your services on physical hardware requires a lot of time, space, money, and overhead. You also need to back up and restore your data, provide for catastrophes, and deploy the best hardware for the job.

With Linux virtualization, you can partition a single physical server into a group of virtual ones. Each virtual server appears like a physical one to system administrators. You can create a separate server instance for each service you want to provide: email, DNS, web serving, and so on. If one fails, you won't mangle the others.

Partitioning the physical host also enables you to create a different configuration for each virtual server on the same physical hardware. In one environment, for example, we created smaller virtual machines (VMs) for our DNS servers and larger ones for email and web serving. This allowed us to spread the workload and maintain the same physical hardware. Figure 9-2 gives a sense of what you can accomplish with a single physical server.

Rapid Provisioning

We first accomplished virtualization on our network by creating a minimal installation of Debian in a VM. Once we got it tuned to our needs, we compressed it and put it on CD-R media. We then set up our additional virtual machines using VMware with different configurations, and copied the compressed image into each directory we specified for a VM.

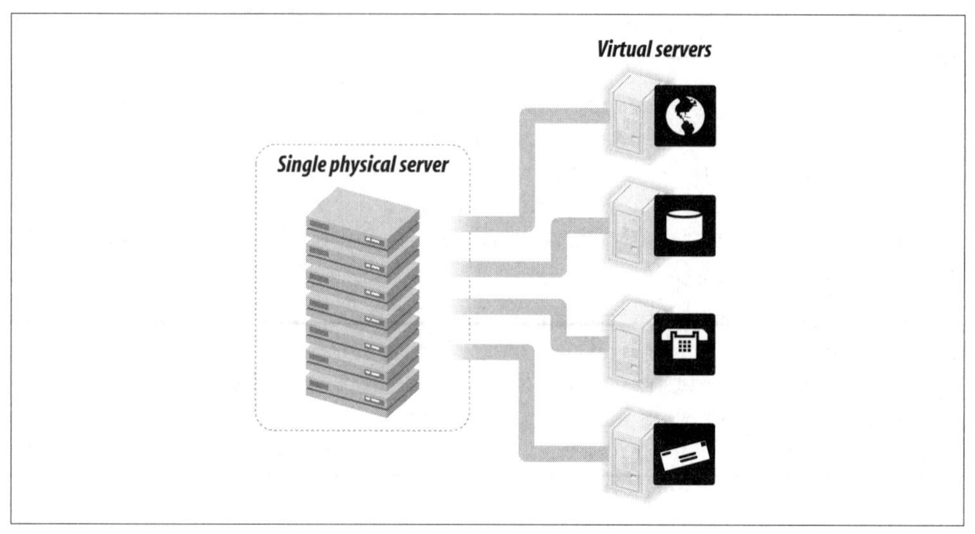

Figure 9-2. Partitioning a single physical server into multiple virtual machines

Each VM lives in a directory. For example, our main directory, */var/lib/vmware/Virtual Machines*, contains several subdirectories such as *debian-31r0a-i386-netinst-kernel2.6*. We simply compressed that subdirectory and used it for deployment to other subdirectories with slightly different names.

We also set up Xen virtual machines using Fedora minimal installations. We then added the components we needed for each service we wanted to provide. For example, our primary DNS server runs in a Xen virtual machine, while our web and mail servers run in separate instances of VMware.

After we got a server (say, email) running, we made a compressed copy of it and burned it to a CD-R. We regularly and systematically back up each virtual server onto visual media such as CDs and DVDs. We also tried moving the images to different distributions of Linux, and they ran just as they had previously.

How Virtualization Helps

What did we accomplish with virtualization? First, we eliminated several physical servers. We deployed our preferred operating system as an image, so we needed to go through the installation process only once. We then created virtual machines on spare hardware and systematically copied our virtual images to allow for instant recovery in case of a system failure.

Virtualization works well for small companies, allowing them to build an infrastructure with free software. Imagine the cost savings just from licensing fees! Now, imagine what kinds of strategies large companies can implement using Linux.

By now, you may be anxious to see how all of this works. So, let's go through the process of installing and configuring Xen and VMware and demonstrate how to virtualize a server network.

Installing Xen on Fedora 5

In this section of the chapter, we'll show you how to install Xen on a single machine to manage two operating systems. As Xen makes its way into the standard Linux distributions, installation will become smoother. But for now, some manual labor is needed.

We're using Fedora Core 5 (FC5) as the Xen host operating system, since it supports Xen 3.0 out of the box. Let's ask *yum* (a package manager similar to Debian's *apt-get* or Red Hat's *up2date*) about Xen:

```
# yum info xen
Loading "installonlyn" plugin
Setting up repositories
core                                                                 [1/3]
updates                                                              [2/3]
extras                                                               [3/3]
Reading repository metadata in from local files
Available Packages
Name   : xen
Arch   : i386
Version: 3.0.2
Release: 3.FC5
Size   : 1.4 M
Repo   : updates
Summary: Xen is a virtual machine monitor
Description:
 This package contains the Xen hypervisor and Xen tools, needed to
run virtual machines on x86 systems, together with the kernel-xen*
packages.  Information on how to use Xen can be found at the Xen
project pages.

Virtualisation can be used to run multiple versions or multiple
Linux distributions on one system, or to test untrusted applications
in a sandboxed environment.  Note that the Xen technology is still
in development, and this RPM has received extremely little testing.
Don't be surprised if this RPM eats your data, drinks your coffee
or makes fun of you in front of your friends.
```

That sounds encouraging. Let's try it, but first check some requirements:

- The system must have at least 256 MB of RAM.
- *grub* must be your boot loader.
- `SELINUX` must be disabled or permissive, but not enforcing.

Run the *system-config-securitylevel* program or edit */etc/selinux/config* to looks as follows:

```
# This file controls the state of SELinux on the system.
# SELINUX= can take one of these three values:
#       enforcing - SELinux security policy is enforced.
#       permissive - SELinux prints warnings instead of enforcing.
#       disabled - SELinux is fully disabled.
SELINUX=Disabled
# SELINUXTYPE= type of policy in use. Possible values are:
#       targeted - Only targeted network daemons are protected.
#       strict - Full SELinux protection.
SELINUXTYPE=targeted
```

If you changed the `SELINUX` value from `enforcing`, you'll need to reboot Fedora before proceeding.

This command will install the Xen hypervisor, a Xen-modified Fedora kernel called *domain 0*, and various utilities:

```
# yum install kernel-xen0
```

The need for a special Xen-modified Linux kernel may disappear in the future as Intel and AMD introduce virtualization support in their chips. Windows Vista is also expected to support virtualization at the processor level.

This adds *xen0* as the first kernel choice in */boot/grub/grub.conf*, but not the default:

```
# grub.conf generated by anaconda
#
# Note that you do not have to rerun grub after making changes to this file
# NOTICE:  You have a /boot partition.  This means that
#          all kernel and initrd paths are relative to /boot/, eg.
#          root (hd0,0)
#          kernel /vmlinuz-version ro root=/dev/VolGroup00/LogVol00
#          initrd /initrd-version.img
#boot=/dev/hda
default=1
timeout=5
splashimage=(hd0,0)/grub/splash.xpm.gz
hiddenmenu
title Fedora Core (2.6.17-1.2157_FC5xen0)
        root (hd0,0)
        kernel /xen.gz-2.6.17-1.2157_FC5
        module /vmlinuz-2.6.17-1.2157_FC5xen0 ro root=/dev/VolGroup00/LogVol00
        module /initrd-2.6.17-1.2157_FC5xen0.img
title Fedora Core (2.6.17-1.2157_FC5)
        root (hd0,0)
        kernel /vmlinuz-2.6.17-1.2157_FC5 ro root=/dev/VolGroup00/LogVol00
        initrd /initrd-2.6.17-1.2157_FC5.img
title Fedora Core (2.6.15-1.2054_FC5)
        root (hd0,0)
```

```
        kernel /vmlinuz-2.6.15-1.2054_FC5 ro root=/dev/VolGroup00/LogVol00
        initrd /initrd-2.6.15-1.2054_FC5.img
default=0
```

To make the Xen kernel the default, change this line:

```
default=1
```

to:

```
default=0
```

Now you can reboot. Xen should start automatically, but let's check:

```
# /usr/sbin/xm list
Name                                      ID Mem(MiB) VCPUs State  Time(s)
Domain-0                                   0      880     1 r-----     20.5
```

The output should show that `Domain-0` is running. Domain 0 controls all the guest operating systems that run on the processor, similarly to how the kernel controls processes in an operating system.

Installing a Xen Guest OS

Xen is now in control of the processor, but you need to add at least one guest operating system. We'll start with installing a Fedora Core 5 guest, because it facilitates the job, and then we'll offer some tips for other variants of Linux.

Fedora Core 5

Fedora Core 5 has a Xen guest installation script that simplifies the process, although it installs only FC5 guests. The script expects to access the FC5 install tree via FTP, the Web, or NFS; for some reason, you can't specify a directory or file. We'll use our FC5 installation DVD and serve it with Apache:

```
# mkdir /var/www/html/dvd
# mount -t iso9660 /dev/dvd /var/www/html/dvd
# apachectl start
```

Now we'll run the installation script and answer its questions:

```
# xenguest-install.py
What is the name of your virtual machine? guest1
How much RAM should be allocated (in megabytes)? 256
What would you like to use as the disk (path)? /xenguest
What is the install location? http://127.0.0.1/dvd
```

At this point, the FC5 installation begins. Choose between text mode and graphic mode (if X is running) via *vnc*. If you choose text mode, you'll be connected to a console. Proceed as you normally would for a Fedora or Red Hat installation. On the IP address screen, give the guest a different address from the host, or use DHCP (if you said `dhcp="dhcp"` in the Xen configuration file, which is explained in the next section). The last screen will ask you to reboot. Unmount the DVD and eject it. You will be rebooting only your new guest system, not Xen or the host.

Xen does not start the guest operating system automatically. You need to type this command on the host:

```
# xm create guest1
```

At this point, you'll have two operating systems (*host1* and *guest1*) operating independently and living in harmony, each with its own filesystems, network connections, and memory. To prove that both servers are running, try these commands:

```
# xm list
Name                                      ID Mem(MiB) VCPUs State  Time(s)
Domain-0                                   0      128     1 r-----   686.0
guest1                                     3      256     1 -b----    14.5
# xentop
xentop - 21:04:38   Xen 3.0-unstable
2 domains: 1 running, 1 blocked, 0 paused, 0 crashed, 0 dying, 0 shutdown
Mem: 982332k total, 414900k used, 567432k free    CPUs: 1 @ 2532MHz
      NAME  STATE   CPU(sec) CPU(%)     MEM(k) MEM(%)  MAXMEM(k) MAXMEM(%) VCPUS NETS
NETTX(k) NETRX(k) SSID
  Domain-0 -----r        686    0.3     131144   13.4   no limit       n/a     1    8
1488528    80298     0
    guest1 --b---         14    0.1     261996   26.7     262144      26.7    1    1
129       131     0
```

To start Xen domains automatically, use these commands:

```
# /sbin/chkconfig --level 345 xendomains on
# /sbin/service xendomains start
```

Other guests

If you want a guest OS other than FC5, you'll need to edit a Xen guest configuration file, which is a text file (actually, a Python script) in the */etc/xen* directory. *xmexample1* and *xmexample2* are commented sample files. For the full file syntax, see:

```
# man xmdomain.cfg
```

When we ran *xenguest-install.py* in the previous section, it generated the Xen guest configuration */etc/xen/guest1*, with a few extra lines:

```
# Automatically generated Xen config file
name = "guest1"
memory = "256"
disk = [ 'file:/xenguest,xvda,w' ]
vif = [ 'mac=00:16:3e:63:c7:76' ]
uuid = "bc2c1684-c057-99ea-962b-de44a038bbda"
bootloader="/usr/bin/pygrub"

on_reboot   = 'restart'
on_crash    = 'restart'
```

This contains some, but not all, of the directives a guest needs. A minimal guest configuration file looks something like this:

1. A unique guest domain name:

```
name="vm01"
```

2. A Xen-enabled kernel image pathname for the guest domain:

```
kernel="/boot/vmlinuz-2.6.12.6-xenU"
```

3. A root device for the guest domain:

```
root="/dev/hda1"
```

4. Initial memory allocation for the guest, in megabytes:

```
memory=128
```

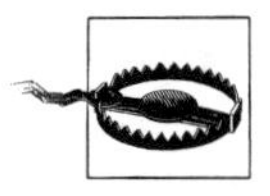

The sum of the memory for all Xen guests must not exceed physical memory minus 64 MB for Xen itself.

5. The disk space for the guest domain. This is defined in one or more disk block device stanzas, each enclosed in single or double quotes:

```
disk = [ 'stanza1', 'stanza2' ]
```

   A stanza consists of a string of three parameters (`'host_dev, guest_dev, mode'`). *host_dev* is the domain's storage area as seen by the host. This may be one of:

   `file:`*pathname*
   : A *loopback* file image (a single local file that Xen treats as a filesystem); this is created when you run *xm create* or the *xen-create-image* program.

   `phy:`*device*
   : A physical device.

   guest_dev is the physical device as seen by the guest domain, and *mode* is `r` for read-only or `w` for read-write. Thus, a sample `disk` directive for two guests is:

```
disk=['file:/vserver/images/vm01.img, hda1, w', 'file:/vserver/images/vm01-swap.
img, hda2, w']
```

6. Network interface information in a `vif` directive. This directive may contain a stanza for each network device. The default network is specified with:

```
vif=[ '' ]
```

   A `dhcp` directive controls whether DHCP is used or the interface information is hard-coded. The following specifies the use of DHCP:

```
dhcp="dhcp"
```

   If the `dhcp` directive is missing or set to `"off"`, you must specify network information statically, as you do when configuring a system:

```
ip="192.168.0.101"
netmask="255.255.255.0"
gateway="192.168.0.1"
hostname="vm01.example.com"
```

The *xm* manpage gives the following example of a minimal guest, with a loopback file image on the host appearing as the root device on the guest:

```
kernel = "/boot/vmlinuz-2.6-xenU"
memory = 128
name = "MyLinux"
root = "/dev/hda1 ro"
disk = [ "file:/var/xen/mylinux.img,hda1,w" ]
```

Once you have a guest configuration file, create the Xen guest with this command:

```
# xm create -c guest_name
```

where *guest_name* can be a full pathname or a relative filename (in which case Xen places it in */etc/xen/guest_name*). Xen will create the guest domain and try to boot it from the given file or device. The *-c* option attaches a console to the domain when it starts, so you can answer the installation questions that appear.

Installing VMware

VMware has made its server available for free, and the code is even open source. You can find it at *http://www.vmware.com/products/server*. We found it robust and user-friendly. You can read about VMware's open source and community source initiatives on its web site.

As we mentioned earlier, startups such as XenSource and Virtual Iron have taken advantage of the Linux kernel's support of hypervisor technology from IBM. Under competitive pressure from Xen, VMware has also submitted its own open source contributions to the kernel developers, realizing that VMware will run better on Linux if VMware gives the Linux kernel a little help.

While we ran Xen using Fedora Core 5, we decided to install VMware on an Ubuntu server as our host and used Debian as our guest operating system. We also managed remote VMware instances from an Ubuntu desktop using the VMware console. Later, we installed FC5 under a VMware virtual machine.

We downloaded *Vmware-server-1.0.1-29996.tar.gz* and decompressed it to an installation directory called *vmware-server-distrib*. Inside the directory we found *vmware-install.pl* and ran it with the command *./vmware-install.pl*. Soon afterward, the installation program began and displayed the following messages:

```
Creating a new installer database using the tar3 format.

Installing the content of the package.

In which directory do you want to install the binary files?
[/usr/bin]
```

VMware Server's installation begins with several questions like this, based on the installation script's sniffing of your operating system and file layouts.

During the installation process, the script asks you to accept VMware's product license. You should read it before accepting it. After you agree to the license, VMware verifies that the compiler and header files on your system are compatible with each other and builds the VMware binaries using your compiler. You will see messages such as:

```
The path "/usr/lib/vmware" does not exist currently. This program is going
to create it, including needed parent directories. Is this what you want?
[yes]
```

Additionally, you will see code compilations like the following example:

```
make[1]: Entering directory '/usr/src/linux-headers-2.6.15-26-k7'
  CC [M]  /tmp/vmware-config0/vmnet-only/driver.o
  CC [M]  /tmp/vmware-config0/vmnet-only/hub.o
  CC [M]  /tmp/vmware-config0/vmnet-only/userif.o
  CC [M]  /tmp/vmware-config0/vmnet-only/netif.o
  CC [M]  /tmp/vmware-config0/vmnet-only/bridge.o
  CC [M]  /tmp/vmware-config0/vmnet-only/procfs.o
  CC [M]  /tmp/vmware-config0/vmnet-only/smac_compat.o
  SHIPPED /tmp/vmware-config0/vmnet-only/smac_linux.x386.o
  LD [M]  /tmp/vmware-config0/vmnet-only/vmnet.o
  Building modules, stage 2.
  MODPOST
```

Toward the end of the installation, the script will inform you that installation of the code has completed and offer you a command you can use if you ever want to uninstall the server:

```
The installation of VMware Server 1.0.1 build-29996 for Linux completed
successfully. You can decide to remove this software from your system at any
time by invoking the following command: "/usr/bin/vmware-uninstall.pl".
```

The installation script will also ask you to run the configuration command:

```
Before running VMware Server for the first time, you need to configure it by
invoking the following command: "/usr/bin/vmware-config.pl". Do you want
this program to invoke the command for you now? [yes]
```

As the installation process ends, you will see the following messages:

```
Starting VMware services:
Virtual machine monitor                             done
Virtual Ethernet                                    done
Bridged networking on /dev/vmnet0                   done
Host-only networking on /dev/vmnet1 (background)    done
Host-only networking on /dev/vmnet8 (background)    done
NAT service on /dev/vmnet8                          done
Starting VMware virtual machines                    done

The configuration of VMware Server 1.0.1 build-29996 for Linux for this
running kernel completed successfully.
```

You can download an existing operating system image, which VMware calls an *appliance*, from *http://www.vmware.com/vmtn/appliances/directory*. We chose *debian-31r0a-i386-netinst-kernel2.6.zip*, which we placed under the */var/lib/vmare/Virtual Machines* directory and decompressed.

Once we had our basic image, we started the VMware management console on a remote Ubuntu desktop behind a firewall at a remote location. We ran the command:

```
$ gksu vmware-server-console
```

We then configured the console to connect to our guest operating system remotely. With the VMware Server Console running, we connected to the remote virtual machine and logged on as *root*, as shown in Figure 9-3.

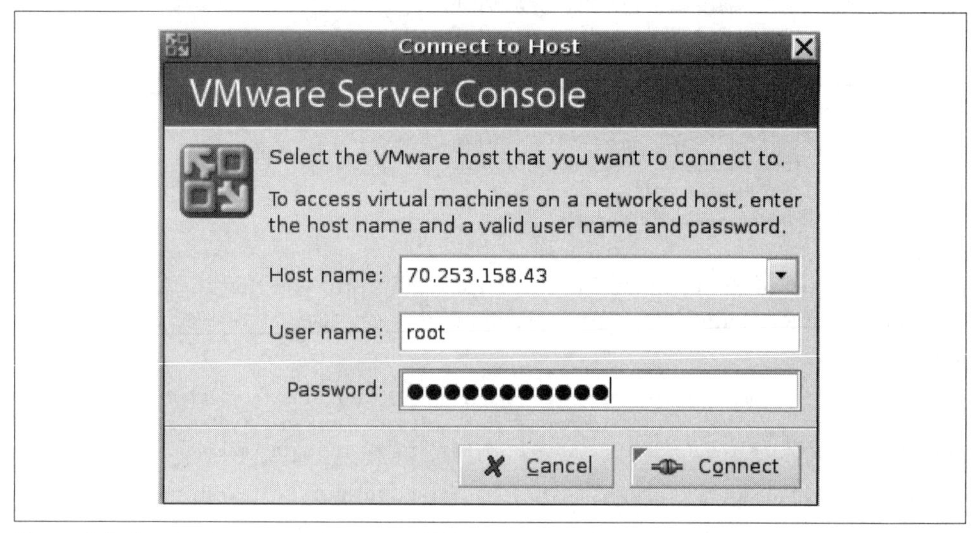

Figure 9-3. Connecting to a remote virtual host

After we connected to the remote host, VMware prompted us to create a virtual machine. Because we'd already created one, we instead clicked on the File menu and opened the directory that contained our existing instance of Debian. This action added Debian to the VM inventory. Our console then appeared similar to Figure 9-4, which gave us an idea of the operating functions available.

We were then able to start Debian. As the system booted, Debian began to run the later phases of its installation script. We let it run, and within a short time we got to the screen in Figure 9-5.

We opted to configure Debian manually instead of choosing one of the predefined configurations. That allowed us to create a default Debian server to deploy in additional instances of VMware Server. Figure 9-6 shows the running Debian system.

The screenshot shows us running the command *ifconfig*. We tested this instance to make sure our virtual Ethernet cards were correctly bound to the IP addresses we set up.

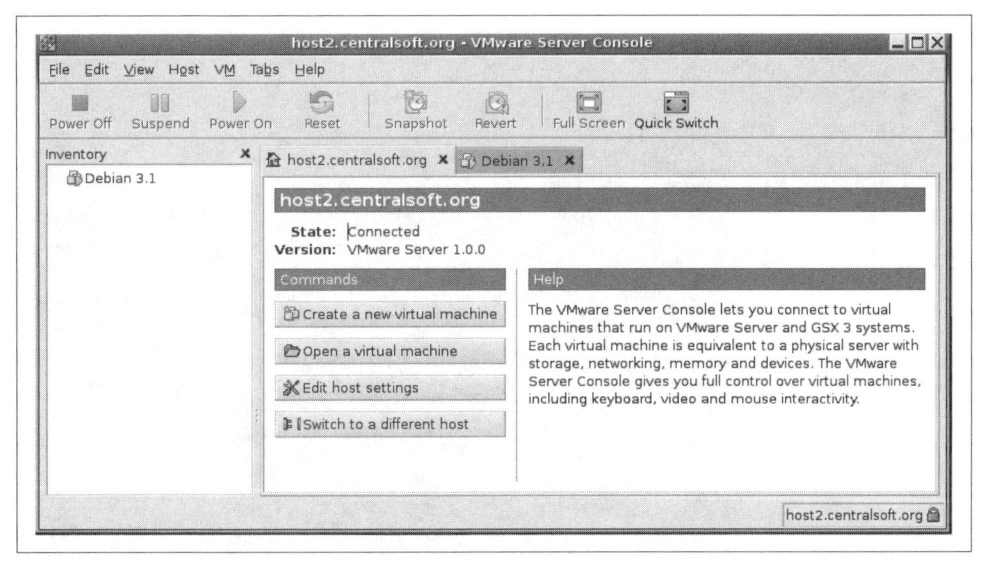

Figure 9-4. Connected to a remote host ready to start up

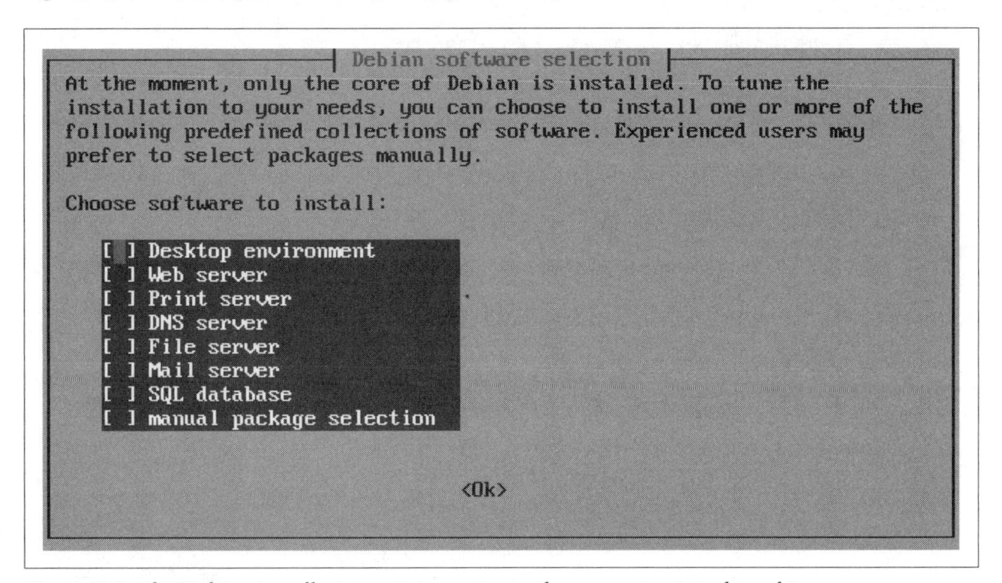

Figure 9-5. The Debian installation script running under a remote virtual machine

Once we had our basic Debian image, we zipped it up and burned it to CD-R media. We then deployed that image on the other hosts, after we'd determined each guest system's role and resource requirements.

Figure 9-7 provides a summary of the Debian image. On the right side of the screen you can see the configuration of the host. We can alter the virtual server dynamically to add memory, disk space, Ethernet cards, processors, and various devices as the need arises and as we set up additional machines.

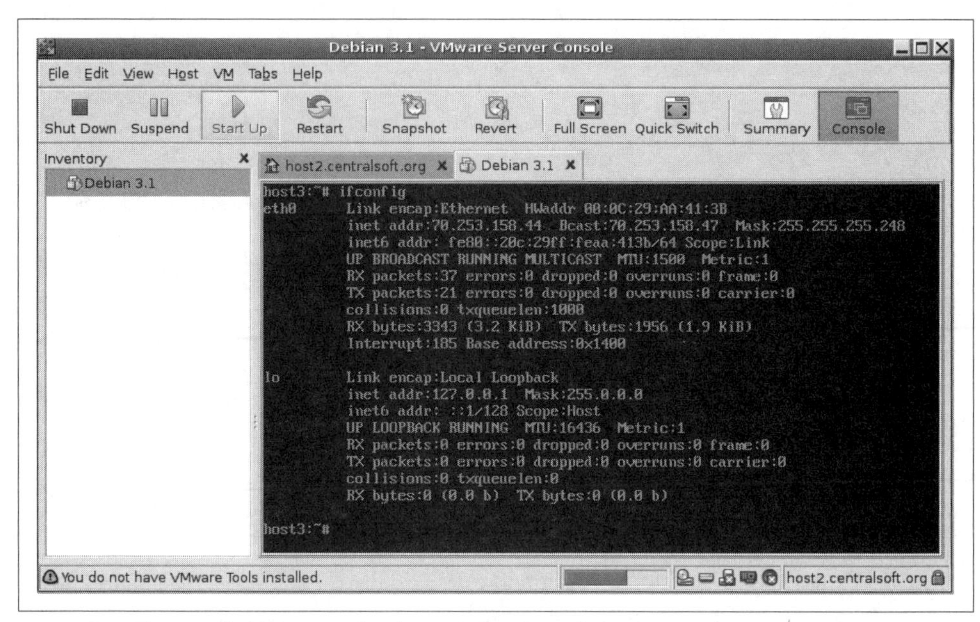

Figure 9-6. The installed instance of Debian on its remote host

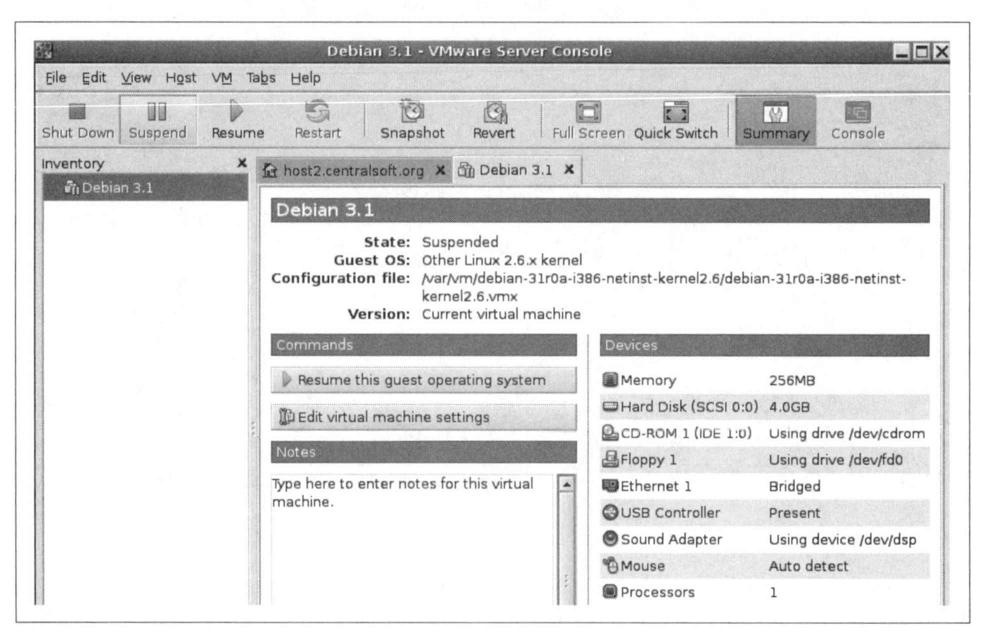

Figure 9-7. Console summary of our basic Debian guest image

Installing a VMware Guest OS

For our final task, installing another operating system, we downloaded Fedora Core 5 from VMware's community site, moved it to the *Virtual Machines* directory, and decompressed it as we did with Debian. Next, we added it to our inventory through the File menu. Figure 9-8 shows a question about a unique identifier; you can keep the existing one.

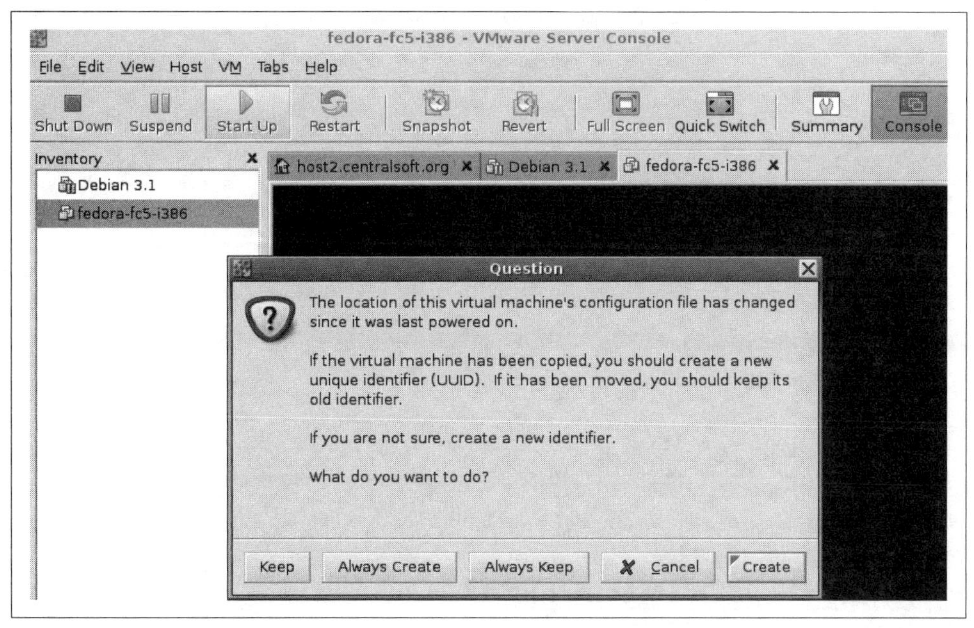

Figure 9-8. VMware asks about a virtual machine image's unique identifier

VMware's management console noticed we added an image. In order to distinguish between possible multiple images, it prompted us for a unique identifier (UUID) in the dialog shown in Figure 9-8. Because we copied Fedora 5 and have all the files making up the image, it did not matter which option we chose from the dialog.

When you open a new virtual machine, VMware gives you a chance to verify the virtual hardware configuration. Figure 9-9 gives you an idea of the virtual hardware inventory available for Fedora Core 5.

In addition to downloading images and loading them into the management console, you can install a Linux operating system from a standard Linux distribution's CD-ROM.

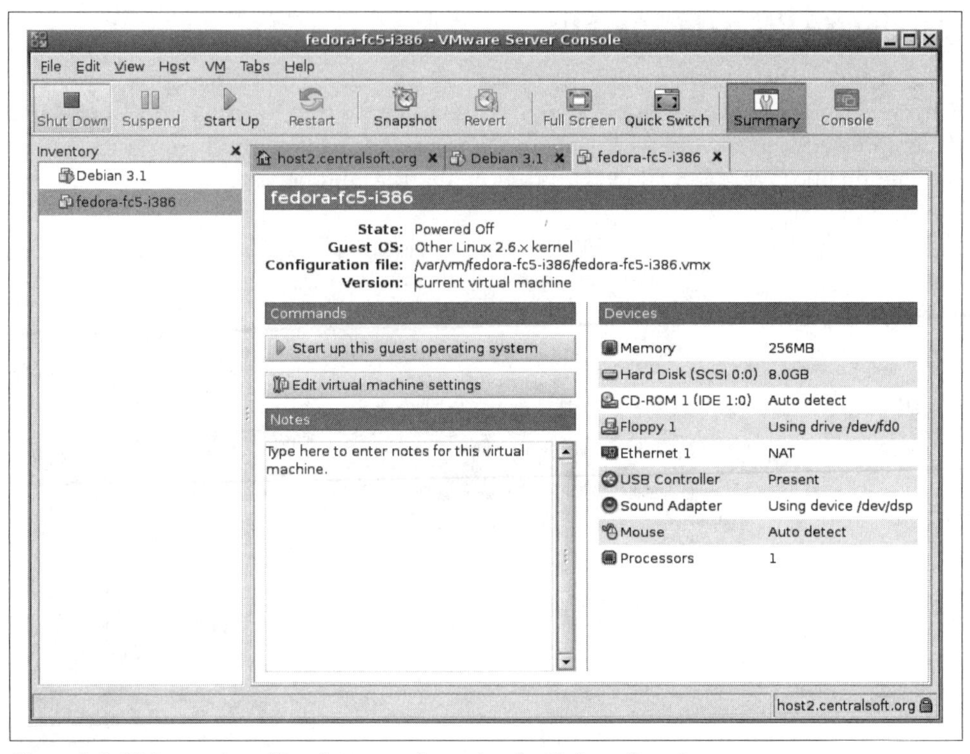

Figure 9-9. VMware virtual hardware configuration for Fedora Core 5

Virtualization: A Passing Fad?

Many analysts say they will sit on the sidelines and wait to see whether Linux virtualization takes hold. As a system administrator, you might want to weigh the risks and rewards of mastering this technology. Virtualization is not the equivalent of IBM's introduction of the PC or Microsoft's introduction of distributed filesystems. The impact of hypervisor technology doesn't even compare to that of ERP programs such as SAP, PeopleSoft, or Oracle Financials.

In any case, technologies such as Xen and VMware have undeniable benefits. Virtualization improves the utilization of servers and reduces overprovisioning of hardware by consolidating system resources. By running your current software in a virtual environment, you can not only preserve your investment in that software but take greater advantage of low-cost, industry-standard servers.

Hopefully, this chapter has provided you with the knowledge and skills you need to implement your own virtualized environments. You now have the opportunity to experiment and have fun with free virtualization technology. Doing so could position you as a specialist in a field few understand.

CHAPTER 10
Scripting

As a Linux system administrator, you'll use two tools more than any others: a text editor to create and edit text files, and a shell to run commands. At some point you'll tire of typing repetitive commands and look for ways to save your fingers and reduce errors. That's when you'll combine the text editor and the shell to create the simplest Linux programs: shell scripts.

Linux itself uses shell scripts everywhere, especially for customizable tasks such as service and process management. If you understand how those system scripts are written, you can interpret the steps they're taking and adapt them for your own needs.

The *shell* (an interface to the operating system) is one of many innovations inherited from Linux's great-grandfather, Unix. In 1978, Bell Labs researcher Stephen Bourne developed the Bourne Shell for Version 7 Unix. It was called *sh* (Unix valued terseness), and it defined the standard features that all shells still display. Shells evolved from that foundation, leading to the development of the Korn shell (*ksh*, or course), the C shell (*csh*), and finally the Bash shell (*bash*) that is now standard on GNU/Linux systems. *bash* is a pun/acronym for *B*ourne-*A*gain *Sh*ell, and it still supports scripts written for the original Bourne shell.

This chapter starts with the *bash* basics: shell prompts, commands and arguments, variables, expressions, and I/O redirection. If you're familiar with these already, you won't miss much by skipping ahead a few pages (except perhaps a cure for insomnia).

Every tool has its limits, and at some point you may find that *bash* is not the best solution to all your problems. Toward the end of this chapter we'll examine a small application written in a number of scripting languages: *bash* as well as Perl, PHP, and Python (the three Ps associated with the LAMP acronym we mentioned in Chapter 6). You can compare their style, syntax, expressiveness, ease of use, and applicability to different domains. Not every problem is a nail, but a big enough hammer can treat it like one.

bash Beginnings

Many operating systems offered command-line interfaces in the early days, and they typically allowed commands to be stored in text files and run as *batch jobs* (a readily understood concept at the time). It soon became natural to introduce ways to submit parameters to scripts and allow the scripts to change their behavior under different conditions. Unix's shell made tremendous leaps in flexibility, turning the shell into a true programming language.

Our interactive examples will show a sample shell *prompt*, a *command* with optional *arguments*, and the command's *output*, like this:

```
admin@server1:~$ date
Thu Aug 24 09:16:56 CDT 2006
```

We'll show the contents of a shell script like this:

```
#!/bin/bash
contents of script...
```

The first line is special in Linux scripts: if it starts with the two characters `#!`, the rest of the first line is the filename of the command to run to process the rest of the script. (If the # character is not followed by a !, it's interpreted as a comment that continues until the end of the line.) This trick lets you use any program to interpret your script files. If the program is a traditional shell like *sh* or *bash*, the file is called a *shell script*. At the end of the chapter we'll show scripts for Perl, PHP, and Python.

Microsoft Windows uses the suffix of the filename to define the file type and what interpreter should run it. If you change a file's suffix, it may stop working. In Linux, filenames have nothing to do with execution (although following conventions can be useful for other reasons).

Use your favorite text editor (or even one you don't care for) to create this three-line file, and save it to a file called *hello*:

```
#!/bin/bash
echo hello world
echo bonjour monde
```

This file is not a working script yet. We'll show how to actually run it in the next section, but first we need to explain some basic syntax rules.

The */bin/bash* shell will interpret this script line by line. It expects each command to be on a single line, but if you end a line with a backslash (\), *bash* will treat the next line as a continuation:

```
#!/bin/bash
echo \
hello\
world
```

This is a good way to make complex lines more readable.

The shell ignores lines filled with whitespace (spaces, tabs, empty lines). It also ignores everything from a comment character (#) to the end of the line. When *bash* reads the second line of this script (`echo hello world`), it treats the first word (`echo`) as the command to run and the other words (`hello world`) as its arguments. The *echo* command just copies its arguments to its output. The third line runs another *echo* command, but with different arguments.

To see what you've put in the file *hello*, you can print its contents to the screen:

```
admin@server1:~$ cat hello
#!/bin/bash
echo hello world
echo bonjour monde
```

Pathnames and Permissions

The *hello* file can be executed by running the *bash* command with a *hello* argument:

```
admin@server1:~$ bash hello
hello world
bonjour monde
admin@server1:~$
```

Now let's try to run *hello* without its *bash* chaperon:

```
admin@server1:~$ hello
bash: hello: command not found
```

Why can't *bash* find it? When you specify a command, Linux searches a list of directories called the *path* for a file of that name and runs the first one it finds. In this case, *hello* was not in any of these directories. If you tell the system what directory *hello* is in, it will run it. The pathname can be absolute (*/home/admin/hello*) or relative (*./hello* means the *hello* file in the current directory). We'll describe how to specify the directories in your path in the next section, but first we have to deal with *permissions*.

A shell script won't run without certain file permissions. Let's check the permissions on *hello*:

```
admin@server1:~$ ls -l hello
-rw-r--r--  1 admin admin 48 2006-07-25 13:25 hello
```

A `-` indicates that the flag is not set. The leading `-` is the directory flag; it's `d` for a directory or `-` for a file. Next come the permissions for the file's owner, the group to which the owner belongs, and everyone else. The owner (*admin*) can read (`r`) and write (`w`) this file, while others in the group (in this case, also named *admin*) and everyone else can only read it (`r--`). No one can execute (run) the file, because the third character in each three-character set is a `-` instead of an `x`.

Now let's try to run *hello* with a relative pathname:

```
admin@server1:~$ ./hello
bash: ./hello: Permission denied
```

This time Linux found it but didn't run it. It failed because the *hello* file does not have executable permissions. You need to decide who will be allowed to execute it: only you (the owner), anyone in your group, and/or users in other groups. This is a practical security decision that administrators must make frequently. If permissions are too broad, others can run your script without your knowledge; if they're too narrow, the script might not run at all.

The command to change permissions is called *chmod* (for change mode), and it can use old-style Unix octal numbers or letters. Let's try it both ways, giving read/write/execute permissions to yourself, read/execute permissions to your group, and nothing to others (what have they ever given you?). For the octal style, read=4, write=2, and execute=1. The user number will be 4+2+1 (7), the group 4+1 (5), and others 0:

```
admin@server1:~$ chmod 750 hello
admin@server1:~$ ls -l hello
-rwxr-x---  1 admin admin 50 2006-08-03 15:44 hello
```

The other style of permission arguments, using letters, is probably more intuitive:

```
admin@server1:~$ chmod u=rwx,g=rx hello
admin@server1:~$ ls -l hello
-rwxr-x---  1 admin admin 50 2006-08-03 15:44 hello
```

To quickly add read and execute permissions for yourself, your group, and others, enter:

```
admin@server1:~$ chmod +xr hello
admin@server1:~$ ls -l hello
-rwxr-xr-x  1 admin admin 50 2006-08-03 15:44 hello
```

Now we can run the script from the command line:

```
admin@server1:~$ ./hello
hello world
bonjour monde
```

The Default Path

The list of directories through which *bash* should search for commands is specified in a shell environment variable called PATH. To see what's in your path, enter:

```
admin@server1:~$ echo $PATH
/bin:/usr/bin
```

Linux reserves the special names . for the current directory and .. for the current directory's parent directory. If you want Linux to always find commands like *hello* in your current directory, add the current directory to PATH:

```
admin@server1:~$ PATH=$PATH:.
```

To make changes such as this one stick, you'll need to make a permanent change to your PATH. This can be done by an individual user in the *.bashrc* file located in the user's home directory, or by the system administrator in a system-wide startup file (usually located in the */etc* directory); just add a statement to the file like the command just shown.

Alternatively, you could move the *hello* script to one of the directories already in the PATH. However, these directories are usually protected so that only the *root* user can put files there, to preserve security.

For a script more complex than *hello* (i.e., almost any script), either method has security implications. If . is in your PATH, you run the risk that if someone else puts a different script named *hello* in another directory and you blunder into that directory and type *hello*, you'll execute the other user's *hello* and not the one you intended.

The correctness of the script is also a concern. We're reasonably sure about what our *hello* script does now, but we might not be after adding a hundred more lines.

A common practice is to put your own scripts in a directory like */usr/local/bin* or a private *~/bin* rather than a system directory like */bin*, */sbin*, or */usr/bin*. To add this directory to your PATH permanently, add a line like the following at the end of your *.bashrc* file:

```
export PATH=$PATH:/usr/local/bin
```

I/O Redirection

I/O redirection and *pipes* are more Unix innovations that Microsoft and many others have copied without shame. The shell gives you access to these features in a very intuitive way.

When you're typing a command at the console or in a text window, your fingers provide the command's *standard input*, and your eyes read the command's *standard output* and *standard error* output. However, you can produce input or capture that output by replacing your fingers or your eyes with a file. Let's run the *ls* command with its standard output going to the screen as usual, and then redirected (with >) to a file:

```
admin@server1:~$ ls
hello
admin@server1:~$ ls > files.txt
admin@server1:~$
```

In the second example, the redirection happens silently. If any errors occurred, however, you would see them on the display rather than in the file (that's why standard error exists):

```
admin@server1:~$ ls ciao > files.txt
ls: ciao: No such file or directory
admin@server1:~$
```

Be aware that if *files.txt* exists before you run these commands, it will be overwritten. If you want to append new content to the file rather than overwriting it, use the append (>>) characters instead:

```
admin@server1:~$ ls -l >> files.txt
```

If *files.txt* does not exist, it will be created before the appending starts.

You can also redirect standard error. Here is a dazzling display that redirects both standard output and standard error at the same time:

```
admin@server1:~$ ls -l > files.txt 2> errors.txt
```

The inelegant `2>` is the standard error redirection magic. Standard error redirection can be useful with long processes such as compilations, so you can review any error messages later rather than hovering over the screen.

If you want to redirect standard output and standard error to the same file, do this:

```
admin@server1:~$ ls -l > files.txt 2>&1
```

The `&1` means "the same place as standard output," which in this case is *files.txt*. A shortcut for the previous command is:

```
admin@server1:~$ ls -l >& files.txt
```

Use >> rather than > anywhere you want to append rather than overwrite.

It's only fair that standard input may also be redirected. Here's a contrived example that searches for filenames containing the string *foo*:

```
admin@server1:~$ ls -l > files.txt
admin@server1:~$ grep foo < files.txt
admin@server1:~$ rm files.txt
```

The first step creates the temporary file *files.txt*. The second step reads from it, and in the third step we practice good disk hygiene and get rid of it. The temporary file's life was short but productive.

We can combine these three steps into one and avoid the temporary file with Unix's best invention, the *pipe*. A pipe connects the output of one command to the input of another command. The pipe symbol is `|`, like a `>` and `<` meeting at great speed. The standard output of the first command becomes standard input for the second command, simplifying our earlier steps:

```
admin@server1:~$ ls -l | grep foo
```

You can also chain pipes together:

```
admin@server1:~$  ls -l | grep foo | wc -l
```

This command will count the number of times the string *foo* appears in any of the files in the current directory.

Variables

bash is a programming language, and programming languages have common features. One of the most basic is the *variable*: a symbol that contains a value. *bash* variables are strings unless you specify otherwise with a `declare` statement. You don't need to declare or define *bash* variables before you use them, unlike with many other languages.

A variable's name is a string starting with a letter and containing letters, numbers, or underscores (_). A variable's value is obtained by putting a `$` character before the variable's name. Here's a shell script that assigns a string value to the variable `hw`, then prints it:

```
#!/bin/bash
hw="hello world"
echo $hw
```

The variable `hw` is created by the assignment in line 2. In line 3, the contents of the variable `hw` will replace the `$hw` reference. Because *bash* and other shells treat whitespace characters (spaces and tabs) as command argument separators rather than normal argument characters, to preserve them you must surround the whole string with double quote (`"`) or single quote (`'`) characters. The difference is that shell variables (and other special shell syntax) are expanded within double quotes and treated literally within single quotes. Look at the difference in output from the two *echo* commands in the following script:

```
admin@server1:~$ cat hello2
#!/bin/bash
hw="hello world"
echo "$hw"
echo '$hw'
admin@server1:~$ ./hello2
hello world
$hw
admin@server1:~$
```

You can assign the standard output of a command to a variable with the `$(`*`command`*`)` or `` ` ``*`command`*`` ` `` (using little grave accents) syntax:

```
admin@server1:~$ cat today
#!/bin/bash
dt=$(date)
dttoo=`date`
echo "Today is $dt"
echo "And so is $dttoo"
admin@server1:~$ ./today
Today is Tue Jul 25 14:56:01 CDT 2006
And so is Tue Jul 25 14:56:01 CDT 2006
admin@server1:~$
```

Special variables represent command-line arguments. The `$` character followed by a number *n* refers to the *n*th argument on the command line, starting from 1. The `$0` variable is the name of the script itself. The $* variable contains all the arguments as one string value. These variables can then be passed along to commands the script runs:

```
admin@server1:~$ cat files
#!/bin/bash
ls -Alv $*
admin@server1:~$ ./files hello hello2 today
-rwxr-xr-x  1 admin admin 48 2006-07-25 13:25 hello
-rwxr-xr-x  1 admin admin 51 2006-07-25 14:45 hello2
-rwxr-xr-x  1 admin admin 45 2006-07-25 14:49 today
admin@server1:~$
```

The special variable $$ contains the current process's process ID. This can be used to create a unique temporary filename. If multiple copies of the same script are running at the same time, each will have a different process ID and thus a different temporary filename.

Another useful variable is $?, which contains the return status of the most recent command executed. We'll use this later in this chapter to check for the success or failure of program execution in a script.

Useful Elements for bash Scripts

We've introduced the basic elements of *bash* that you'll use in the everyday running of interactive commands. Now let's look at some things that will help you write effective scripts.

Expressions

bash expressions contain variables and *operators* such as == (equals) and > (greater than). These are usually used in tests, which can be specified in several ways:

```
test $file == "test"
[ $file == "test" ]
[[ $file == "test" ]]
```

If you use the *test* command, remember that some symbols have multiple meanings (for instance, in an earlier section we used > for output redirection), so they need to be enclosed in quotes. You don't have to worry about the quotes if you use the single or double square bracket syntax. The double brackets do everything the single ones do and a bit more, so it's safest to use double brackets with your expressions.

bash has some useful special built-in operators:

```
-a file    # true if file exists
-d file    # true if file exists and is a directory
-f file    # true if file exists and is a file
-r file    # true if file exists and is readable
-w file    # true if file exists and is writable
-x file    # true if file exists and is executable
```

Arithmetic

bash is heavily weighted toward text such as commands, arguments, and filenames. It can evaluate the usual arithmetic expressions (using +, -, *, /, and other operators) by surrounding them with a pair of double parentheses: ((*expression*)). Because many arithmetic characters—including *, (, and)—are specially interpreted by the shell, it's best to quote shell arguments if they will be treated as math expressions in the script:

```
admin@server1:~$ cat arith
#!/bin/bash
answer=$(( $* ))
echo $answer
admin@server1:~$ ./arith "(8+1)*(7-1)-60"
-6
admin@server1:~$ ./arith "2**60"
1152921504606846976
admin@server1:~$
```

The latest version of *bash* supports 64-bit integers (–9223372036854775808 to 9223372036854775807). Older versions support only 32-bit integers (with a puny range of –2147483648 to 2147483647). Floating-point numbers are not supported. Scripts that need floating-point or more advanced operators can use an external program such as *bc*.

In arithmetic expressions, you can use variables without the $ character that would be used to substitute their values in other settings:

```
admin@server1:~$ cat arithexp
#!/bin/bash
a=$1
b=$(( a+2 ))
echo "$a + 2 = $b"
c=$(( a*2 ))
echo "$a * 2 = $c"
admin@server1:~$ ./arithexp 6
6 + 2 = 8
6 * 2 = 12
admin@server1:~$
```

If...

Given expressions, you can execute different chunks of code depending on the results of tests. *bash* uses the `if ... fi` (backwards `if`) syntax, with optional `elif` (else if) and `else` sections:

```
if expression1 ; then
    (commands)
elif expression2 ; then
    (commands)
        ...
```

```
elif expressionN ; then
    (commands)
else (commands)
fi
```

The `; then` phrase at the end of a line can also be expressed as a plain `then` on the next line:

```
if expression
then
    (commands)
fi
```

If you're in the same directory as the *hello* script you made earlier, try this:

```
admin@server1:~$ if [[ -x hello ]]
> then
> echo "hello is executable"
> fi
hello is executable
admin@server1:~$
```

Here's a fancier script that searches the */etc/passwd* file for an account name:

```
#!/bin/bash
USERID="$1"
DETECTED=$( egrep -o "^$USERID:" < /etc/passwd )
if [[ -n  "${DETECTED}" ]] ; then
    echo "$USERID is one of us    :-)"
else
    echo "$USERID is a stranger   :-("
fi
```

Let's call this script *friendorfoe*, make it executable, and try it with first a known account on our system (*root*) and then a made-up account (*sasquatch*):

```
admin@server1:~$ ./friendorfoe root
root is one of us   :-)
admin@server1:~$ ./friendorfoe sasquatch
sasquatch is a stranger  :-(
```

The first argument is assigned to the shell variable `USERID`. The *egrep* command is run within `$( )` to assign its output to the `DETECTED` shell variable. *egrep -o* prints only the string it matches, rather than the whole line. `"^$USERID:"` matches the contents of the `USERID` variable only if the contents of the variable appear at the start of a line and are immediately followed by a colon. The `if` expression is surrounded with double square brackets to contain it, evaluate it, and return its result. The `-n "${DETECTED}"` expression returns `true` if the shell variable `DETECTED` is a non-empty string. Finally, the variable `DETECTED` is quoted (`"${DETECTED}"`) to treat it as a single string.

Wherever the `if` statement takes an expression, you can put in a command, or even a sequence of commands. If the last command in the sequence succeeds, the `if` statement considers that the expression returned a true result. If the last command in the sequence fails, it's considered that the expression returned a false result, and the `else` expression will be executed. We'll see examples in upcoming sections.

Troubleshooting a Simple Script

Let's perform some surgery on a script that is supposed to delete its argument (a file or a directory) but has a few problems:

```
admin@server1:~$ cat delete
#!/bin/bash
if rm $1
    then
    echo file $1 deleted
else
    if rmdir $1
        then
        echo directory $1 deleted
    fi
fi
```

The script is intended to delete the file passed as an argument using *rm*, and to print a message if it succeeds. If *rm* fails, the script assumes the argument refers to a directory and tries *rmdir* instead.

Here are some results:

```
admin@server1:~$ ./delete hello2
file hello2 deleted
admin@server1:~$ ./delete hello2
rm: cannot remove `hello2': No such file or directory
rmdir: `hello2': No such file or directory
admin@server1:~$ mkdir hello3
admin@server1:~$ ./delete hello3
rm: cannot remove `hello3': Is a directory
directory hello3 deleted
admin@server1:~
```

Using these error messages, let's try to fix the script. First, we'll use I/O redirection to save results to log and error files, which we can review in our copious free time. Next, we'll catch the return value of the *rm* command to generate a success or failure message. We'll also capture the current date and time to include in the output log:

```
admin@server1:~$ cat removefiles
#!/bin/bash
# removefiles deletes either files or directories
echo  "$0 ran at" $(date) >> delete.log
if rm $1 2>> delete-err.log
    then
    echo "deleted file $1" >> delete.log
elif rmdir $1 2>> delete-err.log
    then
    echo "deleted directory $1" >> delete.log
else
    echo "failed to delete $1" >> delete.log
fi
```

The script still has some warts: it doesn't check if the file even exists, and it doesn't distinguish between a file and a directory. We can use some of the built-in operators that we mentioned earlier to fix these problems:

```
admin@server1:~$ cat removefiles
#!/bin/bash
# removefiles deletes either files or directories
echo  "$0 ran at" $(date) >> delete.log
if [ ! -e $1 ]
    then
    echo "$1 does not exist" >> delete.log
elif [ -f $1 ]
    then
    echo -n "file $1 " >> delete.log
    if rm $1 2>> delete-err.log
        then
        echo "deleted" >> delete.log
    else
        echo "not deleted" >> delete.log
    fi
elif [ -d $1 ]
    then
    echo "directory $1 " >> delete.log
    if rmdir $1 2>> delete-err.log
        then
        echo "deleted" >> delete.log
    else
        echo "not deleted" >> delete.log
    fi
fi
```

This looks pretty good, but we have one more curve to throw you: what if the file or directory name contains spaces? (You're guaranteed to see this if you get any files from Windows or Mac systems.) Create a file called *my file*, then try to delete it with our trusty script:

```
admin@server1:~$ ./removefiles my file
```

Then the last line of *delete.log* will contain:

```
my does not exist
```

Since we didn't put quotes around *my file*, the shell split *my* and *file* into the script's `$1` and `$2` variables. So, let's quote *my file* to keep it in `$1`:

```
admin@server1:~$ ./removefiles "my file"
./removefiles: [: my: binary operator expected
./removefiles: [: my: binary operator expected
```

Oops. We got the string *my file* into the shell's `$1` variable, but we need to quote it again *inside* the script to protect it for the name tests and remove commands:

```
admin@server1:~$ cat removefiles
#!/bin/bash
# removefiles deletes either files or directories
```

```
echo  "$0 ran at" $(date) >> delete.log
if [ ! -e "$1" ]
    then
    echo "$1 does not exist" >> delete.log
elif [ -f "$1" ]
    then
    echo -n "file $1 " >> delete.log
    if rm "$1" 2>> delete-err.log
        then
        echo "deleted" >> delete.log
    else
        echo "not deleted" >> delete.log
    fi
elif [ -d "$1" ]
    then
    echo -n "directory $1 " >> delete.log
    if rmdir "$1" 2>> delete-err.log
        then
        echo "deleted" >> delete.log
    else
        echo "not deleted" >> delete.log
    fi
fi
```

Now, at last, when you run the command:

```
admin@server1:~$ ./removefiles "my file"
```

the last line of *delete.log* will be:

```
file my file deleted
```

Loops

If you want to do something more than once, you need a *loop*. *bash* has three flavors: `for`, `while`, and `until`.

The lovely and talented `for` loop has this general appearance:

```
for arg in list
do
commands
done
```

It executes the *commands* action (which can cover as many lines and separate commands as you want) specified between `do` and `done` for each item in *`list`*. When the commands run, they can access the current item from *`list`* through the variable *`$arg`*, The syntax may be a bit confusing at first: in the `for` statement you must specify *`arg`* without the dollar sign, but in the *commands* you must specify *`$arg`* with the dollar sign.

Some simple examples are:

```
admin@server1:~$ for stooge in moe larry curly
> do
```

```
> echo $stooge
> done
moe
larry
curly

admin@server1:~$ for file in *
> do
> ls -l $file
> done
-rw-r--r--  1 admin admin 48 2006-08-26 14:12 hello

admin@server1:~$ for file in $(find / -name \*.gif)
> do
> cp $file /tmp
> done
```

The `while` loop runs while the test condition is true:

```
while expression
do
stuff
done
```

Here's an example script that uses the arithmetic expressions mentioned earlier to create a C-style `while` loop (the indentation isn't necessary, but we like it):

```
#!/bin/bash
MAX=100
((cur=1))  # Treat cur like an integer
while ((cur < MAX))
    do
    echo -n "$cur "
    ((cur+=1)) # Increment as an integer
    done
```

The `until` loop is the opposite of `while`. It loops *until* the test condition is true:

```
until expression
do
stuff
done
```

An example is:

```
#!/bin/bash
gameover="q"
until [[ $cmd == $gameover ]]
    do
    echo -n "Your commmand ($gameover to quit)? "
    read cmd
    if [[ $cmd != $gameover ]]; then $cmd; fi
    done
```

To escape from a loop, use `break`. Let's rewrite our `until` example as a `while` loop with a `break`:

```
#!/bin/bash
gameover="q"
while [[ true ]]
    do
    echo -n "Your commmand ($gameover to quit)? "
    read cmd
    if [[ $cmd == $gameover ]]; then break; fi
    $cmd
    done
```

To skip the rest of the loop and jump back to the start, use `continue`:

```
#!/bin/bash
gameover="q"
while [[ true ]]
    do
    echo -n "Your commmand ($gameover to quit)? "
    read cmd
    if [[ $cmd != $gameover ]]; then $cmd; continue; fi
    break
    done
```

cron Jobs

Shell scripts are often used to glue programs together. A common example in Linux is the definition of *cron jobs*. *cron* is the standard Linux job scheduler. If you want something to happen the third Tuesday of every month at the uncivilized hour of 01:23, you can get *cron* to do it for you without any of the negative feedback that you would get from a person. The *cron* daemon checks every minute to see whether it's time to do something, or if any *cron* job specifications have changed.

You specify *cron* jobs by editing a *crontab* file. You can view the contents of your *crontab*, if any, as follows:

```
admin@server1:~$ crontab -l
no crontab for admin
```

To edit your *crontab*, enter:

```
admin@server1:~$ crontab -e
```

Each line of a *crontab* file contains a day/time specification and a command, in this format:

```
minute hour day_of_month month day_of_week command
```

This requires more than a little explanation:

- *minute* is between `0` and `59`.
- *hour* uses the 24-hour clock and is between `0` and `23`.
- *day_of_month* ranges from `1` to `31`.

- *month* is a number between 1 and 12 or a name such as February.
- *day_of_week* is a number between 0 and 7 (0 or 7 is Sunday, 6 is Saturday) or a name such as Tuesday.
- *day_of_month* and *day_of_week* are ORed together, which may cause surprises. For instance, if each field contains a 1, *cron* will execute the command in January as well as on Mondays. Usually, the *crontab* line puts a specific value in only one of these fields.
- In any field, a value means an exact match; for instance, a 1 in the *month* field means only January.
- An asterisk (*) means *any value*.
- Two values separated by a hyphen indicate a range. Thus, 11-12 in the *month* field means November through December.
- To specify more than one value, separate the values with commas. A *month* list of 2,3,5-6 means February, March, and May through June.
- A *step modifier* may follow values and a slash (/), and it indicates how many units to increment between values. A *month* value of */3 means every third month. A *month* value of 4-9/2 means months 4, 6, and 8.

The shell executes the command, so it can use the features mentioned in this chapter. Some examples using direct commands rather than scripts are:

```
5 * * * * rm /tmp/*.gif # remove all GIF files every 5 minutes
5 * * * * rm -v /tmp/*.gif >> /tmp/gif.log # the same, logged
```

When *cron* runs the command, it emails its standard output and standard error to the owner of the *crontab*. To prevent being pelted with such emails, you can redirect the standard output and standard error to a place where the sun doesn't shine:

```
command > /dev/null 2>&1
```

Scripting Language Shootout

The main use of a shell is to run commands and expand filename patterns, and shells were designed to make these operations easy. Other tasks, such as performing arithmetic calculations, are harder, because their text needs to be protected from word splitting and * expansion. In complex shell scripts, the pile of parentheses, brackets, and other symbols begins to resemble a cartoon character swearing.

In the old days ("We had zeroes and ones then, and we were lucky to have ones!"), how-to articles often featured long shell scripts to add users, download and build packages, back up files, and so on. Nowadays you may prefer to carry out these tasks using a more advanced scripting language, for several reasons:

- Over time, applications such as *adduser* and *apt-get* have automated some traditional shell-script tasks.
- Shell scripts don't scale well, and they get hard to maintain.

- Shell scripts run slower.
- Shell syntax is icky.

Perl initially filled the gap as administrators looked for more productive tools, but now PHP has migrated out of its web niche, and Python has gained a reputation for productivity. We'll write one application in each of these languages; several others, such as Ruby and Tcl, are also available on Linux.

Our application will search the */etc/passwd* file for name, user ID, hat size, or whatever else we can find in there. You'll see how to open a file, read records, parse formats, search for patterns, and print results. Then we'll look at ways to avoid some of this work, because sweat != productivity. You'll be able to apply these techniques to other files, such as logs or web pages. This is an example of *data munging*, and you're probably doing a lot of it already.

Let's invent some requirements for our application and express them with this pseudocode:

```
read a search string from the user
open the places file
for each line:
    parse the fields (columns)
    search the name field for a match
    if there's a match:
        print the other fields in a readable format
```

By now, many programmers would have rushed in and started typing (some without having read the data format or requirements). Readers of this book are more disciplined, though, as well as better looking. They've had to fix the messes that the other programmers have made and don't want to make the same mistakes themselves.

Data Format: The /etc/passwd File

The password file usually contains standard system accounts such as the mighty *root*, application accounts such as *apache*, and user accounts. Here are snips of such a file:

```
# System
root:x:0:0:root:/root:/bin/bash
bin:x:1:1:bin:/bin:/sbin/nologin
daemon:x:2:2:daemon:/sbin:/sbin/nologin
...
# Applications
postgres:x:26:26:PostgreSQL Server:/var/lib/pgsql:/bin/bash
apache:x:48:48:Apache:/var/www:/bin/false
...
# Users
adedarc:x:500:500:Alfredo de Darc:/home/adedarc:/bin/bash
rduxover:x:501:501:Ransom Duxover:/home/rduxover:/bin/bash
```

```
cbarrel:x:502:502:Creighton Barrel:/home/cbarrel:/bin/bash
cmaharias:x:503:503:C Maharias:/home/cmaharias:/bin/bash
pgasquette:x:504:504:Papa Gasquette:/home/pgasquette:/bin/bash
bfrapples:x:505:505:Bob Frapples:/home/bfrapples:/bin/bash
```

The colon-separated fields are:

- Account name
- Encrypted password, or x if */etc/shadow* is used
- User ID (*uid*)
- Group ID (*gid*)
- Full name or description
- Home directory
- Shell

We're interested in the fifth field (full name or description). In the ancient Unix scrolls, this was called the *gecos* field, for reasons that were obsolete even then. The name persists, and it's useful to know.

Script Versions

We'll start each of the following sections with a minimal script that searches for a string anywhere in the */etc/passwd* file and prints the matching line. We know this is too broad, but we want to get the script working before we get too fancy.

Next, we'll split the input lines into fields and restrict the pattern matching to the *gecos* field that contains our users' names.

Then we'll further restrict the search to lines in which the value of the *uid* field is greater than 500. In our case, normal user IDs start at 501, so this will exclude system accounts and other automatons.

By this point we'll be pretty tired of the previous steps, so we'll look for some tools that can do some of this work for us.

The bash script

Most languages provide function libraries for various tasks. Programs fill this role for the shell, and experienced shell scripters are familiar with the most useful Linux utilities (*cat*, *head*, *tail*, *awk*, *cut*, *grep*, *egrep*, and others). We'll use some of these for our *bash* script.

Here's a quick and dirty version (*finduser.sh*) that reads the user's search string as its argument, searches for a case-independent match anywhere on the line, and prints any matching line verbatim:

```
#!/bin/bash
grep -i "$1" /etc/passwd
```

```
admin@server1:~$ chmod +x finduser.sh
admin@server1:~$ ./finduser.sh alf
adedarc:x:500:500:Alfredo de Darc:/home/adedarc:/bin/bash
```

This wasn't any faster than just typing:

```
admin@server1:~$ grep -i alf /etc/passwd
```

But what if *alf* had also matched a system account named *gandalf*, or a string in some other field? If we want to restrict the search to the name field and to normal user accounts (i.e., accounts with user IDs greater than 500), our script is going to grow a bit.

Digging through *bash* documentation reveals that *bash* can split its input on characters other than whitespace, using its `IFS` variable. In the following version of the script, we read */etc/passwd* line by line, splitting each line into field variables. If we find a match, we need to rebuild the line to print it in its original form:

```
#!/bin/bash
pattern=$1
IFS=":"
while read account password uid gid name directory shell
    do
    # Exact case-sensitive matches only!
    if [[ $name == $pattern ]]; then
        echo "$account:$password:$uid:$gid:$name:$directory:$shell"
        fi
        done < /etc/passwd
```

But now we run into a problem with matching: unlike *grep*, *bash* does not have a built-in case-insensitive partial string match. We'll have to put in more sophisticated pattern matching with an external helper, *egrep*:

```
#!/bin/bash
pattern=$1
IFS=":"
while read account password uid gid name directory shell
    do
    if [[ $(echo $name | egrep -i -c "$pattern") -gt 0 ]]; then
        echo "$account:$password:$uid:$gid:$name:$directory:$shell"
        fi
        done < /etc/passwd
```

For our final script, let's add our check on the *uid* numbers:

```
#!/bin/bash
pattern=$1
IFS=":"
while read account password uid gid name directory shell
    do
    # Exact matches only!
    if [[ $uid -gt 500 && $(echo $name | egrep -i -c "$pattern") -gt 0 ]]; then
        echo "$account:$password:$uid:$gid:$name:$directory:$shell"
        fi
        done < /etc/passwd
```

If you run a shell script with a *-v* or *-x* option, *bash* will print each command before executing it. This can help you see what the script is actually doing.

The Perl script

Perl is terse, and it's really, really good at text. A Perl equivalent of our first *bash* script is:

```
admin@server1:~$ perl -ne 'print if /alf/i' /etc/passwd
```

The */pattern/* matches *pattern* while the following `i` ignores case. Here's an equivalent script version that we'll use to beef up the program to meet our other requirements:

```
#!/usr/bin/perl
my $pattern = shift;
while (<>) {
    if (/$pattern/i) {
        print;
    }
}
```

Many elements of Perl syntax are cryptic, but some are reminiscent of shell syntax (or other common Unix tools) and therefore not too hard to remember once you know those tools. In particular, you can see `while` and `if` statements in the previous script, and they behave as you might expect having learned about the shell equivalents. The `<>` syntax is also reminiscent of the `<` and `>` of shell redirection; it causes each iteration of the `while` loop to read one line of input. Note that unlike with *bash*, variables in Perl require the initial `$` even when you're assigning values. The `print` statement displays what `<>` finds.

Perl has an alternative backward `if` syntax that saves a few characters:

```
#!/usr/bin/perl
my $pattern = shift;
while (<>) {
    print if /$pattern/i;
}
```

The script (call it *finduser.pl*) assumes the password file is read from standard input, so you would run it like this:

```
admin@server1:~$ ./finduser.pl alf < /etc/passwd
```

The next version opens the password file directly:

```
#!/usr/bin/perl
my $fname = "/etc/passwd";
my $pattern = shift;
open(FILE, $fname) or die("Can't open $fname\n");
while (<FILE>) {
    if (/$pattern/i) {
        print;
    }
}
close(FILE);
```

To restrict matches to the name field as we did in the *bash* section, we play to Perl's strengths:

```
#!/usr/bin/perl
my $fname = "/etc/passwd";
my $pattern = shift;
open(FILE, $fname) or die("Can't open $fname\n");
while (<FILE>) {
    $line = $_;
    @fields = split/:/;
    if ($fields[4] =~ /$pattern/i) {
        print $line;
    }
}
close(FILE);
```

An argument supplied by the user is read into the `$pattern` variable using the `shift` statement. The script also defines another kind of variable: an array named `@fields`. Perl's `split` function puts each colon-separated element of a line into a single element of the array. We can then extract element number 4 (which is really the fifth element, because elements are numbered starting from 0) and compare it in a case-insensitive manner to the user's argument.

All of these scripts have involved reading text input lines and matching patterns. Because */etc/passwd* is such an important file in Linux, you'd think someone would have automated some of this work by now. Fortunately, someone has: good old Perl provides a built-in function called `getpwent` that returns the contents of */etc/passwd* a line at a time as an array of strings. In the following version of our script, we assign each field its own variable; in the subsequent version, we'll use the array `@list` to hold all of them. In each case, we want the *gecos* field (called *gcos* in the Perl documentation). Note that this is field 6 as returned by `getpwent`, not field 4, because `getpwent` supports two other fields that appear in the *passwd* files on some systems:

```
#!/usr/bin/perl
$pattern = shift;
while (($name,$passwd,$uid,$gid,
       $quota,$comment,$gcos,$dir,
       $shell,$expire) = getpwent) {
    if ($gcos =~ /$pattern/i) {
        print "$gcos\n";
    }
}

#!/usr/bin/perl
$pattern = shift;
while (@fields = getpwent) {
    if ($fields[6] =~ /$pattern/i) {
        print "$fields[6]\n";
    }
}
```

For our final bit of self-torture, let's restrict searches to normal users (*uid* > 500). It's an easy addition:

```
#!/usr/bin/perl
$pattern = shift;
while (@fields = getpwent) {
    if ($fields[6] =~ /$pattern/i and $fields[2] > 500) {
        print "$fields[6]\n"
    }
}
```

The PHP script

PHP can be run by a web server (using CGI) or on its own (using the CLI). We'll use the CLI version. If you don't have the CLI version, you can install it on Debian-based systems with *apt-get install php4-cli*.* Our first PHP script will look like our early Perl scripts:

```
#!/usr/bin/php
<?
$pattern = $argv[1];
$file = fopen("/etc/passwd", "r");
while ($line = fgets($file, 200)) {
    if (eregi($pattern, $line))
        echo $line;
}
fclose($file);
?>
```

Thanks to its origin as an accompaniment to web pages, PHP makes the unusual assumption that the default content of the file to be interpreted is plain text, and that PHP code is recognized only between an opening <? or <?php tag and a closing ?> tag. It echoes text to standard output. The `eregi` function does a regular-expression comparison in a case-insensitive manner.

Because PHP has borrowed a lot from Perl, it's not surprising that it has a `split` function:

```
#!/usr/bin/php
<?
$pattern = $argv[1];
$file = fopen("/etc/passwd", "r");
while ($line = fgets($file, 200)) {
    $fields = split(":", $line);
    if (eregi($pattern, $fields[4]))
        echo $line;
}
fclose($file);
?>
```

* Or *php5-cli*, when it's available.

But can we call a function like Perl's getpwent to slice and dice the password file for us? PHP doesn't appear to have an equivalent, so we'll stick with the parsing approach to restrict the search to *uid* values over 500:

```
#!/usr/bin/php
<?
$pattern = $argv[1];
$file = fopen("/etc/passwd", "r");
while ($line = fgets($file, 200)) {
    $fields = split(":", $line);
    if (eregi($pattern, $fields[4]) and $fields[2] > 500)
        echo $line;
}
fclose($file);
?>
```

The Python script

Python scripts look different from Perl and PHP scripts, because statements are terminated with whitespace rather than C-style semicolons or curly braces. Tab characters are also significant. Our first Python script, like our earlier attempts in the other languages, searches the password file and prints any line that contains the matching text:

```
#!/usr/bin/python
import re, sys
pattern = "(?i)" + sys.argv[1]
file = open("/etc/passwd")
for line in file:
    if re.search(pattern, line):
        print line
```

Python has *namespaces* (as does Perl) to group functions, which is why the functions in this script are preceded by the strings sys. and re.. This helps keep code modules a little more, well, modular. The "(?i)" in the third line of the script makes the match case-insensitive, similar to /i in Perl.

The next iteration, which splits the input line into fields, involves a straightforward addition to the first:

```
#!/usr/bin/python
import re, sys
pattern = "(?i)" + sys.argv[1]
file = open("/etc/passwd")
for line in file:
    fields = line.split(":")
    if re.search(pattern, fields[4]):
        print line
```

Python has an equivalent to Perl's getpwent function that enables us to restrict the search to the field that contains names. Save the following script as *finduser.py*:

```
#!/usr/bin/python
import re, sys, pwd
pattern = "(?i)" + sys.argv[1]
for line in pwd.getpwall( ):
    if re.search(pattern, line.pw_gecos):
        print line
```

Now let's see how it works:

```
admin@server1:~$ ./finduser.py alf
('adedarc', 'x', 501, 501, 'Alfredo de Darc', '/home/adedarc', '/bin/bash')
```

In this script, the line we printed was a Python list rather than a string, and it was pretty-printed. To print the line in its original format, use this:

```
#!/usr/bin/python
import re, sys, pwd
pattern = "(?i)" + sys.argv[1]
for line in pwd.getpwall( ):
    if re.search(pattern line.pw_gecos):
        print ":".join(["%s" % v for v in line])
```

The last line is needed to turn each field into a string (pw_uid and pw_gid are integers) before joining them into one long, colon-separated string. Although Perl and PHP let you treat a variable as a string or a number, Python is stricter.

The final step is to restrict the searches to accounts with *uid* > 500:

```
#!/usr/bin/python
import re, sys, pwd
pattern = "(?i)" + sys.argv[1]
for line in pwd.getpwall( ):
    if line.pw_uid > 500 and re.search(pattern line.pw_gecos):
        print ":".join(["%s" % v for v in line])
```

Choosing a Scripting Language

The choice of a programming language, like the choice of a text editor or operating system, is largely a matter of taste. Some people find Perl unreadable, and others resist Python's whitespace rules. Often the comparison goes no further; if you don't like beets, why eat them?

If you're comfortable with the style of the language, the most important criterion is productivity for the task. *bash* is a quick way to create one-liners and short scripts, but it drags when scripts get over a hundred lines or so. Perl can be hard to read, but it's powerful and has the benefit of the huge CPAN library. PHP looks like C, lacks namespaces, easily mingles code and output, and has some good libraries. Python may be the easiest to read and write, which is a special advantage for large scripts.

Further Reading

Appendix contains some longer *bash* scripts that may be useful to system administrators. *Linux Shell Scripting with Bash* by Ken Burtch (Sams) and the *Advanced Bash-Scripting Guide* (*http://www.tldp.org/LDP/abs/html*) are good resources. If you venture into the other scripting languages, any computer book with an animal on the cover should be a safe bet (unless you find *Curious George Learns COBOL* in the children's section).

CHAPTER 11

Backing Up Data

Computers fail—disks break, chips fry, wires short circuit, and drinks dribble into the cases. Sometimes computers are stolen or are victims of human error. You may lose not only hardware and software but, more importantly, data. Restoring lost data takes time and money. In the meantime, your customers will be unhappy, and the government may take an interest if the data is needed for compliance with regulations. Making backup copies of all important data is cheap insurance against potentially expensive disasters, and business continuity requires a backup and recovery plan.

In this chapter we'll cover several tools for backing up data that can be useful in different circumstances:

rsync
: Sufficient for most user files; transfers files efficiently over a network to another system, from which you can retrieve them if disaster strikes the local system

tar
: Traditional Unix program for creating compressed collections of files; creates convenient bundles of data that you can back up using other tools in this chapter

cdrecord/cdrtools
: Records files to CD-Rs or DVDs

Amanda
: Automates backups to tape; useful in environments with large amounts of data

MySQL tools
: Provide ways to solve the particular requirements of databases

Backing Up User Data to a Server with rsync

The most critical data to back up is data that is impossible, or very costly, to re-create. Usually this is *user data* that has grown over months or years of work. You can typically restore *system data* relatively easily by reinstalling from the original distribution media.

We'll focus here on making backups of user data from Linux desktop computers. A backup server needs enough disk space to store all of your user files. A dedicated machine is recommended. For a large office, disks may have a *RAID* (Redundant Array of Independent Disks) configuration to further protect against multiple failures.

The Linux utility *rsync* is a copy program designed to replicate large quantities of data. It can skip previously copied files and fragments and encrypt data transfers with *ssh*, making remote backups with *rsync* faster and more secure than they are with traditional tools like *cp*, *cpio*, or *tar*. To check whether *rsync* is on your system, enter:

```
# rsync --help
bash: rsync: command not found
```

If you see that message, you have to get the *rsync* package. To install it in Debian, enter:

```
# apt-get install rsync
```

Usually, you'll want your backups to preserve the original ownership and permissions. Thus, you'll need to ensure that all users have accounts and home directories on the backup server.

rsync Basics

The syntax of the *rsync* command is:

```
rsync options source destination
```

The major command-line options for *rsync* are:

-a
: Archive. This option fulfills most of the previously mentioned requirements, and it's easier to type and pronounce than its equivalent, *-Dgloprt*.

-b
: Make backup copies of already existing destination files instead of replacing them. You usually won't want to use this option unless you want to keep old versions of every file. It can result in the backup servers being filled up very quickly.

-D
: Preserve devices. This option is used when replicating system files; it is not needed for user files. Works only when *rsync* is run as *root*. Included in *-a*.

-g
: Preserve the group ownership of files being replicated. This is important for backups. Included in *-a*.

-H
: Preserve hard links. If two names being replicated refer to the same file inode, this preserves the same relationship in the destination. This option slows down *rsync* somewhat, but its use is recommended.

-l
: Copy symlinks as symlinks. You'll almost always want to include this option; without it, a symlink to a file would be copied as a regular file. Included in *-a*.

-n
: Dry run: see what files would be transferred, but don't actually transfer them.

-o
: Preserve the user ownership of files being replicated. This is important for backups. Included in *-a*.

-p
: Preserve file permissions. This is important for backups. Included in *-a*.

-P
: Enable *--partial* and *--progress*.

--partial
: Enable partial file transfers. If *rsync* is aborted, it will be able to complete the remainder of the file transfer when it resumes later.

--progress
: Display file transfer progress.

-r
: Enable recursion, transferring all subdirectories. Included in *-a*.

--rsh='ssh'
: Use SSH for file transfer. This is recommended because the default transfer protocol (*rsh*) is not secure. You can also set the `RSYNC_RSH` environment variable to `ssh` to get the same effect.

-t
: Preserve the modification times on each file. Included in *-a*.

-v
: List the files being transferred.

-vv
: Like *-v*, but also list the files being skipped.

-vvv
: Like *-vv*, but also print *rsync* debugging info.

-z
: Enable compression; more useful over the Internet than on a high-speed LAN.

There are many more *rsync* options that may come in useful in specialized situations. You can find these on the manpage.

After the options, the arguments are the source and destination. Both *source* and *destination* can be paths to local files on the computer where *rsync* is running, *rsync* server designations (generally used for download file servers), or *user@host:path* designations for *ssh*. Because *rsync* takes so many options and long arguments that won't regularly change, next we'll write a *bash* script to run it.

Making a User Backup Script

This section presents a simple *bash* script that makes a backup from a user's desktop to the backup server. The name of the backup server is assigned to the variable `dest` in this script. The variable user is assigned the username of the account that runs the script by running the *whoami* command and capturing the output as a string. The *cd* command changes the current directory to the user's home directory. The logical-OR test condition that follows the *cd* command aborts the script if there is a failure. The one dot (`.`) all by itself specifies the current directory as the *source* argument. For the *destination* argument, we specify the username and hostname to log in as via *ssh*, followed by a dot to specify the current home directory on the destination host.

Here's the script:

```
#!/bin/bash
export RSYNC_RSH=/usr/bin/ssh
dest=backup1
user=$(whoami)
cd || exit 1
rsync -aHPvz . "${user}@${dest}:."
```

The `RSYNC_RSH` environment variable contains the name of the shell that *rsync* will use. The default is */usr/bin/rsh*, so we change it to */usr/bin/ssh* here. Running this script replicates all the files in the home directory of the user who runs it into that user's home directory on the backup server. Let's take a look at how this works by running it for our sample user (after logging into her desktop):

```
amy@desk12:~$ ./backup
Password:
building file list ...
14 files to consider
./
new-brochure.sxw
       37412 100%  503.91kB/s    0:00:00  (1, 62.5% of 16)
sales-plan-2006-08.sxw
       59513 100%    1.46MB/s    0:00:00  (2, 68.8% of 16)
sales-plan-2006-09.sxw
       43900 100%  691.47kB/s    0:00:00  (3, 75.0% of 16)
sales-plan-2006-10.sxw
       41285 100%  453.00kB/s    0:00:00  (4, 81.2% of 16)
```

```
vacation-request.sxw
       15198 100%  154.60kB/s    0:00:00  (5, 87.5% of 16)

sent 185942 bytes  received 136 bytes  24810.40 bytes/sec
total size is 210691  speedup is 1.13
amy@desk12:~$
```

rsync tells us that it is considering 14 files. It backs up only five files, though, because the other nine files are already on the backup server and have not been changed. This output shows the progress output as 100 percent when the files are complete and indicates how long each transfer took. On a high-speed LAN the transfer time will usually be less than one second for small or medium-sized files. On slower connections or for very large files, you will see a progress status that gives the size and percentage transferred so far, and an estimate of time to completion.

Listing Files on the Backup Server

rsync can also provide a list of the files on the backup server. This is useful for verifying whether new and important files are really there, as well as for finding files that need to be restored because they've been lost or because the user needs to recover an old version.

To get this listing, omit the *`options`* and *`destination`* arguments. Here's a simple *bash* script that obtains the desired results:

```
#!/bin/bash
dest=server1
user=$(whoami)
cd || exit 1
rsync "${user}@${dest}:." | more
```

Running this script produces results similar to the following:

```
amy@desk12:~$ ./backlist
Password:
drwx------  4096 2006/08/09 13:20:41 .
-rw------- 10071 2006/08/09 12:35:21 .bash_history
-rw-r--r--   632 2006/07/27 23:03:06 .bash_profile
-rw-r--r--  1834 2006/07/26 19:59:08 .bashrc
-rwxr-xr-x   108 2006/07/27 23:06:51 .path
-rwxr-xr-x    79 2006/08/09 13:18:34 backlist
-rwxr-xr-x   137 2006/08/09 13:19:29 backrestore
-rwxr-xr-x    88 2006/08/09 13:03:46 backup
-rw-r--r-- 37412 2006/07/17 14:40:52 new-brochure.sxw
-rw-r--r-- 59513 2006/07/19 09:16:41 sales-plan-2006-08.sxw
-rw-r--r-- 43900 2006/07/19 22:51:54 sales-plan-2006-09.sxw
-rw-r--r-- 41285 2006/07/17 16:24:19 sales-plan-2006-10.sxw
-rw-r--r-- 15198 2006/07/10 14:42:23 vacation-request.sxw
drwx------  4096 2006/08/09 13:12:25 .ssh
amy@desk12:~$
```

Restoring Lost or Damaged Files

No backup system is any good if lost files cannot be restored. Not only must we must be ready in case disaster strikes, but we must also test our recovery and restoration plans to make sure they will work when they are most needed.

Our restoration script is just slightly more complicated than the previous script. We've added a way to specify individual files to be restored:

```
#!/bin/bash
dest=server1
user=$(whoami)
cd || exit 1
for file in "$@" ; do
    rsync -aHPvz "${user}@${dest}:./${file}" "./${file}"
done
```

To restore files, we simply run the script, passing the names of the files to be restored as arguments on the command line. In the following example, we will intentionally remove one of our files and then watch it be restored:

```
amy@desk12:~$ rm sales-plan-2006-10.sxw
amy@desk12:~$ ./backrestore sales-plan-2006-10.sxw
Password:
receiving file list ...
1 file to consider
sales-plan-2006-10.sxw
       41285 100%    6.56MB/s    0:00:00  (1, 100.0% of 1)

sent 42 bytes  received 39299 bytes  6052.46 bytes/sec
total size is 41285  speedup is 1.05
amy@desk12:~$
```

We can also restore all the files at once by using a dot as the filename.

Automated Backups

Backups can be automated using scripts similar to these run as *cron* jobs (discussed in Chapter 10). SSH requires the user's password to be entered, so you'll need to include your users' public keys in their SSH configurations in order to make the SSH logins work when the users are not present (say, nightly at 3 A.M.).

You have many options for creating backups. You might want to run a *cron* job script on the server daily or weekly, to make backups on another server. Businesses with remote offices may want to make regular backups of data from those offices over the Internet. Backups can also be burned to CD-Rs, DVDs, or tape, to make long-term archival copies that can be transported offsite.

tar Archives

The *tar* command creates an archive file from one or more specified files or directories. It can also list the contents of an archive, or extract files and directories from an archive. A *tar archive* file is also known as a *tarfile* or a *tarball*.

A *tar* archive file offers several advantages over a directory of separate files. For example, it makes sending a whole directory by email a lot easier. Directories containing lots of similar files can be compressed more efficiently when the compression operates on all the data in a single file.

A common use for a *tar* archive is to aid in the distribution of the source program files for free or open source software. In most cases, the *tar* archives are compressed with the *gzip* or *bzip2* programs. However, if all the files being archived are already compressed (which is usually true of audio, video, and OpenOffice.org files), compressing the archive itself will not have much benefit.

You can name a *tar*red file anything you want, but certain file extensions are conventionally used to tell recipients how to unpack the file. The most common extensions are:

.tar
: For uncompressed *tar* archives

.tar.gz or .tgz
: For *tar* archives that have been compressed with the *gzip* compression program

.tar.bz2 or .tbz
: For *tar* archives that have been compressed with the *bzip2* compression program

The syntax of a *tar* command is:

```
tar options arguments
```

The options are traditionally given as single letters without a dash (-) character, although many versions of *tar* also accept a dash. The most useful options are:

-b
: Specify the block size (the default is units of 512 bytes).

-c
: Create (write) a new archive.

-f filename
: Read from or write to the archive *filename*. If *filename* is omitted or is -, the archive file is written to standard output or read from standard input.

-j
: Compress or uncompress the archive using *bzip2* or *bunzip2*. Archives compressed with *bzip2* usually have the *.bz2* suffix.

-p

Preserve file permissions.

-t

List the files in an existing archive.

-v

When creating or unpacking archives, list the contents. With the *-t* option, provide more detail about the listed files.

-x

Extract (read) files from an existing archive.

-z

Compress or uncompress the archive using *gzip* or *gunzip*. Archives compressed with *gzip* usually have the *.gz* suffix.

Creating a New Archive

You can create a *tar* archive just to save a group of files for your own archiving purposes, to send them to someone else by email, or to make them available to the public (for example, on an FTP server). Some typical commands to archive the directory *work-docs* are as follows:

- To create the archive *work-docs.tar* from the directory *work-docs*:

```
$ tar -cf work-docs.tar work-docs
```

- To create the compressed archive *work-docs.tar.gz* from the directory *work-docs*:

```
$ tar -czf work-docs.tar.gz work-docs
```

- To create the compressed archive *work-docs.tar.bz2* from the directory *work-docs*:

```
$ tar -cjf work-docs.tar.bz2 work-docs
```

Extracting from an Archive

At different times, you may need to extract files from an archive you created earlier (such as a backup), from an archive someone has mailed to you, or from an archive you have downloaded from the Internet (say, the source code for some software you need).

Before you extract an archive, you should list and review its contents. You don't want to accidentally replace existing files on your system with files from the archive, nor do you want to wind up with a mess of files that you have to clean up.

Files in an archive should be arranged inside a directory, but not everyone does this, so you need to be careful to avoid extracting files into your current directory. It is usually a good idea to create a new directory on your computer in which to extract a *tar* archive. This keeps the extracted files apart from your other files, so they don't get mixed up. It can also prevent the extraction from overwriting existing files.

The *-t* option lists the names of the files in the archive and the directories they'll be in when the archive is unpacked. Adding the *-v* option increases the verbosity to give details about each file in the *tar* archive, including the size of each file and its last modification time. Here are some example commands:

- To list the files in the archive *collection.tar*:

  ```
  $ tar -tf collection.tar
  ```

- To list the files in the archive *collection.tar.bz2* with extra details:

  ```
  $ tar -tvjf collection.tar.bz2
  ```

  To extract the files in *collection.tar* into the current directory, while preserving the original permissions:

  ```
  $ tar -xpf collection.tar
  ```

  The *-x* option extracts the files into the current directory. *tar* works silently unless the *-v* option is also used to list the files. The *-p* option preserves the original permissions, so the extracted files will have the same permission settings as the files that were archived.

- To extract the files in *collection.tar.gz* into the current directory, while preserving the original permissions:

  ```
  $ tar -xpzf collection.tar.gz
  ```

- To extract the files in *collection.tar.bz2* into the current directory, while preserving the original permissions:

  ```
  $ tar -xpjf collection.tar.bz2
  ```

- To list and extract the files in *collection.tar.bz2* into the current directory, while preserving the original permissions:

  ```
  $ tar -xpvjf collection.tar.bz2
  ```

A Complete Example of Packing and Unpacking with tar

The following shell session demonstrates the creation of a *tar* archive from a directory of files:

```
amy@desk12:~$ ls -dl monthly-reports
drwxr-xr-x  2 amy amy 4096 2006-08-11 14:15 monthly-reports
amy@desk12:~$ ls -l monthly-reports
total 228
-rw-r--r--  1 amy amy 50552 2006-05-09 11:09 mr-2006-04.sxw
-rw-r--r--  1 amy amy 51284 2006-06-06 15:44 mr-2006-05.sxw
-rw-r--r--  1 amy amy 51428 2006-07-06 14:30 mr-2006-06.sxw
-rw-r--r--  1 amy amy 54667 2006-08-07 10:06 mr-2006-07.sxw
amy@desk12:~$ tar -czf monthly-reports-aug.tar.gz monthly-reports
amy@desk12:~$ ls -l monthly-reports-aug.tar.gz
-rw-r--r--  1 amy amy 199015 2006-08-14 12:46 monthly-reports-aug.tar.gz
```

The following shell session demonstrates listing the contents of the *tar* archive:

```
amy@desk12:~$ ls -l monthly-reports-aug.tar.gz
-rw-r--r--  1 amy amy 199015 2006-08-14 12:46 monthly-reports-aug.tar.gz
```

```
amy@desk12:~$ tar -tzf monthly-reports-aug.tar.gz
monthly-reports/
monthly-reports/mr-2006-04.sxw
monthly-reports/mr-2006-05.sxw
monthly-reports/mr-2006-06.sxw
monthly-reports/mr-2006-07.sxw
amy@desk12:~$ tar -tvzf monthly-reports-aug.tar.gz
drwxr-xr-x amy/amy          0 2006-08-11 14:15:12 monthly-reports/
-rw-r--r-- amy/amy      50552 2006-05-09 11:09:12 monthly-reports/mr-2006-04.sxw
-rw-r--r-- amy/amy      51284 2006-06-06 15:44:33 monthly-reports/mr-2006-05.sxw
-rw-r--r-- amy/amy      51428 2006-07-06 14:30:19 monthly-reports/mr-2006-06.sxw
-rw-r--r-- amy/amy      54667 2006-08-07 10:06:57 monthly-reports/mr-2006-07.sxw
amy@desk12:~$
```

The following shell session demonstrates extracting the contents of a *tar* archive:

```
amy@desk12:~$ mkdir extract.dir
amy@desk12:~$ cd extract.dir
amy@desk12:~/extract.dir$ tar -xzf ../monthly-reports-aug.tar.gz
amy@desk12:~/extract.dir$ tar -xvzf ../monthly-reports-aug.tar.gz
monthly-reports/
monthly-reports/mr-2006-04.sxw
monthly-reports/mr-2006-05.sxw
monthly-reports/mr-2006-06.sxw
monthly-reports/mr-2006-07.sxw
amy@desk12:~/extract.dir$ tar -xvvzf ../monthly-reports-aug.tar.gz
drwxr-xr-x amy/amy          0 2006-08-11 14:15:12 monthly-reports/
-rw-r--r-- amy/amy      50552 2006-05-09 11:09:12 monthly-reports/mr-2006-04.sxw
-rw-r--r-- amy/amy      51284 2006-06-06 15:44:33 monthly-reports/mr-2006-05.sxw
-rw-r--r-- amy/amy      51428 2006-07-06 14:30:19 monthly-reports/mr-2006-06.sxw
-rw-r--r-- amy/amy      54667 2006-08-07 10:06:57 monthly-reports/mr-2006-07.sxw
amy@desk12:~/extract.dir$ cd
amy@desk12:~$
```

Summary

The most important things to remember about *tar* are:

- *-c* reads from your files and *creates* (writes to) a *tar* file.
- *-x extracts* (reads from) a *tar* file and writes to your files.

Most Unix and Linux administrators have mixed up these options at least once.

Saving Files on Optical Media

Recordable CD and DVD media, called CD-Rs, DVD-Rs, and DVD+Rs, allow you to save files in a convenient and compact form. They can be used for making backups that can be stored offsite, and for distributing software or data to users or customers. A CD-R can hold upwards of 700 MB of data, while a DVD-R or DVD+R can hold upward of 4.7 GB. A dual-layer version of DVD+R also exists, with a capacity of 8.55 GB.

The difference between a DVD-R and a DVD+R is the technology used to locate the laser into the track groove for recording. The two methods are incompatible, so if your drive supports only either DVD-R or DVD+R, you must use matching recordable media. (Drives do exist that support both, allowing the use of either recordable DVD media type.)

Recording files on a CD or DVD is not as straightforward or flexible as saving files on a hard disk. Rewritable media can get around some of the limitations, but they have a higher cost and reduced compatibility. In this section, we'll focus on saving files on CD-Rs. The methods for DVDs are similar.

A data CD consists of an array of sectors of 2048 bytes each. A special filesystem known as *ISO-9660* is used to organize the files on the CD so that it can be read on a wide range of computers and other devices. Newer CD music players also support data CDs written in the ISO-9660 format, so they can access music files in compressed formats such as MP3. DVDs use a newer filesystem called Universal Disk Format (UDF).

To record data, all CD and most DVD recorders require that the data be streamed to the drive continuously. If the data cannot be made available when the laser is trying to record it, the laser will have to stop, which breaks up the continuity of the recording. The methods used to record a CD were designed for slower computer systems, to maximize the reliability of these recordings. Today's faster computers still face the challenge of providing data nonstop to today's faster recording devices; however, many recorders now support Buffer Underrun Free technologies that enable them to continue the writing process even if the data buffer becomes empty at some point.

The files to be recorded are typically first collected into a file called an *ISO image file*, which usually has the extension *.iso*. This file is then recorded directly to the CD-R. It is possible to record files directly to a CD-R without creating an *.iso* file first, but this method increases the risk that something else running on your computer could slow things down at the wrong time.

The software needed to record a CD or DVD on Linux is located in a package called *cdrecord* (note that this package is undergoing a name change to *cdrtools*). If this package is not yet installed on your system, you should install it now using the methods you have already learned. On Debian Sarge, you would run the command:

```
# apt-get install cdrecord mkisofs
```

Debian 4.0 forked the *cdrecord* package to one called *wodim*. Other packages include *dvd+rw-tools* (described at *http://www.debianhelp.co.uk/burningdvd.htm*) and *K3b* (*http://www.k3b.org*).

Accessing Your CD-R Drive

Linux supports recording on IDE ATAPI CD-R drives through a special driver called *ide-scsi*. Most Linux distributions also include this driver in the kernel. If your system does not have the driver, you will need to load the driver module (installing it if needed), or possibly recompile your kernel.

The *ide-scsi* driver emulates a SCSI device for software that is designed just for SCSI devices. Your IDE ATAPI CD drive and DVD drive will appear as if they are SCSI devices when the *ide-scsi* driver is active.

The following command will list the SCSI devices on your system, so you can locate the emulated SCSI device number for your CD-R drive. It may list other devices as well, including any real SCSI devices if your computer actually has them. Run the command as *root*:

```
# cdrecord -scanbus
```

The output might look similar to this:

```
Cdrecord-Clone 2.01 (i686-pc-linux-gnu) Copyright (C) 1995-2004 J&#246;rg Schilling
scsidev: 'ATA'
devname: 'ATA'
scsibus: -2 target: -2 lun: -2
Linux sg driver version: 3.5.27
Using libscg version 'schily-0.8'.
scsibus1:
        1,0,0   100) 'SONY    ' 'CD-RW  CRX195E1 ' 'ZYS5' Removable CD-ROM
        1,1,0   101) 'DVD-16X ' 'DVD-ROM BDV316E ' '0052' Removable CD-ROM
        1,2,0   102) *
        1,3,0   103) *
        1,4,0   104) *
        1,5,0   105) *
        1,6,0   106) *
        1,7,0   107) *
```

Look for the device description that matches your CD-R recorder. If you have more than one device, the brand name and model should help identify the correct device. The output should at least list CD-R or CD-RW in the description. In this example, our CD recorder is on emulated SCSI device *1,0,0*.

If the *ide-scsi* driver is not installed or not active, you may get output like this:

```
Cdrecord-Clone 2.01 (i686-pc-linux-gnu) Copyright (C) 1995-2004 J&#246;rg Schilling
cdrecord: No such file or directory. Cannot open '/dev/pg*'. Cannot open SCSI driver.
cdrecord: For possible targets try 'cdrecord -scanbus'.
cdrecord: For possible transport specifiers try 'cdrecord dev=help'.
cdrecord:
cdrecord: For more information, install the cdrtools-doc
cdrecord: package and read /usr/share/doc/cdrecord/README.ATAPI.setup .
```

If you get this kind of output, you will need to activate the *ide-scsi* driver before doing the actual recording step.

Setting Defaults

A number of *cdrecord* parameters can be configured. For instance, you can configure *cdrecord* to recognize names for recording devices (so you don't have to memorize the device numbers), and you can designate a default device. To configure *cdrecord*, log in as (or use *su* - to switch to) *root*. Then create a text file with your editor:

```
# vi /etc/default/cdrecord
```

We will put the following lines of text in this file to match the devices shown in our previous *cdrecord -scanbus* output. You will need to change these values to match the values for your own devices. Use any names you choose in place of `cd` and `dvd`. The whitespace between the fields on each line must be tabs, not spaces:

```
CDR_DEVICE=cd
cd=1,0,0        -1          -1          ""
dvd=1,1,0       -1          -1          ""
```

If your Linux kernel is Version 2.6, you will most likely need to specify the device with the prefix `ATA:`, due to a redesign of the driver. In this case, the configuration file may look like this:

```
CDR_DEVICE=cd
cd=ATA:1,0,0    -1          -1          ""
dvd=ATA:1,1,0   -1          -1          ""
```

You can also set the default recording speed for each device, right after the device number. `-1` indicates that the default value should be used. The next number is the FIFO buffer size; once again, `-1` specifies the default on the Linux system. The last item on the line allows you to pass a driver-specific option; we left it as an empty string.

Newer versions of *cdrecord* support the option `driveropts=burnfree` to protect against buffer underruns.

Preparing Files to Record on a CD-R

The *mkisofs* command creates an ISO filesystem image file. It should contain all the files to be recorded on the CD-R. There are a lot of options for this command, but these are the important ones that we will use:

-J
: Include Joliet names for Windows compatibility.

-r
: Include Rock Ridge names for Unix/Linux compatibility.

-v
: Set verbose mode to show the progress status.

-V *`id_string`*
: Specify a volume ID to name the disc to be created.

-o filename
: Specify the filename of the ISO image being created.

Here is a sample command to include all the files from a specified directory:

```
# mkisofs -JrvV "disc name" -o backup.iso /home/amy
```

You will see a lot of output from this command. The output is useful for large file collections to indicate an estimate of how much time remains. If you prefer not to have this output, omit the *-v* option from the command.

Recording the CD-R

You can now record a CD-R with the ISO image you created. To perform the actual recording, log in as (or use *su -* to switch to) *root*. Root permissions are needed by the *cdrecord* program to access the raw SCSI layer, to modify process priorities, and to lock buffer space into RAM to avoid swapping. CD writing has critical timing dependencies, so it helps to keep the rest of the system as idle as possible.

If you are using a rewritable CD-RW disc in a CD-RW drive, you need to erase (blank) the CD-RW before doing the recording:

```
# cdrecord blank=fast padsize=63s -pad -dao -v -eject
```

Some drives require the media to be ejected to reset the drive for the next operation. Unless you have discovered that your drive does not need this, use the *-eject* option, as shown here.

To record the ISO image created in the previous section, enter:

```
# cdrecord padsize=63 -pad -dao -v -eject backup.iso
```

Avoid doing any other work on a computer that is recording a CD or DVD.

Some modern drives have special features such as burnfree that help avoid problems when the computer is not operating fast enough. Discs recorded with these fix-ups taking place may not be compatible with some older devices. If you find that your recordings sometimes fail, do them at a slower speed. You can change the speed by including the *speed=* option, which is documented in the *cdrecord* manpage. Slowing down the recording speed may be particularly important if the image file being recorded is on a network filesystem.

Padding is necessary for some IDE ATAPI CD readers to work correctly with read-ahead operations that Linux and other systems usually do. You may find that omitting the padding works with newer drives, but because the problem occurs during reading, you should include padding to ensure that older drives will be able to read the CD-Rs you record. Otherwise, you may find that your critical backup files are not readable on a temporary replacement computer.

Verifying the Recording

After you've recorded a CD or DVD, it's a good idea to verify that the recording reads back correctly. The media may be defective, or the computer may have been bumped during the recording, causing the laser to be moved out of the groove.

The correct way to verify a recording is to either compare the sectors recorded with the sectors on the hard disk or generate checksums of those sectors and compare them. Both methods must be used only with the actual data sectors, not the padding sectors. The following *bash* shell script makes this verification easy when the original ISO image file is available:

```
#!/bin/bash
if [[ $# -lt 1 ]] ; then
    echo "usage: isomd5 <file_or_device> ..." 1>&2
    exit 1
fi
for name in "$@" ; do
    isoinfo -di "${name}" 1>/dev/null || exit 1
done
for name in "$@" ; do
    count=( $( isoinfo -di "${name}"     \
        | egrep "^Volume size is: " ) )
    count="${count[3]}"
    bsize=( $( isoinfo -di "${name}"     \
        | egrep "^Logical block size is: " ) )
    bsize="${bsize[4]}"
    md5=$( dd                            \
        if="${name}"                     \
        ibs="${bsize}"                   \
        obs=4096 count="${size}"         \
        2>/tmp/isomd5.$$.err             \
        | md5sum )
    if [[ $? != 0 ]] ; then
        cat /tmp/isomd5.$$.err
        rm -f /tmp/isomd5.$$.err
        exit 1
    fi
    rm -f /tmp/isomd5.$$.err
    echo "${md5:0:32}" "" "${name}"
done
```

This script works by obtaining the number of sectors used by the ISO filesystem in the image file. It limits the number of sectors read into the MD5 checksum hashing program to exactly the number used. This avoids reading any padding sectors, which could vary in number.

We call this script *isomd5*. Give it the name of the ISO image file, as well as the name of the CD device normally used to read CD-Rs (with the newly recorded CD-R reinserted). You should get a result similar to this:

```
amy@desk12:~$ isomd5 backup.iso /dev/sr0
d41d8cd98f00b204e9800998ecf8427e  backup.iso
```

```
d41d8cd98f00b204e9800998ecf8427e  /dev/sr0
amy@desk12:~$
```

The checksum from the MD5 program is the 32-character hexadecimal part. If it is not the same for both the ISO image file and the contents of the CD-R drive, the recording is defective.

A failed recording is derisively called a "coaster." You can use it to protect your coffee table from unsightly rings, but unlike a real drinks coaster, it'll explode into a shower of sharp fragments and sparks in a microwave.

When a write to disc fails, try in turn:

1. Repeating the recording with another blank disc
2. Recording at a slower speed
3. Using a different batch or different brand of blank discs

If failures persist, you may have a defective recording drive.

DVD Backups

The steps shown in this section are specific to CD media, but DVD media can be recorded in similar ways, using the same software in the *cdrecord* or *cdrtools* package. Some DVD media—notably, the rare DVD-RAM—can operate much like hard drives, but these require a special drive that supports this mode of operation.

Backing Up and Archiving to Tape with Amanda

Tape is still a popular backup medium. The *Advanced Maryland Automated Network Disk Archiver* (Amanda) is an open source package that manages tape backups. Developed at the University of Maryland, it's included in many distributions of Linux, including Debian. Amanda's features include:

- The use of traditional Unix backup formats such *tar* and *dump*
- Operation over a LAN, backing up client data to a central tape server
- Support for backing up Windows clients via file shares
- Support for standard tape devices and many tape changers, jukeboxes, and stackers
- Ability to balance full backups over a multi-day backup cycle
- Support for incremental backups to write daily changes
- Data compression on either the client or the server, or via devices that include hardware compression
- Prevention of accidental overwriting of the wrong media

- A holding disk strategy that allows for staged or delayed writing to media
- Authentication through Kerberos or its own authentication scheme
- Data encryption for protection over unsafe networks

Installing Amanda

Amanda has client and server components. The client is used on systems that have data that needs to be backed up. The server is used on systems that perform the backup work and write data to tape.

Run the following command to install Amanda on the backup server:

```
# apt-get install amanda-server
```

Run the following command to install Amanda on each client Linux machine:

```
# apt-get install amanda-client
```

When you install these packages, the other packages that are needed will be included. If you wish to use the *amplot* program in Amanda, you will need to also install the *gnuplot* package.

Amanda uses files in many different directories. These settings are configurable, but the defaults are:

/etc/amanda
: Configuration files (server)

/root
: The file */root/.amandahosts*

/usr/man/man8
: Manpages

/usr/share/doc/amanda-common
: Documentation files

/usr/share/doc/amanda-client
: Client-specific documentation files

/usr/lib
: Shared libraries used by Amanda programs

/usr/lib/amanda
: Daemon programs and internal utilities

/usr/sbin
: Command programs

/var/lib/amanda
: Running state, log, and other files

Configuring Amanda

The */etc/services* file should already have entries with the following names and port numbers. If these entries are not present, edit the */etc/services* file and add them at the end. The comments are optional:

```
/etc/services:
amanda          10080/udp       # amanda backup services
amandaidx       10082/tcp       # amanda backup services
amidxtape       10083/tcp       # amanda backup services
```

You may also need to edit the */etc/inetd.conf* file, which should contain the following entries:

```
/etc/inetd.conf: (for clients)
amanda    dgram  udp wait   backup /usr/sbin/tcpd /usr/lib/amanda/amandad

/etc/inetd.conf: (for server)
amandaidx stream tcp nowait backup /usr/sbin/tcpd /usr/lib/amanda/amindexd
amidxtape stream tcp nowait backup /usr/sbin/tcpd /usr/lib/amanda/amidxtaped
```

The first entry, named *amanda*, is needed on all clients. The other two entries are needed only on the server. If these lines are not present, edit the */etc/inetd.conf* file and add them at the end.

Amanda uses random ports after the initial communication. You should use Amanda over the Internet only through a VPN. This prevents the need to open a wide range of ports from the Internet into your LAN.

Amanda runs as the user *backup* with *disk* group permissions. You will need to set access permissions for all files that you want to back up so that they can be read by Amanda.

The Amanda server needs to be well connected to the local network, with sufficient bandwidth for the volume of data to be transferred. It should have a very large holding disk, with enough space to hold twice the largest per-run dump size. A fast CPU is also needed if the server will be performing software compression.

Amanda supports multiple configurations. Each configuration consists of a set of three files in a subdirectory of */etc/amanda*:

amanda.conf
: The main configuration file. You edit this to specify the *disklist* (see next item), tape device, backup frequency, your email address, reporting formats, and a huge array of other options.

disklist
: This file specifies the hosts and disks to be backed up.

tapelist
: This file lists active tapes, including dates when each was written. Amanda manages this file, so you can look at it but shouldn't edit it.

Reporting the full details of all of Amanda's options would take several pages, so we'll leave their exploration up to you. Sample files with useful comments are provided in the */etc/amanda/DailySet1* directory when you install the Debian *amanda-server* package. For details on these configuration files, see the Amanda manpage or *http://wiki.zmanda.com*.

Amanda produces a report for each backup run. These detailed reports are sent by email to the user specified in the `mailto` option in the *amanda.conf* configuration file. You should review the reports regularly, particularly checking for errors and reviewing runtimes.

Restoring Files Backed Up by Amanda

Amanda uses standard Unix backup formats (*tar* or *dump*), which you specify in the configuration file. This allows backup tapes to be used to restore system files even if the Amanda system is not present. This can be crucial when restoring files after a complete disk failure.

Amanda also provides indexed recovery tools to allow restoring of selected files. Be sure to configure `index  yes` to have Amanda create the needed index files. The *amrecover* manpage provides full details.

Backing Up MySQL Data

Until now, we've been backing up files and directories. Databases have some special quirks that we need to address. Our examples use MySQL, but the same principles apply to PostgreSQL and other relational databases.

If your MySQL server does not need to be available 24x7, a fast and easy offline raw backup method is:

1. Stop the MySQL server:

   ```
   # /etc/init.d/mysqld stop
   ```

2. Copy MySQL's data files and directories. For example, if your MySQL data directory is */var/lib/mysql* and you want to save it to */tmp/mysql-backup*:

   ```
   # cp -r /var/lib/mysql /tmp/mysql-backup
   ```

   Instead of *cp*, you can use *rsync*, *tar*, *gzip*, or other commands mentioned earlier in this chapter.

3. Start the server again:

   ```
   # /etc/init.d/mysqld start
   ```

Online backups are trickier. If you have mutually independent MyISAM tables (no foreign keys or transactions), you could lock each one in turn, copy its files, and unlock it. But you may have InnoDB tables, or someone could write a transaction involving multiple tables. Fortunately there are several reasonable noncommercial solutions, including *mysqlhotcopy*, *mysqlsnapshot*, replication, and *mysqldump*.

mysqlhotcopy is a Perl script that does online raw backups of ISAM or MyISAM tables. The manpage includes many options, but here's how to back up a single database named *drupal*:

```
# mysqlhotcopy -u user -p password drupal /tmp
Locked 57 tables in 0 seconds.
Flushed tables (`drupal`.`access`, `drupal`.`accesslog`, `drupal`.`aggregator_
category`, `drupal`.`aggregator_category_feed`, `drupal`.`aggregator_category_item`,
`drupal`.`aggregator_feed`, `drupal`.`aggregator_item`, `drupal`.`authmap`, `drupal`.
`blocks`, `drupal`.`book`, `drupal`.`boxes`, `drupal`.`cache`, `drupal`.`client`,
`drupal`.`client_system`, `drupal`.`comments`, `drupal`.`contact`, `drupal`.`file_
revisions`, `drupal`.`files`, `drupal`.`filter_formats`, `drupal`.`filters`,
`drupal`.`flood`, `drupal`.`forum`, `drupal`.`history`, `drupal`.`locales_meta`,
`drupal`.`locales_source`, `drupal`.`locales_target`, `drupal`.`menu`, `drupal`.
`node`, `drupal`.`node_access`, `drupal`.`node_comment_statistics`, `drupal`.`node_
counter`, `drupal`.`node_revisions`, `drupal`.`permission`, `drupal`.`poll`,
`drupal`.`poll_choices`, `drupal`.`poll_votes`, `drupal`.`profile_fields`, `drupal`.
`profile_values`, `drupal`.`role`, `drupal`.`search_dataset`, `drupal`.`search_
index`, `drupal`.`search_total`, `drupal`.`sequences`, `drupal`.`sessions`, `drupal`.
`system`, `drupal`.`term_data`, `drupal`.`term_hierarchy`, `drupal`.`term_node`,
`drupal`.`term_relation`, `drupal`.`term_synonym`, `drupal`.`url_alias`, `drupal`.
`users`, `drupal`.`users_roles`, `drupal`.`variable`, `drupal`.`vocabulary`,
`drupal`.`vocabulary_node_types`, `drupal`.`watchdog`) in 0 seconds.
Copying 171 files...
Copying indices for 0 files...
Unlocked tables.
mysqlhotcopy copied 57 tables (171 files) in 1 second (1 seconds overall).
```

mysqlsnapshot is even easier. It backs up all the ISAM or MyISAM tables on your server to one *tar* file per database:

```
# ./mysqlsnapshot -u user -p password -s /tmp --split -n
checking for binary logging... ok
backing up db drupal... done
backing up db mysql... done
backing up db test... done
snapshot completed in /tmp
```

You'll find *mysqlsnapshot* at *http://jeremy.zawodny.com/mysql/mysqlsnapshot*.

If you've set up MySQL replication for 24x7 availability, you can back up from a slave server using one of the methods just decribed. You'll also need to save replication info (logs, configuration files, and so on). See Chapters 7 and 9 of *High Performance MySQL* by Jeremy D. Zawodny and Derek J. Balling (O'Reilly) for the gritty details.

For extra protection from hardware corruption (but not human error), set up replication and provide your slave (and/or master) with RAID 1 (mirrored) disks.

Many MySQL sites migrate data from MyISAM to InnoDB tables to get true database transactions and better write performance. The authors of the InnoDB module have a commercial product for online InnoDB backups named InnoDB Hot Backup, which you can order from *http://www.innodb.com/order.php*.

The last method is usually the first mentioned in most documentation: *mysqldump*. Rather than a raw (verbatim) copy, *mysqldump* produces an ASCII dump of the specified databases and tables. It works with all MySQL table types, including InnoDB. It's relatively slow and the text files it produces are large, although they compress fairly well. It's useful to create these dumps from time to time, because they contain a straightforward script for re-creating your databases and tables from scratch. You can use editors, *grep*, and other text tools to search through or modify the dump files.

To lock all of your tables and dump them to a single file, enter:

```
# mysqldump -u user -ppassword -x --all-databases > /tmp/mysql.dump
```

You can pipe the output through *gzip* to save some time and space:

```
# mysqldump -u user -ppassword -x --all-databases | gzip > /tmp/mysql.dump.gz
```

A new open source tool (free download, pay for support) called *Zmanda Recovery Manager for MySQL* provides a useful frontend to many of these alternatives. The Zmanda web site (*http://www.zmanda.com/backup-mysql.html*) has the details, but we'll mention some of the notable features here:

- Has a command-line interface.
- Backs up local databases, or remote databases over SSL.
- Emails the status of the backup procedure.
- Handles all table types, including InnoDB.
- Does not provide any new backup methods. Instead, it chooses among *mysqldump*, *mysqlhotcopy*, MySQL replication, or LVM snapshots.
- Supports recovery to a particular transaction or point in time.

Zmanda provides *.tar.gz* and *.rpm* files for many Linux distributions. For an installation how-to for Debian, see *http://www.howtoforge.com/mysql_zrm_debian_sarge*.

APPENDIX

bash Script Samples

This appendix contains several scripts that can be useful to you in your daily work, as well as serving as models for writing other scripts. You can download the scripts from *http://www.centralsoft.org*.

Adding Users

If you have a lot of turnover (such as in a university, where new students enter in bunches once or several times a year), this script can help you add them to your system quickly. It reads a file listing information about each user and invokes *useradd* with the proper arguments (see the section "User Management" in Chapter 8 for details about *useradd* and its variants):

```
#!/bin/bash

expiredate=2009-02-18

if [[ -z "$1" ]] ; then
    echo ""
    echo "Please give exactly one file name."
    echo "The file will have one user per line."
    echo "Each line will have:"
    echo "    username"
    echo "    group"
    echo "    personal real name"
    echo ""
    echo "Sample line:
    echo "alfredo marketing Alfredo de Darc"
    exit 1
fi

cat "$1" | while read username groupname realname
do
    # Skip blank lines.
    if [[ -z $username || -z $groupname || -z $realname ]]; then
        continue
    fi
```

```
    # Check whether the user already exists.
    # If so, report this and skip this user.
    result=$( egrep "^$username:" < /etc/passwd )
    if [[ -n "$result" ]] ; then
        echo "User '$username' already exists"
        continue
    fi

    # Check whether the group already exists.
    # If not, add the group.
    result=$( egrep "^$groupname:" < /etc/group )
    if [[ -z "$result" ]] ; then
        groupadd "$groupname"
    fi

    # Add the user.
    useradd    -c "$realname" \
        -d "/home/$username"  \
        -e "$expiredate"      \
        -f 365                \
        -g "$groupname"       \
        -m                    \
        -s /bin/bash          \
        "$username"

    if [[ $? == 0 ]]; then
        echo "Successfully added user '$username'."
    else
        echo "Error adding user '$username' (group \
             '$groupname', real name '$realname')"
        exit 1
    fi

done
```

Random Password Generator

Here's a script that generates a password of any requested length, in ASCII characters:

```
#!/bin/bash
n="$1"
[[ -n "$n" ]] || n=12
if [[ $n -lt 8 ]]; then
    echo "A password of length $n would be too weak"
    exit 1
fi
p=$( dd if=/dev/urandom bs=512 count=1 2>/dev/null \

    | tr -cd 'a-zA-Z0-9' \
    | cut -c 1-$n )

echo "${p}"
```

If this makes perfect sense to you as it stands, you deserve a reward.* While you're out, the rest of us will look a bit more closely at the inherent flaws in this code.

This code is typical of something you might inherent from a previous developer: no comments, unhelpful variable names, and some magic incantations. Since you want to make the world a better place, there are a few things you can do when writing scripts like this one.

At the very least, you can leave comments describing the code's purpose. These comments should be split into two parts: an overview right in the header (for example, indicating what the arguments passed to the script should specify, and any defaults), and explicit explanations in close proximity to difficult-to-understand processes. Don't waste time just running through the basic commands used, because the maintainer can look those up if he's unfamiliar with them. However, where you employ a more exotic variant of a command, you should explicitly describe its effect and how you achieve it.

Overall, you should aim to document the *results* you're seeking with command sets, and why you're pursuing those results in the manner you've chosen.

Now, here's the explanation of the code for the password generator, in detail you're unlikely to see in the real world. The script begins with the usual starting comment that tells the system to run the *bash* interpreter. Next, we assign the first argument string to the variable `n`, which will be the number of characters to generate. We put this in quotes because it may be a null string when the script is run with no arguments. That string is then tested to determine whether it actually is null. The *-n* argument means "non-zero length," so the test is actually true if a string is given.

The two vertical bars will execute the assignment that follows if the test fails. This forces a default length of 12 for our password. The next four lines check to see whether the given length is too small; we have decided (based on classic recommendations by security experts) that the minimum length should be 8.

The first statement in the loop body uses three system commands in a pipeline to generate one trial password. All three lines in the pipeline are placed inside `$( )` to capture the output as a string that is then assigned to the variable `p`.

To generate a random password, we need a source of random data; the system provides that by combining a variety of sources of statistics into the */dev/urandom* pseudodevice. The *dd* command reads some binary data from the device. The *tr* command with the *-cd* option deletes all characters that are not in the ranges `a-z`, `A-Z`, and `0-9`. The last command in the pipeline, *cut*, extracts the desired number of characters.

* Go to Starbucks. Order a Venti Mocha Frappuccino. Tell them it's on the house. Run.

Don't try to execute this command at your terminal and view the results on the screen. You'll go blind for 10 minutes and your dog will start meowing. Did you give in to the temptation to do so? You may have to execute an *stty sane* command to restore the screen to a useful state.

Authoritative DNS Lookup

This script uses the *dig* command introduced in Chapter 3 to do DNS lookups, bypassing the cache of the local DNS caching server. One feature of this script is that it uses its own name to specify what DNS record type to look up. If the script is named *a*, it looks up DNS `A` records. If it is named *soa*, it looks up DNS `SOA` records. The name *ptr* is a special case that takes an IPv4 address and converts it to the proper `in-addr.arpa` form to do the actual lookup. You should make a copy of this script with the appropriate name for each of the common DNS record types you may need to look up: *a*, *aaaa*, *mx*, and so on. You can also use hard links or symlinks to create the aliases.

Regardless of the name, the script takes a list of hostnames to look up as arguments:

```
#!/bin/bash
#-----------------------------------------------------------------
# Copyright &#169; 2006 - Philip Howard - All rights reserved
#

# script  a, aaaa, cname, mx, ns, ptr, soa, txt
#
# purpose Perform direct DNS lookups for authoritative DNS
#         data. This lookup bypasses the local DNS cache
#         server.
#
# syntax  a       [ names ... ]
#         aaaa    [ names ... ]
#         any     [ names ... ]
#         cname   [ names ... ]
#         mx      [ names ... ]
#         ns      [ names ... ]
#         ptr     [ names ... ]
#         soa     [ names ... ]
#         txt     [ names ... ]
#
# author  Philip Howard
#-----------------------------------------------------------------

# For use with ptr query.
function inaddr {
    awk -F. '{print $4 "." $3 "." $2 "." $1 ".in-addr.arpa.";}'
}
```

```
query_type=$( exec basename "${0}" )

# Get and query for each host.
for hostname in "$@" ; do
    if [[ "${query_type}" == ptr ]] ; then
    # A typical scripting trick: when a case can begin
    # with a numeral, place a dummy character such as x in
    # front because the case syntax expects an alphanumeric
    # character.
    case "x${hostname}y" in
        ( x[0-9]*\.[0-9]*\.[0-9]*\.[0-9]*y )
        hostname=$( echo "${hostname}" | inaddr )
        ;;
        ( * )
        ;;
    esac
    fi

    # Execute the query.
    dig +trace +noall +answer "${query_type}" "${hostname}" | \
        egrep "^${hostname}"
done
exit
```

Sending Files Between Shell Sessions

You can use the script presented in this section to send a file, or a directory of files (including all subdirectories), from one system to another using a shell session on each system. The script works by creating an *rsync* daemon (*rsync* is discussed in Chapter 11) in the foreground to send the specified file or directory. It displays a few different forms of *rsync* commands that could be used to receive that file or directory. This script does not need to exist on the receiving system, so it can even be used to send a copy of itself. The *rsync* package, however, must be installed on both systems.

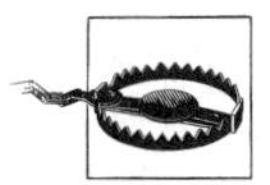

The sending system must have network access open for the port number it uses to accept incoming *rsync* connections. The port number is chosen at random from the range 12288 through 28671. You can override the random port selection by using the *-p* option followed by a port number. If your firewall rules only allow one or a few ports to be connected, you must use those port numbers with this script.

To transfer data, first run this script on the sending system. Once it outputs the sample commands, select which command would be appropriate to use based on the IP address or hostname that can reach the sending system, and the target location where the file or directory is to be stored on the receiving system. Copy the selected command line, and paste that command into the shell of the receiving system to execute the *rsync* command that receives the data. The daemon will continue to run when the transfer is complete, allowing you to transfer a file or directory multiple times to different computers. Stop the daemon when the transfers are complete by pressing Ctrl-C in the sending system's shell window.

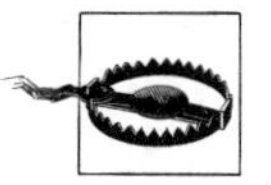

This script has no security. Anyone who can reach the address and port number on which it's listening can retrieve the data being transferred. You should not use this script to transfer confidential or secret data; try *scp* or *sftp* instead. Be sure to terminate the daemon once the desired transfers are completed.

The suggested name for this script is *rsend*:

```
#!/bin/bash
#-------------------------------------------------------------
# Copyright &#169; 2006 - Philip Howard - All rights reserved
#

# script  rsend
#
# purpose To start an rsync daemon in the shell foreground
#         to send a specified directory or file when
#         retrieved using one of the rsync command lines
#         shown, by pasting it in a shell session on another
#         host.
#
# usage   rsend [options] directory | file
#
# options -c include checksum in the rsync command lines
#         -d change daemon to the specified directory
#         -n include dryrun in the rsync command lines
#         -p use the specified port number, else random
#         -s include sparse in the rsync command lines
#         -u user to run as, if started as root
#         -v show extra information
#
# author  Philip Howard
#-------------------------------------------------------------
umask 022
hostname=$( exec hostname -f )
whoami=$( exec whoami )
uid="${whoami}"

#-------------------------------------------------------------
# Set defaults.
#-------------------------------------------------------------
checksum=""
delete=""
delmsg=""
dryrun=""
padding="-------"
port=""
sparse=""
```

```
verbose=""

bar1="--------------------------"
bar1="#${bar1}${bar1}${bar1}"

bar2="##########################"
bar2="#${bar2}${bar2}${bar2}"

#-----------------------------------------------------------------
# Include paths for ifconfig.
#-----------------------------------------------------------------
export PATH="${PATH}:/usr/sbin:/sbin"

#-----------------------------------------------------------------
# Scan options.
#-----------------------------------------------------------------
while [[ $# -gt 0 && "x${1:0:1}" = "x-" ]]; do
    case "x${1}" in
    ( x-c | x--checksum )
    checksum="c"
    ;;
    ( x--delete )
    delete=" --delete"
    delmsg="/delete"
    padding=""
    ;;
    ( x-d | x--directory )
    shift
    cd "${1}" || exit 1
    ;;
    ( x--directory=* )
    cd "${1:12}" || exit 1
    ;;
    ( x-n | x--dry-run )
    dryrun="n"
    ;;
    ( x-p | x--port )
    shift
    port="${1}"
    ;;
    ( x--port=* )
    port="${1:7}"
    ;;
    ( x-s | x--sparse )
    sparse="S"
    ;;
    ( x-u | x--user )
    shift
    uid="${1}"
    ;;
    ( x--user=* )
    uid="${1:7}"
    ;;
```

```
    ( x-v | x--verbose )
    verbose=1
    ;;
    esac
    shift
done

#-----------------------------------------------------------------
# Get a random number for a port.
#-----------------------------------------------------------------
if [[ -z "${port}" || "${port}" = 0 || "${port}" = . ]]; then
    port=$( dd if=/dev/urandom ibs=2 obs=2 count=1 2>/dev/null \
        | od -An -tu2 | tr -d ' ' )
    port=$[ $port % 16384 ]
    port=$[ $port + 12288 ]
fi

#-----------------------------------------------------------------
# Make up names for temporary files to be used.
#-----------------------------------------------------------------
conffile="/tmp/rsync-${whoami}-${port}-$$.conf"
lockfile="/tmp/rsync-${whoami}-${port}-$$.lock"

#-----------------------------------------------------------------
# This function adds quotes to strings that need them.
# Add single quotes if it has one of these: space $ " `
# Add double quotes if it has one of these: '
# Note: not all combinations will work.
#-----------------------------------------------------------------
function strquote {
    local str

    str=$( echo "${1}" | tr -d ' $"`' )
    if [[ "${str}" != "${1}" ]]; then
    echo "'${1}'"
    return
    fi
    str=$( echo "${1}" | tr -d "'" )
    if [[ "${str}" != "${1}" ]]; then
    echo '"'"${1}"'"'
    return
    fi
    echo "${1}"
    return 0
}

#-----------------------------------------------------------------
# Only one name can be handled.
#-----------------------------------------------------------------
if [[ $# -gt 1 ]]; then
    echo "Only one name (directory or file)" 1>&2
    exit 1
```

```
elif [[ $# -eq 1 ]]; then
    name="${1}"
else
    name=$( exec pwd )
fi


#-----------------------------------------------------------------
# Set up a temporary config file.
#
# Arguments:
#    $1    Directory transferred, or where transfer is starting
#    $2    Not used (AO: Should be removed)
#    $3    File transferred (if single file specified)
#-----------------------------------------------------------------
function configout {
    echo "lock file = ${lockfile}"
    echo "log file = /dev/stderr"
    echo "use chroot = false"
    echo "max connections = 32"
    echo "socket options = SO_KEEPALIVE"
    echo "list = yes"
    echo "[.]"
    echo "path = ${1}"
    echo "read only = yes"
    echo "uid = ${uid}"
    echo "comment = ${2}"
    if [[ -n "${3}" ]]; then
    echo "include = **/${3}"
    echo "exclude = **"
    fi
}

#-----------------------------------------------------------------
# Get directory and file.
#-----------------------------------------------------------------
if [[ ! -e "${name}" ]]; then
    echo "does not exist:" $( strquote "${name}" ) 1>&2
    exit 1
elif [[ -d "${name}" ]]; then
    p=$( exec dirname "${name}" )
    b=$( exec basename "${name}" )
    d="${name}"
    f=""
    r=$( cd "${name}" && exec pwd )
    announce="${d}"
    rsyncopt="-a${checksum}${dryrun}H${sparse}vz${delete}"
    configout "${d}/." "directory:${d}/" >"${conffile}"
elif [[ -f "${name}" ]]; then
    p=$( exec dirname "${name}" )
    b=$( exec basename "${name}" )
    d="${p}"
    f="${b}"
    r=$( cd "${p}" && exec pwd )
```

```
    r="${r}/${b}"
    announce="${d}/${f}"
    rsyncopt="-a${checksum}${dryrun}${sparse}vz"
    configout "${d}/." "file:${d}/${f}" >"${conffile}"
elif [[ -L "${name}" ]]; then
    p=$( exec dirname "${name}" )
    b=$( exec basename "${name}" )
    d="${p}"
    f="${b}"
    r=$( cd "${p}" && exec pwd )
    r="${r}/${b}"
    announce="${d}/${f}"
    rsyncopt="-a${checksum}v"
    configout "${d}/." "symlink:${d}/${f}" "${f}" >"${conffile}"
fi

#-----------------------------------------------------------------
# Show config file if verbose is requested.
#-----------------------------------------------------------------
if [[ -n "${verbose}" ]]; then
    echo "${bar2}"
    ls -ld "${conffile}"
    echo "${bar2}"
    cat "${conffile}"
fi

#-----------------------------------------------------------------
# This function outputs example receive commands.
#-----------------------------------------------------------------
function showrsync {
    echo -n "rsync ${rsyncopt} "
    if [[ -n "${oldfmt}" ]]; then
    echo "--port=${port}" $( strquote "${1}::${2}" ) $( strquote "${3}" )
    else
    echo $( strquote "rsync://${1}:${port}/${2}" ) $( strquote "${3}" )
    fi
    return
}

#-----------------------------------------------------------------
# These functions show rsync commands for hostname and IP address.
#-----------------------------------------------------------------
function getip {
    case $( exec uname -s ) in
    ( SunOS )
    netstat -i -n | awk '{print $4;}'
    ;;
    ( Linux )
    ifconfig -a | awk '{if($1=="inet")print substr($2,6);}'
    ;;
    ( * )
    netstat -i -n | awk '{print $4;}'
    ;;
    esac
    return
```

```
}

function ipaddr {
    getip                       \
    | egrep '^[0-9]*\.[0-9]*\.[0-9]*\.[0-9]*$'     \
    | egrep -v '^0\.|^127\.'                \
    | head -2                        \
    | while read ipv4 more ; do
    showrsync "${ipv4}" "$@"
    done
    return
}

function showcmd {
    ipaddr "${2}" "${3}"
    showrsync "${1}" "${2}" "${3}"
    return
}

#-----------------------------------------------------------------
# Announce the shell commands to receive this data.
#-----------------------------------------------------------------
echo "${bar2}"
echo "# sending ${announce}"
echo "# paste ONE of these commands in a remote shell to receive"

if [[ -d "${name}" ]]; then
    echo "${bar1}"
    showcmd "${hostname}" . .

    echo "${bar1}"
    showcmd "${hostname}" . "${b}"

    if [[ "${d}" != "${b}" && "${d}" != "${r}" ]]; then
    echo "${bar1}"
    showcmd "${hostname}" . "${d}"
    fi

    echo "${bar1}"
    showcmd "${hostname}" . "${r}"
else
    echo "${bar1}"
    showcmd "${hostname}" "./${f}" "${b}"

    s=$( exec basename "${d}" )
    s="${s}/${f}"
    if [[ "${s}" != "${b}" ]]; then
    echo "${bar1}"
    showcmd "${hostname}" "./${f}" "${s}"
    fi

    if [[ "${name}" != "${b}" \
       && "${name}" != "${s}" \
       && "${name}" != "${r}" ]]; then
```

```
    echo "${bar1}"
    showcmd "${hostname}" "./${f}" "${name}"
    fi

    echo "${bar1}"
    showcmd "${hostname}" "./${f}" "${r}"
fi

echo "${bar1}"
echo "# press ^C here when done"
echo "${bar2}"

#----------------------------------------------------------------
# Start rsync in daemon mode.
#----------------------------------------------------------------
s="DONE"
trap 's="SIGINT ... DONE"' INT
trap 's="SIGTERM ... DONE"' TERM
rsync --daemon --no-detach "--config=${conffile}" "--port=${port}"
rm -f "${conffile}" "${lockfile}"
echo "${s}"
```

Integrating ssh and screen

You should already be familiar with the *ssh* command, which connects to another computer and starts a shell there in a secure manner. The *screen* command is a useful tool that allows such a shell session to be held in an active state, with its screen contents intact, when you disconnect from the remote computer. The held shell session can then be reconnected later, even from a different computer. It is also possible to have two or more connections to the same shell session.

The following script makes an *ssh* connection and starts a named screen session in one command. The benefit of using this script is quicker connecting and disconnecting when working with multiple servers.

This script is used much like the *ssh* command. The *ssh* syntax that specifies the username and hostname of the remote session is expanded to also include a session name. You can create multiple sessions on the remote host under the same username with different session names. The session name is optional. If it is not given, this script runs the *ssh* command in the normal way, without running *screen*. The full syntax of this script, including the *ssh* options it supports, can be seen in the script's comments.

The suggested name for this script is *ss*:

```
#!/usr/bin/env bash
#----------------------------------------------------------------
# Copyright &#169; 2006 - Philip Howard - All rights reserved
#
```

```
# command ss (secure screen)
#
# purpose Establish a screen based background shell session
#         via secure shell communications.
#
# syntax  ss  [options]  session/username@hostname
#         ss  [options]  session@username@hostname
#         ss  [options]  username@hostname/session
#         ss  [options]  username@hostname  session
#
# options -h hostname
#         -h=hostname
#         -i identity
#         -i=identity
#         -l loginuser
#         -l=loginuser
#         -m Multi-display mode
#         -p portnum
#         -p=portnum
#         -s session
#         -s=session
#         -t Use tty allocation (default)
#         -T Do NOT use tty allocation
#         -4 Use IPv4 (default)
#         -6 Use IPv6
#         -46 | -64 Use either IPv6 or IPv4
#
# requirements The local system must have the OpenSSH package
#         installed. The remote system must have the
#         OpenSSH package installed and have the sshd
#         daemon running. It must also have the screen(1)
#         program installed. Configuring a .screenrc
#         file on each system is recommended.
#
# note    The environment variable SESSION_NAME will be set
#         in the session created under the screen command
#         for potential use by other scripts.
#
# author  Philip Howard
#------------------------------------------------------------
whoami=$( exec whoami )
hostname=$( exec hostname )

h=""
i=( )
m=""
p=( )
s=''
t=( -t )
u="${whoami}"
v=( -4 )

#------------------------------------------------------------
# Parse options and arguments.
#------------------------------------------------------------
```

```
while [[ $# -gt 0 ]]; do
    case "x${1}" in
    ( x*/*@* )
    # Example: session1/lisa@centrhub
    u=$( echo "x${1}" | cut -d @ -f 1 )
    u="${u:1}"
    s=$( echo "x${u}" | cut -d / -f 2 )
    u=$( echo "x${u}" | cut -d / -f 1 )
    u="${u:1}"
    h=$( echo "x${1}" | cut -d @ -f 2 )
    shift
    break
    ;;
    ( x*@*/* )
    # Example: lisa@centrhub/session1
    u=$( echo "x${1}" | cut -d @ -f 1 )
    u="${u:1}"
    h=$( echo "x${1}" | cut -d @ -f 2 )
    s=$( echo "x${h}" | cut -d / -f 2 )
    h=$( echo "x${h}" | cut -d / -f 1 )
    h="${h:1}"
    shift
    break
    ;;
    ( x*@*@* )
    # Example: session1@lisa@centrhub
    s=$( echo "x${1}" | cut -d @ -f 1 )
    s="${s:1}"
    u=$( echo "x${1}" | cut -d @ -f 2 )
    h=$( echo "x${1}" | cut -d @ -f 3 )
    shift
    break
    ;;
    ( x*@* )
    # Example: lisa@centrhub
    u=$( echo "x${1}" | cut -d @ -f 1 )
    u="${u:1}"
    h=$( echo "x${1}" | cut -d @ -f 2 )
    # Next argument should be session name.
    shift
    if [[ $# -gt 0 ]]; then
        s="${1}"
        shift
    fi
    break
    ;;
    ( x-h=* )
    h="${1:3}"
    ;;
    ( x-h )
    shift
    h="${1}"
    ;;
    ( x-i=* )
```

```
i="${1:3}"
if [[ -z "${i}" ]]; then
    i=( )
else
    i=( -i "${1:3}" )
fi
;;
( x-i )
shift
i=( -i "${1}" )
;;
( x-l=* | x-u=* )
u="${1:3}"
;;
( x-l | x-u )
shift
u="${1}"
;;
( x-m | x--multi )
m=1
;;
( x-p=* )
p="${1:3}"
if [[ -z "${p}" ]]; then
    p=( )
else
    p=( -p "${1:3}" )
fi
;;
( x-p )
shift
p=( -p "${1}" )
;;
( x-s=* )
s="${1:3}"
;;
( x-s )
shift
s="${1}"
;;
( x-t )
t=( -t )
;;
( x-T )
t=( )
;;
( x-4 )
v=( -4 )
;;
( x-6 )
v=( -6 )
;;
( x-46 | x-64 )
v=()
;;
```

```
    ( x-* )
    echo "Invalid option: '${1}'"
    die=1
    ;;
    ( * )
    echo "Invalid argument: '${1}'"
    die=1
    ;;
    esac
    shift
done

#-----------------------------------------------------------------
# Make sure essential information is present.
#-----------------------------------------------------------------
if [[ -z "${u}" ]]; then
    echo "User name is missing"
    die=1
fi

if [[ -z "${h}" ]]; then
    echo "Host name is missing"
    die=1
fi

[[ -z "${die}" ]] || exit 1

#-----------------------------------------------------------------
# Run screen on the remote only if a session name is given.
#-----------------------------------------------------------------
c=( ssh "${v[@]}" "${i[@]}" "${p[@]}" "${t[@]}" "${u}@${h}" )
if [[ -n "${s}" ]]; then
    o="-DR"
    [[ -n "${m}" ]] && o="-x"
    x="exec /usr/bin/env SESSION_NAME='${s}' screen ${o} '${s}'"
    c=( "${c[@]}" "${x}" )
fi
exec "${c[@]}"
```

Index

Symbols

A

B

We'd like to hear your suggestions for improving our indexes. Send email to *index@oreilly.com*.

C

D

E

F

G

H

I

K

L

M

About the Authors

Tom Adelstein began his career in investment banking, where his technical skills helped financial service companies become industry leaders. He is now a full-time system administrator and a technical writer.

Bill Lubanovic started developing software with Unix in the 1970s, GUIs in the 1980s, and the Web in the 1990s. He now does web visualization work for a wind energy company.

Colophon

The image on the cover of *Linux System Administration* is a cowboy running cattle.

The cover image and chapter opening images are from the Dover Pictorial Archive. The cover font is Adobe ITC Garamond. The text font is Linotype Birka; the heading font is Adobe Myriad Condensed; and the code font is LucasFont's TheSans Mono Condensed.

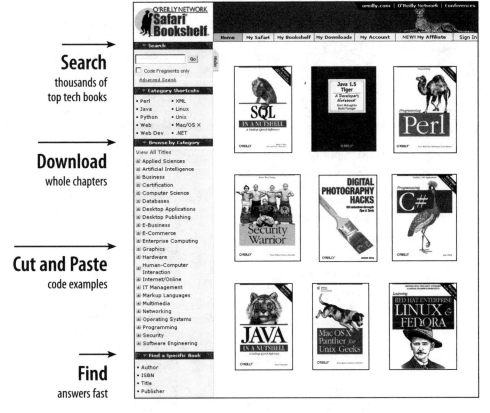

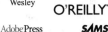

Related Titles from O'Reilly

Linux

Building Embedded Linux Systems

Building Linux Distributions

Building Secure Servers with Linux

The Complete FreeBSD, *4th Edition*

Even Grues Get Full

Exploring the JDS Linux Desktop

Extreme Programming Pocket Guide

Fedora Linux

GDB Pocket Reference

Knoppix Hacks

Knoppix Pocket Guide

Learning Red Hat Enterprise Linux and Fedora, *4th Edition*

Linux Annoyances for Geeks

Linux Cookbook

Linux Desktop Hacks

Linux Desktop Pocket Guide

Linux Device Drivers, *3rd Edition*

Linux in a Nutshell, *5th Edition*

Linux in a Windows World

Linux iptables Pocket Reference

Linux Kernel in a Nutshell

Linux Multimedia Hacks

Linux Network Administrator's Guide, *3rd Edition*

Linux Pocket Guide

Linux Security Cookbook

Linux Server Hacks, *Volume 2*

Linux System Administration

Linux System Programming

Linux Unwired

LPI Linux Certification in a Nutshell, *2nd Edition*

Managing RAID on Linux

OpenOffice.org Writer

Producing Open Source Software

Programming with Qt, *2nd Edition*

Root of all Evil

Running Linux, *5th Edition*

Samba Pocket Reference, *2nd Edition*

SUSE Linux

Test Driving Linux

Ubuntu Hacks

Understanding Linux Network Intervals

Understanding the Linux Kernel, *3rd Edition*

Understanding Open Source & Free Software Licensing

User Friendly

Using Samba, *2nd Edition*

Version Control with Subversion

O'REILLY®